GED® Mathematical Reasoning Test
FOR DUMMIES®
A Wiley Brand

by Murray Shukyn, BA
and Achim K. Krull, BA, MAT

FOR DUMMIES®
A Wiley Brand

GED® Mathematical Reasoning Test For Dummies®

Published by: **John Wiley & Sons, Inc.,** 111 River Street, Hoboken, NJ 07030-5774, www.wiley.com

Copyright © 2015 by John Wiley & Sons, Inc., Hoboken, New Jersey

Published simultaneously in Canada

For general information on our other products and services, please contact our Customer Care Department within the U.S. at 877-762-2974, outside the U.S. at 317-572-3993, or fax 317-572-4002. For technical support, please visit www.wiley.com/techsupport.

Wiley publishes in a variety of print and electronic formats and by print-on-demand. Some material included with standard print versions of this book may not be included in e-books or in print-on-demand. If this book refers to media such as a CD or DVD that is not included in the version you purchased, you may download this material at http://booksupport.wiley.com. For more information about Wiley products, visit www.wiley.com.

Library of Congress Control Number: 2015945227

ISBN 978-1-119-03008-9 (pbk); ISBN 978-1-119-03011-9 (ebk); ISBN 978-1-119-03010-2 (ebk)

Manufactured in the United States of America

10 9 8 7 6 5 4 3 2 1

Contents at a Glance

Table of Contents

Introduction

•••

You've decided to take the General Education Development (GED) test to earn the equivalent of a high school diploma. Good for you. You have the fortitude and certitude to clear a major hurdle standing between you and your educational and professional goals. But now you realize that you need extra guidance and practice in mathematics to tackle the Mathematical Reasoning test. Perhaps you took the test once or even twice and didn't do so well, or you've done an honest self-assessment and now realize that math was never your favorite or best subject. Whatever the reason, you need to quickly review the fundamentals and practice solving math problems similar to those you'll encounter on the test. You want to know what to expect, so you're not blindsided on test day.

Welcome to *GED Mathematical Reasoning Test For Dummies* — your key to excelling on the GED Mathematical Reasoning test. Here, you find everything you need to do well on the test, from instruction on basic addition and subtraction all the way up to strategies for solving word problems and dealing with quadratic equations. We also pepper you with plenty of practice questions to reinforce your newly acquired knowledge and skills.

About This Book

As we were writing *GED Test For Dummies,* 3rd edition (Wiley), we didn't have the space to cover all four sections of the GED test in great detail. In that book, we provided a general overview of the GED test and two full-length practice tests that covered all four sections — Reasoning through Language Arts (RLA), Mathematical Reasoning, Science, and Social Studies.

Knowing that each section of the GED test can be taken separately and that test-takers probably need more guidance in some subject areas than in others, we decided to develop a separate book for each section — four books, each with a balance of instruction and practice. In this book, we focus exclusively on the GED Mathematical Reasoning test. Our goal is to prepare you to solve any math problem you're likely to encounter on the test.

We begin by giving you a sneak peek at the test format and an overview of what's on the test. We then provide a diagnostic test that presents you with math problems that challenge your knowledge and skills across the entire spectrum of high school mathematics to identify your unique strengths and weaknesses. The diagnostic test and the self-assessment form following the test guide you to specific chapters for instruction and practice. When you feel ready, you can then tackle the full-length practice test in Chapter 10 and turn to Chapter 11 for answers and explanations.

We wrap up with two Part of Tens chapters — one to help you avoid ten common mistakes and the other to guide you in solving ten tricky math problems.

Foolish Assumptions

When we wrote this book, we made a few assumptions about you, dear reader. Here's who we think you are:

✔ You're serious about earning a high-school diploma or GED endorsement for existing qualifications as quickly as you can.

✔ You're looking for additional instruction and guidance, specifically in mathematics, not English, science, or social studies.

✔ You've made earning a high-school diploma and an endorsement a priority in your life because you want to advance in the workplace or move on to college.

✔ You're willing to give up some activities so you have the time to prepare, always keeping in mind your other responsibilities, too.

✔ You meet your state's requirements regarding age, residency, and the length of time since leaving school that make you eligible to take the GED test. (See Chapter 1 for details.)

✔ You have sufficient English language skills to handle the test. Yes, you will encounter plenty of word problems.

✔ You want a fun and friendly guide that helps you achieve your goal.

If any of these descriptions sounds like you, welcome aboard. We've prepared an enjoyable tour of the GED test.

Icons Used in This Book

Icons — little pictures you see in the margins of this book — highlight bits of text that you want to pay special attention to. Here's what each one means:

Whenever we want to tell you a special trick or technique that can help you succeed on the GED Mathematical Reasoning test, we mark it with this icon. Keep an eye out for this guy.

This icon points out information you want to burn into your brain. Think of the text with this icon as the sort of stuff you'd tear out and put on a bulletin board or your refrigerator.

Take this icon seriously! Although the world won't end if you don't heed the advice next to this icon, the warnings are important to your success in preparing to take the GED Mathematical Reasoning test.

We use this icon to flag example questions that are much like what you can expect on the actual GED Mathematical Reasoning test. So if you just want to get familiar with the types of questions on the test, this icon is your guide.

Beyond the Book

In addition to the book content, you can find valuable free material online. We provide you with a Cheat Sheet that addresses things you need to know and consider when getting ready for the GED Mathematical Reasoning Test. You can access this material at www.dummies.com/cheatsheet/gedmathtest.

We also include additional articles at www.dummies.com/extras/gedmathtest that provide even more helpful tips and advice to help you score your best on the GED Mathematical Reasoning Test.

Where to Go from Here

Some people like to read books from beginning to end. Others prefer to read only the specific information they need to know now. Here we provide a road map so you can find your way around.

Chapter 1 starts off with an overview of the GED test and how to register for the exam. Chapter 2 brings you up to speed on what the Mathematical Reasoning test covers. Chapter 3 is a must-read — a diagnostic test followed by a self-assessment to target areas where you need the most guidance and practice. Based on your self-assessment, you'll know which chapters to focus on in Part II of this book.

The chapters in Part II are the meat and potatoes — instruction and practice across the entire spectrum of high school mathematics:

- **Basics:** In Chapter 5, you hone your basic math skills — addition, subtraction, multiplication, division, fractions, and so on — which you need to solve nearly every math problem you're likely to encounter on the test.

- **Quantitative problems:** In Chapter 6, you find out how to approach word problems and solve quantitative problems, such as those dealing with unit rates (such as miles per hour), ratios, proportions, and percentages.

- **Measurement problems:** Chapter 7 covers basic geometry — calculating the perimeter and area of flat shapes and the volume and surface area of three-dimensional objects. In this chapter, you also come to master the Pythagorean theorem; the concepts of mean, median, and mode; and approaches to solving probability problems, which are very handy if you ever plan to become a high roller in Las Vegas.

- **Expressions and equations:** Chapter 8 turns your attention to algebra, where you discover how to solve expressions and equations, deal with polynomials and quadratic equations, and solve real-world problems that involve inequalities. If your head is spinning just from reading that last sentence, Chapter 8 is a must-read.

- **Graphs and functions:** Chapter 9 helps you navigate the transition from higher level math to the coordinate plane, where you can see math in action, as it's used to describe points and lines. Here, you may also have your first encounter with mathematical *functions* — relationships or expressions that contain one or more variables, such as x and y. Don't worry; in the course of a single chapter, you'll know all you need to know about solving math problems that contain variables.

When you're ready to dive into a full-length practice test that mimics the real GED Mathematical Reasoning test, check out Part III, and then check your answers with the detailed answer explanations we provide for the practice test (but be sure to wait until *after* you take the practice test to look at the answers!).

If you need a break, turn to the chapters in Part IV, where we help you steer clear of ten common math mistakes and show you how to solve ten tricky math problems.

Part I

Getting Started with the GED Mathematical Reasoning Test

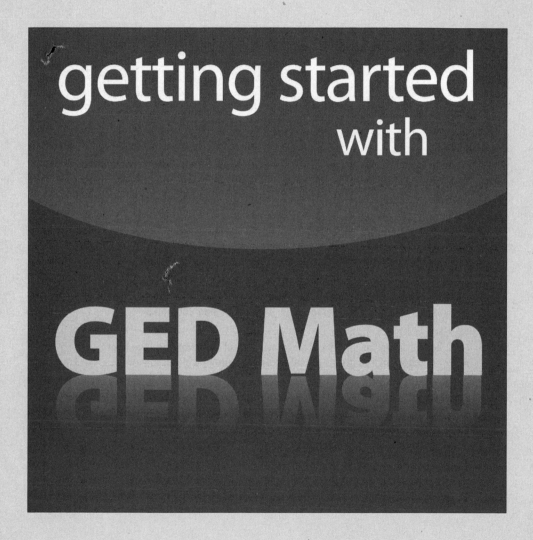

In this part . . .

✔ Get oriented to the test format, question types, test scheduling, and scoring, and find out what steps to take if English isn't your first language.

✔ Find out what's on the GED Math test and the knowledge and skills you'll be required to demonstrate on the test.

✔ Take a diagnostic test to identify your strengths and weaknesses and highlight the areas where you may need additional practice.

✔ Prepare for the actual test day and find out what you should or shouldn't do on the day(s) before and the day of the test and during the exam.

Chapter 1

Taking a Quick Glance at the GED Mathematical Reasoning Test

In This Chapter
▶ Warming up to the GED test format
▶ Checking out what's covered on the GED Math test
▶ Registering to take the test
▶ Completing the GED test when English isn't your first language
▶ Understanding what your scores mean and how they're determined

The GED test offers high-school dropouts, people who leave school early, and people who were educated outside the United States an opportunity to earn the equivalent of a United States (U.S.) high-school diploma without the need for full-time attendance in either day or night school. The GED test is a recognized standard that makes securing a job or college placement easier.

The GED test complies with current Grade 12 standards in the United States and meets the College and Career Readiness Standards for Adult Education. The GED test also covers the Common Core Standards, used in most states in the country. These standards are based on the actual expectations stated by employers and postsecondary institutions.

The GED test measures whether you understand what high-school seniors across the country have studied before they graduate. Employers need better-educated employees. In addition, some colleges may be uncertain of the quality of foreign credentials. The GED diploma provides those assurances. When you pass the GED test, you earn a high-school equivalency diploma. That can open many doors for you — perhaps doors that you don't even know exist at this point.

The new GED test is now given on a computer and has taken advantage of many different formats that the computer can create. Most of them are variations of multiple choice. You can see examples of all these formats and how they would appear on the computer screen by looking at *GED Test For Dummies*, 3rd Edition (published by Wiley).

You're permitted to take the GED in sections, so you can take the Reasoning Through Language Arts (RLA), Mathematical Reasoning, Science, and Social Studies tests in separate testing sessions. This flexibility enables you to focus your studies and practice on one section of the test at a time, and this book supports your efforts to do just that.

Ready to get started? This chapter gives you the basics of the GED Mathematical Reasoning section: how the test is administered and what it looks like, how to schedule the test, including whether you're eligible, and how your score is calculated (so you know what you need to focus on to pass).

The diagnostic test in Chapter 3 helps you discover your weaknesses and strengths so that with additional practice, you can convert your weaknesses into strengths.

Knowing What to Expect: The GED Test Format

A computer administers the GED test. That means that all the questions appear on a computer screen, and you enter all your answers into a computer. You read, evaluate, analyze, and write everything on the computer. Even when drafting an essay, you don't use paper. Instead, the test center provides you with an erasable tablet. If you know how to use a computer and are comfortable with a keyboard and a mouse, you're ahead of the game. If not, practice your keyboarding. Also, practice reading from a computer screen, because reading from a screen is very different from reading printed materials. At the very least, you need to get more comfortable with computers, even if that means taking a short course at a local learning center. In the case of the GED test, the more familiar you are with computers, the more comfortable you'll feel taking the computerized test. (For guidance on how to more effectively read and comprehend content on a computer screen, check out *GED Test For Dummies*, 3rd Edition [Wiley].)

Under certain circumstances, as a special accommodation, the sections are available in booklet format. Check with the GED Testing Service to see what exceptions are acceptable.

The computer-based GED test allows for speedy, detailed feedback on your performance. When you pass (yes, we said *when* and not *if,* because we believe in you), the GED Testing Service provides both a diploma and a comprehensive transcript of your scores, similar to what high-school graduates receive. They're available online at www.gedtestingservice.com within a day of completing the test. You can then send your transcript and diploma to an employer or college. Doing so allows employers and colleges access to a thorough outline of your scores, achievement, and demonstrated skills and abilities. This outline is also a useful tool for you to review your progress. It highlights areas where you did well and areas where you need further work. If you want to (or have to) retake the test, these results provide a detailed guide to what you should work on to improve your scores. Requests for additional copies of transcripts are handled online and also are available within a day.

Reviewing the GED Mathematical Reasoning Test

The Mathematical Reasoning section presents you with two general areas of mathematics: 45 percent quantitative, consisting of problem solving involving number operations and geometrical thinking, and 55 percent algebraic problem solving. See Chapter 2 for a more detailed description of the subject matter that the Mathematical Reasoning section covers.

The computer version of the test provides an on-screen calculator for all except the first five questions. If you prefer, you can use a hand-held calculator, but the GED Testing Service is very specific about the make and model of the hand-held calculator you're allowed to use. If you bring your own hand-held calculator, you must store it in a secure location while you answer the first five questions; then you're permitted a couple of minutes to retrieve it for use on the rest of the test.

Visit www.gedtestingservice.com/testers/calculator to view a video demonstration of the on-screen calculator provided during the test and to find out which make and model of hand-held calculator is permitted.

If you're comfortable with on-screen calculators, use the one provided. If you're not sure of your comfort level, practice using the calculator on your computer or a calculator online. If you aren't comfortable with on-screen calculators, consider purchasing the approved hand-held calculator.

Questions are presented in four formats:

- **Multiple choice:** Multiple choice provides you with four possible answers, only one of which is correct. In this book, we provide explanations for all four answers, so you understand why the right answer is correct and why the other three answer choices are incorrect. On the diagnostic test especially, this can provide you with some insight into which math skills you need to practice most.

- **Drag and drop:** Drag-and-drop items provide you with a list of possible answers, only one of which is correct. On the computer, you choose the correct answer by dragging it to a designated spot with the mouse. This is very similar to playing solitaire on the computer.

- **Fill in the blank:** Fill-in-the-blank items provide you with no answer choices. You use the keyboard to type the correct answer in the blank.

- **Hot spot:** Hot-spot items are typically used for questions that require you to plot a point on a graph or coordinate plane. If you've ever played the game Battleship on a computer, you're aware of winning points by clicking a space on the screen with your mouse. If you click the correct spot, you win. If you click anywhere else on the screen, you lose.

It's a Date: Scheduling the Test

To take the GED test, you schedule it based on the available testing dates. Each state or local testing center sets its own schedule for the GED test, which means that your state decides how and when you can take each section of the test. It also determines how often you can retake a failed section and how much such a retake will cost. Because a computer administers the test, many testing centers allow you to schedule an individual appointment. Your test starts when you start and ends when your allotted time is completed. The test centers are small computer labs, often containing no more than 15 seats, and actual testing facilities are located in many communities in your state.

You book your appointment through the GED Testing Service (www.gedtestingservice. com). Your local GED test administrator can give you all the information you need about scheduling the test. In addition, local school districts and community colleges can provide information about local test centers in your area.

Sending a specific question or request to www.gedtestingservice.com may come with a charge for the service. To save money, you're better off asking a person at your local testing center. That way, you don't have to pay for the privilege of asking a question, and your answer will be based on rules and conditions specific to your area.

The following sections answer some questions you may have before you schedule your test date, including whether you're even eligible to take the test, when you can take the test, and how to sign up for the test.

Determining whether you're eligible

Before you schedule your test, make sure you meet the requirements to take it. You're eligible to apply to take the GED test only if

✔ **You're not currently enrolled in a high school.** If you're currently enrolled in a high school, you're expected to complete your diploma there. The purpose of the GED test is to give people who aren't in high school a chance to get an equivalent high-school diploma.

✔ **You're not a high-school graduate.** If you're a high-school graduate, you should have a diploma, which means you don't need to take the GED test. However, if you did not complete high school, you can use the GED to upgrade or update your skills and to present a diploma that shows that you're ready for further education and training.

✔ **You meet state requirements regarding age, residency, and the length of time since leaving high school.** Check with your local GED test administrator to determine your state's requirements concerning these criteria. Residency requirements are an issue because you may have to take the test in a different jurisdiction, depending on how long you've lived at your present address.

Knowing when you can take the test

If you're eligible, you can take the GED test whenever you're prepared. You can apply to take the GED test as soon as you want. Just contact your local testing center or www.gedtestingservice.com for a test schedule. Pick a day that works for you.

You can take all four sections of the GED test together. That takes about seven hours. However, the test is designed so that you can take each section separately, whenever you're ready. In most areas, you can take the test sections one at a time, even in the evening or on weekends, depending on the individual testing center. If you pass one test section, that section of the GED test is considered done, no matter how you do on the other sections. If you fail one section, you can retake it at any time. The scheduling and administration of the test varies from state to state, so check with www.gedtestingservice.com or your local high-school guidance office.

Because the test starts when you're ready and finishes when you've used up the allocated time, you should be able take it alone and not depend on other people. You may be able to find locations that offer the testing on evenings or weekends as well as during regular business hours. Even better, because you don't have to take the test with a group, you may be able to set an individual starting time that suits you.

If circumstances dictate that you must take the paper version of the test, you'll probably have to forgo the flexibility afforded by the computer. Check well in advance to see what the rules are for you.

You can also apply to take the test if you're not prepared, but if you do that, you don't stand a very good chance of passing. If you do need to retake any section of the test, use your time before your next test date to get ready. You can retake the test three times in a year without waiting, but after the third failed attempt you must wait 60 days. In most jurisdictions, taking the test costs money (check with your local testing center to find out specifics for your area). The GED Testing Service does offer a discounted retake up to twice a year, but these promotions change. Some states include free retakes in the price of the test. Check with the GED Testing Service or your state to find out what special discounts may be available. To save time and money, prepare well before you schedule the test. Refer to the later section "Retaking the test(s) if you score poorly" for details.

Are special accommodations available?

If you need to complete the test on paper or have a disability that makes it impossible for you to use the computer, your needs can be accommodated. However, other specifics apply: Your choice of times and testing locations may be much more restricted, but times to complete a test may be extended. Remember also that if accommodation is required, the GED testing centers will ask for documentation of the nature of the accommodation required.

The GED testing centers make every effort to ensure that all qualified people have access to the tests. If you have a disability, you may not be able to register for the tests and take them the same week, but, with some advanced planning, you can probably take the tests when you're ready. Here's what you need to do:

- ✔ Check with your local testing center or check out www.gedtestingservice.com/testers/accommodations-for-disability.

- ✔ Contact the GED Testing Service or your local GED test center and explain your disability.

- ✔ Request any forms that you have to fill out for your special circumstances.

- ✔ Ensure that you have a recent diagnosis by a physician or other qualified professional.

- ✔ Complete all the proper forms and submit them with a medical or professional diagnosis.

- ✔ Start planning early so that you're able to take the tests when you're ready.

Note that, regardless of your disability, you still have to be able to handle the mental and emotional demands of the test.

The GED Testing Service in Washington, D.C., defines specific disabilities, such as the following, for which it may make special accommodations, provided the disability severely limits your ability to perform essential skills required to pass the GED test:

- ✔ Medical disabilities, such as cerebral palsy, epilepsy, or blindness

- ✔ Psychological disabilities, such as schizophrenia, major depression, attention deficit disorder, or Tourette's syndrome

- ✔ Specific learning disabilities, including perceptual handicaps, brain injury, minimal brain dysfunction, dyslexia, and developmental aphasia

Signing up

When you're ready to sign up for the test, follow these steps:

1. **Contact your local GED test administrator or go to** www.gedtestingservice.com **to make sure you're eligible.**

   Refer to the earlier section "Determining whether you're eligible" for some help.

2. **Ask the office for an application (if needed) or an appointment.**

3. **Complete the application (if needed).**

4. **Return the application to the proper office, with payment, if necessary.**

   Testing fees vary state by state, so contact your local administrator or testing site to find out the fee amount. In some states, low-income individuals may be eligible for financial assistance.

Note: You can do all this online, including submitting the payment, with your computer, tablet, or smartphone. Go to www.gedtestingservice.com to start the process.

Never send cash by mail to pay for the GED test. Most local administrators have payment rules and don't accept cash.

Working with unusual circumstances

If you feel that you may have a special circumstance that prevents you from taking the GED test on a given day, contact the GED test administrator in your area. If, for example, the test is going to be held on your Sabbath, the testing center may make special arrangements for you.

When applying for special circumstances, keep the following guidelines in mind:

- Document everything in your appeal for special consideration.
- Contact the GED test administrator in your area as early as you can.
- Be patient. Special arrangements can't be made overnight. The administrator often has to wait for a group with similar issues to gather so arrangements can be made for the entire group.
- Ask questions. Accommodations can be made if you ask. For example, allowances include extended time for various special needs, large print and Braille for visual impairments, and age allowance for individuals older than 60 who feel they may have a learning disability.

Taking the GED Test When English Isn't Your First Language

English doesn't have to be your first language for you to take the GED test, because it's offered in English, Spanish, and French. If you want to take the test in Spanish or French, contact your local GED test administrator to apply or see www.gedtestingservice.com/testers/special-test-editions-spanish or www.gedtestingservice.com/testers/special-test-editions-french. However, individuals who speak another language as their first language must take the test in English.

If English, Spanish, or French isn't your first language, you must decide whether you can read and write English as well as or better than 40 percent of high-school graduates, because you may be required to pass an English as a Second Language (ESL) placement test. If you write and read English well, prepare for and take the test in English. If you don't read or write English well, take additional classes to improve your language skills until you think you're ready. An English Language Proficiency Test (ELPT) is also available for people who completed their education in other countries. If you're not sure of your English language skills, consider taking an ELPT to assess your language skills before taking the GED test.

In many ways, the GED test is like the Test of English as a Foreign Language (TOEFL) comprehension test. If you've completed the TOEFL test with good grades, you're likely ready to take the GED test. If you haven't taken the TOEFL test, enroll in a GED test-preparation course to see whether you have difficulty understanding the subjects and skills assessed on the test. GED test courses provide you with some insight into your comprehension ability with a teacher to discuss your skills and struggles.

Websites that can help you plan to take the GED test

The Internet is a helpful and sometimes scary place. Some websites are there to help you in your GED test preparation, while others just want to sell you something. You have to know how to separate the good from the bad. Here are a couple of essential websites (most are accessible through www.gedtestingservice.com):

✔ adulted.about.com/od/getting yourged/a/stateged.htm links to the GED test eligibility requirements and testing locations in your state.

✔ usaeducation.info/Tests/GED/ International-students.html explains GED test eligibility for foreign students.

If you're curious and want to see what's out there, type in "GED test" into any search engine and relax while you try to read about millions of results, ranging from the helpful to the misleading. We suggest leaving this last activity until after you've passed the tests. As useful as the Internet can be, it still provides the opportunity to waste vast amounts of time. And right now, you need to spend your time preparing for the test — and leave the rest for after you get your diploma.

Taking Aim at Your Target Score

To pass the GED test, you need to score a minimum of 150 on each section: Reasoning Through Language Arts, Mathematical Reasoning, Science, and Social Studies. If you achieve a passing score, congratulate yourself: You've scored better than at least 40 percent of today's high-school graduates, and you're now a graduate of the largest virtual school in the country. And if your marks are in the honors range, you're ready for college or career training.

Be aware that some colleges require scores higher than the minimum passing score. If you plan to apply to postsecondary schools or some other form of continuing education, check with their admissions office for the minimum admission score requirements.

The following sections address a few more points you may want to know about how the GED test is scored and what you can do if you score poorly on one or more of the test sections.

Identifying how scores are determined

Correct answers may be worth one, two, or more points, depending on the item and the level of difficulty.

Because you don't lose points for incorrect answers, make sure you answer all the items on each test. After all, a guessed answer can get you a point. Leaving an answer blank, on the other hand, guarantees you a zero. The information and practice in this book provides you with the knowledge and skills you need to answer most questions on the Mathematical Reasoning section with confidence and to narrow your choices when you're not quite sure which answer choice is correct.

Retaking the test(s) if you score poorly

If you discover that your score is less than 150 on any test section, start planning to retake the test(s) and make sure you leave plenty of time for additional study and preparation.

Retake the diagnostic test in Chapter 3 and carefully review the answers and explanations to determine your weaknesses and strengths. Concentrate on understanding your weaknesses and try several more GED sample tests to make sure. If none of this helps, enroll in a preparation course or a study group. Remember that you are trying to complete several years of high school in a concentrated time. Don't get discouraged.

As soon as possible after obtaining your results, contact your local GED test administrator to find out the rules for retaking the failed section of the test. Some states may require that you wait a certain amount of time and/or limit the number of attempts each year. Some may ask that you attend a preparation course and show that you've completed it before you can retake the GED. Some may charge you an additional fee. However, you need to retake only those sections of the test that you failed. Any sections you pass are completed and count toward your diploma. Furthermore, the detailed evaluation of your results will help you discover areas of weakness that need more work before repeating any section of the test.

One advantage of taking the GED test on a computer is that you can receive, within a day, detailed feedback on how you did, which includes some specific recommendations of what you need to do to improve your scores.

No matter what score you receive on your first round of the section, don't be afraid to retake any section that you didn't pass. After you've taken it once, you know what you need to work on, and you know exactly what to expect on test day.

Chapter 2

What's on the Mathematical Reasoning Test?

In This Chapter

▶ Identifying the skills you need for the Math test

▶ Getting a handle on the test format

▶ Preparing for the test using a few tried-and-true strategies

▶ Getting familiar with the calculator and formula sheet

▶ Doing a little math to help manage your time on the test

The Mathematical Reasoning test gauges your understanding of mathematical concepts and your ability to apply them to situations you may find in the real world. To prepare for the test, you need to know what's on it, familiarize yourself with the different question formats, and shift your brain into mathematical problem-solving mode. This chapter gets you started by revealing what's on the Mathematical Reasoning test and providing some tips and tricks for tackling the different types of questions you'll encounter.

Looking at the Skills the Math Test Covers

To do well on the Math test, you need to have a general understanding of numbers, their relationships to one another, measurements, geometry, data analysis and statistics, probability, patterns, functions, and algebra. (To find out more about these terms and concepts, turn to the chapters in Part II.) In essence, to be successful on this test, you need to have the mathematical knowledge base that most high-school graduates have, and you need to know how to apply it to solve real-life problems.

The GED Math test provides a formula sheet for you to use during the test. Keep in mind that you may not need all the formulas provided, and you may not need a formula for every question. Part of the fun of math is knowing which formula to use for which problems and figuring out when you don't need one at all.

The Math test assesses four areas: number operations and number sense; measurement and geometry; data analysis, statistics, and probability; and algebra, functions, and patterns. The following sections describe these areas in greater detail.

The formulas you memorized and understand are instantly available to you. The formulas you have to look up and ponder take time that could be used answering questions or checking answers.

Number operations and number sense

Surprise, surprise — these problems deal with numbers. Here's a breakdown of the two topics in this category:

- *Number operations* are the familiar actions you take in math problems and equations, such as addition, subtraction, multiplication, and division. You probably mastered these operations in grade school; now all you have to do is practice them.

- *Number sense* is the ability to understand numbers. You're expected to be able to recognize numbers (not a difficult task), know their relative values (that 5 is larger than 3, for example), and know how to use them (which takes us back to number operations). In addition, number sense includes the ability to *estimate* (or approximate) the result of number operations — which is always a handy skill on a timed test.

For more about operations and number sense, head to Chapters 5 and 6.

Measurement and geometry

Here, you get a chance to play with mathematical shapes and manipulate them in your head. You get to use the Pythagorean relationship (or theorem) to do all sorts of interesting calculations, and you get to use measurements to do things like find the volume of ice cream in a cone or the amount of paint you need to cover a wall. If you relax, you can have fun with these questions and then maybe even use a lot of the knowledge in real life. This category breaks down into two topics:

- *Measurement* involves area, volume, time, and the distance from here to there. Measurement of time is a good thing to know when taking any test because you want to make sure you run out of questions before you run out of time!

- *Geometry* is the part of mathematics that deals with measurement. It also deals with relationships and properties of points, lines, angles, and planes. This branch of math requires you to draw, use, and understand diagrams.

To find out more about solving measurement problems, check out Chapter 7.

Data analysis, statistics, and probability

If you pay attention and practice the concepts in this category, you'll be able to think more clearly about the next political poll that shows that every representative of the party sponsoring the poll is good and all others are evil. This category breaks down into the following types:

- *Data analysis* allows you to analyze data. You probably already practice this skill without realizing it. When you read about stock performance or lack of performance, calculate or read about baseball statistics, or figure out how many miles per gallon your car gets, you're doing data analysis.

- *Statistics and probability* are part of data analysis. *Statistics* is the interpretation of collections of random numbers and can be used to prove one thing or another; *probability* tells you how often an event is likely to happen.

See Chapter 7 for guidance on how to solve math problems related to data analysis, statistics, and probability.

Algebra, functions, and patterns

You most likely use these concepts in everyday life, although you may not realize that you do. Here's a breakdown of the three types in this category:

- *Algebra* is a form of mathematics used to solve problems by using letters to represent unknown numbers, creating equations from the information given, and solving for the unknown numbers — thus, turning them into known numbers. If you ever said something like, "How much more does the $10 scarf cost than the $7.50 one?" you were really solving this equation: Let the difference in cost be x, $\$7.50 + x = \$10.00$.

- *Function*s are part of mathematics. They involve the concept that one number can be determined by its relationship with another. A dozen always consists of 12 units, for example. If you were buying two dozen eggs, you'd be buying $12 \times 2 = 24$ eggs.

- *Patterns* are the predictable repeat of a situation. For example, if someone told you the first four numbers in a pattern were 1, 2, 3, and 4 and asked you what the next number was, you'd say "5" pretty fast. This simple pattern involves adding 1 to each number to get the next one. Patterns on the test are more complicated than this one, but, if you keep your wits about you, you can figure out how to solve them.

For additional information and guidance on solving problems related to algebra, functions, and patterns, see Chapter 8.

Warming Up to the Test Format

The Mathematical Reasoning test is 115 minutes long and consists of four different question formats, including multiple-choice, drag-and-drop, fill-in-the-blank, and hot-spot items. In the sections that follow, we describe these question types in detail and provide sample questions to make you more familiar with each question type. For more about responding to GED test questions on a computer, check out *GED Test For Dummies*, 3rd Edition (Wiley), which covers the topic in some detail.

To get ready for the Math test, relax and realize that math is your friend — perhaps not a lifetime friend but a friend at least until you finish the test. You also need to consider that you've been using math all your life without ever realizing it. When you tell a friend that you'll be over in 20 minutes, for example, you use math. When you see a sale sign in the store and mentally figure out whether you can afford the sale-priced item, you use math. When you complain about the poor mileage your car gets (and can prove it), you use math. You already know more math than you thought, and we show you the rest in this chapter.

Answering multiple-choice and drag-and-drop questions

The multiple-choice questions on the Math test are pretty straightforward. You're given some information or a figure and asked to answer the question based on that info. The question provides four answer choices, and you must select the correct answer. Here are a couple examples of multiple-choice questions.

Because you're not penalized for guessing, if you don't know the answer to a multiple-choice or drag-and-drop question, go ahead and guess, but don't make a wild guess. To improve your chances of guessing the correct answer, try to eliminate as many obviously wrong answers as possible before guessing. If you can eliminate two of the four answer choices, you have a 50/50 chance of guessing correctly. With a wild guess, your chances are only one in four, or 25 percent.

Milton wanted to be taller than his father, who was 2 yards tall. Milton was 5 feet 10 inches tall even when he stretched. How much taller would Milton have to grow to be taller than his father by at least an inch?

(A) 1 inch

(B) 2 inches

(C) 3 inches

(D) 4 inches

The first thing you have to do with questions like this one is make sure all measurements are in the same format. Two yards equals 6 feet (1 yard equals 3 feet). So Milton is 2 inches shorter than his father. The question asks how much he would have to grow to be at least 1 inch taller than his father. If he were to grow 3 inches, he would have reached that goal. Choice (C) is correct.

Samantha was a super salesperson and by far the best salesperson at Industrial Chemical and Explosives Ltd. She was so good that she knew that she had to work for only three months, not only to beat the sales records of her fellow salespeople but also to boost the total sales for the company substantially. The following chart appeared in the company's annual report. In which quarter do you think Samantha made all her sales?

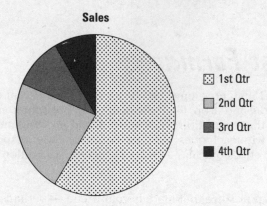

Sales

- ▨ 1st Qtr
- ▢ 2nd Qtr
- ▨ 3rd Qtr
- ■ 4th Qtr

(A) first

(B) second

(C) third

(D) fourth

The graph shows that the majority of sales were made in the first quarter, and if Samantha's boasts were correct, the majority of those sales would have been made by her. In the other nine months of the year, without her sales, the sales slipped considerably. In a graph such as this one, the area of the segment of the circle represents the data. Choice (A) is correct.

Providing the answer in fill-in-the-blank items

Fill-in-the-blank items require that you fill in the answer without the benefit of four answer choices to choose from. Often, they involve some calculation, using the information provided in the item. We walk you through answering two fill-in-the-blank questions in this section.

Demitri wanted to buy a new TV set. His old one had a diagonal measurement of 32 inches, but he wanted to buy a 50-inch diagonal set. The new TV set would be [   ] inches wider, measured diagonally.

To answer this question, you have to find the difference between the two TV sets. The new set would be 50 – 32 = 18 inches wider, measured diagonally.

Carol found a part-time job to augment her scholarship. She was paid $13.45 an hour and was promised a 15% raise after three months. Business had been very poor during that period, and the owner of the business called Carol in to explain that he could afford only an 11% raise but would reassess the raise in the next quarter, depending on how business was. With this raise, Carol's new hourly rate would be [   ].

Carol's new salary would be calculated at the rate of $13.45 times 11%, or $13.45 × 1.11 = $14.93 (to the nearest penny). If you want to calculate the amount of an 11% raise, you can multiply by 111% (100% + 11% = 111%, or 1.11 expressed as a decimal).

Responding to hot-spot questions

Hot spots are areas on the computer screen that record or respond to mouse clicks. On the computer version of the GED Mathematical Reasoning test, hot-spot questions typically ask you to plot a point on a graph or a coordinate plane. You simply move the mouse pointer to where you want the point to appear and click the left mouse button. To change your answer, you can remove a point by moving the mouse pointer over it and clicking the left mouse button. In this book, you simply darken the circle for the point you want to select, as in the following example:

Herb's Nutritional Supplements' profits increased 50% in its second year of business as compared to its first year. In its third year, profits increased 20% over the previous year's profits. If profits were $10 million in its first year, plot the point on the graph indicating the profits for the third year.

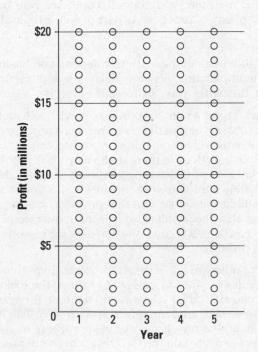

By the way, the correct answer is profits were $18 million in the third year, so your graph should look like the one below.

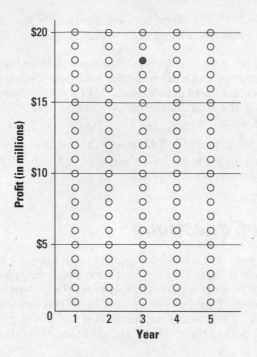

Getting Your Brain in the Game

Even if you were a math whiz at some point in your educational journey, math questions can paralyze a brain that's unaccustomed to dealing with them. To optimize your performance, you need a refresher course and plenty of practice. As part of your preparation, this book helps you do the following:

✔ **Master arithmetic fundamentals.** About half of the Math test depends on basic arithmetic (addition, subtraction, multiplication, division, decimals, and fractions). The better you know the fundamentals, the better you can do on the test.

✔ **Understand how to solve problems.** To get a handle on how to solve basic mathematical problems, do a lot of practice problems before the test. The more problems you solve, the more natural solving problems will become. Borrow or buy as many math books as you can, and use the sample questions in them to develop your problem-solving skills. (Be sure to get one that also provides the answers so you can check your work.) Check every answer immediately after you work the question. If you answered it incorrectly, figure out why. If you still have trouble with that problem, ask someone to explain the solution to you. You can also check online for free math quiz websites that provide worksheets with answers. YouTube is a good place to look for lessons on how to handle a particular type of math problem.

✔ **Understand the rules of math.** Textbooks are full of rules, theorems, hypotheses, and so on. Read over as many of these rules as you can, and try to explain the main ones to a friend. If you can explain a particular rule (the Pythagorean Theorem, for example) to a friend and she understands it, you've mastered the rule. If you can't explain it, ask someone to help you better understand the rule. If you're not sure where to start, begin by looking at the formula sheet provided on the GED test (check out an example in Chapter 3 or 10). Try to explain what each formula does and how it works.

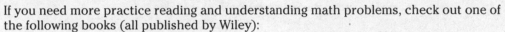

✔ **Sign up for a math prep class or a math study group.** The loneliest time is sitting in a room staring at a wrong answer without anyone to ask why it's wrong. If you're having trouble with math, swallow your pride and enroll in a math class or study group where you can get some help and have access to someone who can answer your questions.

✔ **Take practice tests and check your answers.** Chapter 3 provides a diagnostic test, and Chapter 10 features a full-length practice test. As you take these tests, answer every question and adhere to the time limits. Then, be sure to check your answers. Going through the answer explanations can help you figure out which areas you need more work on. Even if you get an answer correct, reading the explanation can be helpful.

The only part of the test you can't duplicate is the feeling of sitting in the examination room just before you start the test. But the more practice tests you take, the more comfortable you'll be when test day finally arrives.

✔ **Get familiar with the calculator ahead of time.** You're probably familiar with calculators that add, subtract, multiply, and divide. The calculator included on-screen in the GED Math test is a scientific calculator, which means it does all those operations and a whole lot more, such as calculating fractions, percentages, exponents, and problems involving parentheses. For more about the calculator, see the later section "Solving questions with and without a calculator."

If you need more practice reading and understanding math problems, check out one of the following books (all published by Wiley):

- *Basic Math and Pre-Algebra For Dummies,* by Mark Zegarelli

- *Basic Math and Pre-Algebra Workbook For Dummies,* by Mark Zegarelli

- *Math Word Problems For Dummies,* by Mary Jane Sterling

Reading and Deciphering Math Questions

What all the GED test sections have in common is that they all assess, in one way or another, reading comprehension; if you can't read and understand the items, you can't answer them. But reading the words isn't always enough — you need to grasp the meaning of what you read and be able to extract the information necessary to answer the question. In the following sections, we explain how to extract the information you need from a math question and offer guidance on what to do if the question contains too much information or doesn't have the information you need to answer it.

Practice reading problems in old math textbooks. Don't worry about the grade level or even the content. If it's full of problems to solve, it'll work.

Extracting the info you need

When reading a math problem, be an active reader. Ask yourself the following questions and jot down your answers on the scratchpad provided by the testing center:

✔ What does this problem want me to find?

✔ What details does it provide to help me find the answer?

✔ How can I calculate the answer?

✔ What is the answer in general terms?

Here's an example:

Jennifer wants an area rug to cover the floor of her bedroom, which is 16 feet by 14 feet, leaving a space of 1 foot from each wall. What is the perimeter of the rug?

Granted, this is a fairly easy question to answer, but you could get tripped up if you misread the question or didn't read it to the end and assumed that the question was asking you to calculate the square footage of the rug. The question actually asks you to determine the *perimeter,* the distance around the rug. It provides you with the floor's dimensions, 16 feet by 14 feet. To calculate the answer, you need to subtract 2 feet from the length and width of the room to leave a 1-foot space around the rug. You then add the adjusted width and length together and multiply by 2: $(14+12) \times 2 = 26 \times 2 = 52$

If possible, draw a picture to illustrate the problem. Illustrations enable you to envision the problem you're being asked to solve and how the information provided fits into the picture.

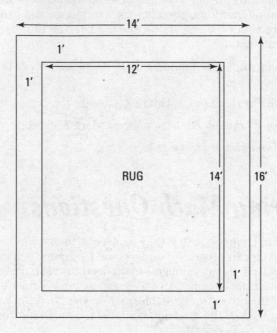

Ignoring extraneous information

Some of the questions on the Math test may have extra information that you don't need; in those cases, just ignore it. The people who write the test questions include extra information for a reason — extra information can make guessing more difficult and separate the test-takers who are paying attention from those who aren't. Sometimes, extra information is put in to make the question a bit more realistic. You don't want to disregard anything essential to solving the problem.

While reading the following question, try to visualize the situation and consider where the plot takes an extreme turn. This is usually the place where the information turns from important to irrelevant, or vice versa.

Kenny, Dharma, and Sophie went out for a snack after school. The wall of their favorite burger place has the following menu:

Item	Calories (kcal)	Fat (g)	Cost ($)
Hamburger	780	44	4.09
Bacon Cheeseburger	1,340	75	6.09
Chicken Wrap	450	25	1.69
French Fries	360	17	1.59
Chocolate Muffin	450	15	2.10
Chocolate Chip Cookie	160	7	1.00
Soda	220	0	1.49

Their total bill came to $24.31, and after a long discussion, they decided to tip the server 15%. What was the server's tip?

(A) $2.92

(B) $3.00

(C) $3.65

(D) $4.86

The first part of this item may be interesting, but it's irrelevant. The relevant information is the part that asks about the server's tip. The only important information is the amount of the bill and the percentage of the tip. So you multiply the total bill by 15% to get the tip: $24.31 \times .15 = \$3.65$ rounded to the nearest penny, Choice (C).

Deciding what to do when you don't have enough info

Some questions may not give you enough information to solve the problem. For example, a question may ask for a conclusion that you can't make from the information given. Even if you know some information that would help you solve the problem, don't use it.

You bring with you to the test the knowledge of what the basic operations are and how to use them. You aren't expected to know the dimensions of some fictional character's room or how well a character does on his reading scores. You're expected to know how to solve problems and to leave the specifics of the problems to the GED test-makers.

Not every question on the GED Math test is solvable. If you come across a question that doesn't include enough information to solve the problem or can't be answered with the information given, don't panic! Reread the question to make sure it can't be answered and then choose the appropriate answer choice, which is usually "not enough information given" or some variation.

Don't assume that when a question includes the answer choice "not enough information given," it's a clue to mean that you don't have enough information, because some questions that can be solved include this answer choice to make you think. Use this choice only when you've already determined that the question can't be solved.

Carmen bought a new Thunderbolt 8 as a gift to himself. He was impressed with its shiny aluminum wheels, all-electronic dashboard, and ventilated leather seats. The acceleration made him feel like a race car driver. He opted for rustproofing and a deluxe GPS and sound system. He negotiated with the salesperson for several hours to get a monthly payment he could barely afford. What were his annual insurance premiums if he was under 25?

(A) $4,159

(B) $4,638

(C) $5,200

(D) not enough information given

This question includes a lot of information; unfortunately, none of it enables you to answer the question, so Choice (D) is the only answer possible.

Using the Mathematical Reasoning Test's Special Features

During the Mathematical Reasoning test, you can use the on-screen calculator provided by the GED Testing Service for all but the first five questions. Before you start celebrating, remember that the calculator is an instrument that makes calculations easier. It doesn't solve problems or perform other miracles. You still have to solve the problems, using the computer between your ears.

The test also has a formula sheet. This feature also isn't a miracle to work out problems for you. It's just a memory aid if you don't remember the formulas. And as a special treat, the Math test also provides symbols for you to use in the fill-in-the blank items as needed. We explore all these features in the following sections.

Solving questions with and without a calculator

For all but the first five items on the Math test, you can use a calculator. You have to finish the first five items before you go on to questions that use the calculator. To pull up the calculator on the computerized GED Math test, click on the calculator icon. A calculator — a Texas Instruments TI-30XS calculator to be exact — appears on-screen.

If you prefer, you can bring your own calculator, but it must be the make and model approved by the GED Testing Service. Visit www.gedtestingservice.com/testers/calculator to find out which make and model of hand-held calculator is permitted. This site also contains a link to watch a video demonstration of the calculator. We strongly encourage you to watch the video. It's a good idea to get familiar with the calculator before taking the GED test.

Often, solving a problem without a calculator is easier, especially with multiple-choice questions where you have four answer choices to choose from. And the more questions you practice in your head, the easier it will be. Here are some ways to practice solving problems in your head (without a calculator):

- When you go shopping, add up the items as you put them in the cart.

- Calculate discounts off items you see or buy when you shop.

- Be the first at your table in a restaurant to figure out the tip. And for bonus practice, figure out different tip percentages on your bill, such as 10, 15, 18, and 20 percent tips.

For multiple-choice questions, sometimes estimating the answer to a question is easier and faster. For example, 4.2×8.9 is almost 4×9, which equals 36. If you see only one answer choice that's close to 36, that answer is probably correct. If you see that all the answer choices are close to 36, however, you need to spend time calculating the exact answer. Although you may be able to solve problems in your head, always work them out to verify you have the correct answer.

Refreshing your memory with the formula sheet

The GED Math test includes a formula sheet with a list of formulas you may need for the test. You simply click on the formula icon to make the page of formulas appear. Unfortunately, no genie will appear to tell you which formula to use. Figuring out which formula you need is your job.

To get familiar with the formulas you may need on the GED test, study the formulas in this book (you can find a list of formulas in the practice tests in Chapters 3 and 10), and make sure you know their purpose. Then make sure you understand what kind of problem you can use each formula for. For example, if you have a formula for the volume of a rectangular cube and the question asks you how many cubic feet of water a swimming pool contains, you know this formula will let you work out the answer. If the question asks you how many tiles it'd take to go around the rim of the pool, you need another formula.

Inserting special symbols

When answering fill-in-the-blank items, you sometimes need special symbols. Fortunately, the Math test provides such symbols on the screen behind the special icon. These symbols are mainly math operators, such as plus and minus signs, greater than or less than signs, and so on. You have to know what they mean and how to use them. To make a symbol appear in the fill-in-the-blank box on the test, click the symbols icon, and then click the symbol you want to include in the box.

Managing Your Time for the Math Test

Try not to be intimidated by the word *math* or the subject as a whole. A math teacher once said that mathematicians are lazy people — they always use the easiest way to find the right answer. We don't want to insult or irritate any mathematicians by calling them lazy, but finding the easiest way to solve a problem is usually the right way. If your way is too long and complicated, it's probably not right.

The Mathematical Reasoning test allows you 115 minutes to complete 46 to 50 questions. You must answer the first five items without using the calculator. The rest of your time is yours to divide any way you see fit. Just remember that you have to answer a question to get a mark.

On the computerized GED test, each question is given a specific number of points depending on how difficult it is. That means that each version of the test may have a different number of questions, but each test has the same number of points. Don't worry if you find out after you leave that you had fewer or more items than a friend. It will all work out.

To help you manage your time for the Math test, check out the following suggestions:

✔ **Stay on schedule.** Being able to manage your time is the most important indicator of success on the Math test. If you can keep to your schedule of less than 1½ minutes per question, you'll have enough time to go over your answers and make any changes necessary after you finish solving all the questions.

With such a tight schedule for taking the Math test, you have no time to panic. Aside from the fact that panicking distracts you from your overall goal, it also takes time — and you have very little time to spare. So relax and just do your best — save the panicking for another day.

✔ **Know when to move ahead.** If you don't see what's being asked by a question within a few seconds, reread the question and try again. If it still isn't clear, go on to the next question. Spending all your time trying to solve one problem at the expense of the others isn't a good idea. If you have time left at the end, you can always go back.

✔ **Keep an eye on the time.** The timer on the computer screen is your only time-management tool. You're not allowed to bring any electronics into the testing area.

Chapter 3

Uncovering Your Strengths and Weaknesses with a Diagnostic Test

• •

*B*efore committing to any serious training regimen for the GED Mathematical Reasoning (Math) test, take the diagnostic test in this chapter and check the answers and explanations to identify the skills you need to work on most. This approach enables you to focus your efforts on your weakest areas, so you don't waste a lot of time on what you already know.

Taking the Diagnostic Test

The GED Mathematical Reasoning test comprises 50 questions intended to measure general mathematics skills and problem-solving ability. The questions are based on short readings that may include a graph, chart, or figure. The test generally takes about 115 minutes to complete. The good news is that the diagnostic test in this chapter isn't quite that long and requires less of a time commitment. However, if you need more time, consider whether the extra time you need is in reading and deciphering the questions or in performing the necessary computations.

If your problem is reading, try some simple techniques to speed up your reading. You can enter "speed reading" in your favorite search engine to find guidance.

If your time issue is with computations, practice, practice, practice. Doing computations is like mental athletics: You'll improve with practice. You may not make the Mathematical Olympics, but you'll improve enough to pass this test.

Simply follow the instructions to mark your answer choices. When you're done, check your answers and read the answer explanations that immediately follow the test. Although you can simply look at the answer key to check which questions you answered correctly and which ones you missed, we encourage you to read the answer explanations for all questions to make sure that you understand how to approach similar problems. Because this is a diagnostic test, wrong answers are actually more valuable than correct answers because your mistakes shed light on areas where you need the most preparation. A few extra minutes on the answers and explanations can make all the difference on the actual GED test.

Formulas you may need are given on the page before the first test question. Only some of the questions require you to use a formula, and you may not need all the formulas provided. *Note:* If you can memorize the formulas and understand how to use them before beginning the test, you'll save a bit of time; you then can use that time for review or for more challenging questions.

Unless you require accommodations, you'll be taking the actual GED test on a computer instead of marking your answers on a separate answer sheet, as you do for the diagnostic and practice tests in this book. You'll see clickable ovals and fill-in-the-blank text boxes, and you'll be able to click with your mouse and drag and drop items where indicated. We formatted the questions and answer choices in this book to make them appear as similar as possible to the real GED test, but we had to retain A, B, C, and D choices for marking your answers, and we provide a separate answer sheet for you to do so.

You can get a good idea of what the tests look like on a computer by going to www.gedtestingservice.com/educators/freepracticetest. While you're there, check out the FAQ.

Answer Sheet for Mathematical Reasoning Diagnostic Test

1. Ⓐ Ⓑ Ⓒ Ⓓ	21. Ⓐ Ⓑ Ⓒ Ⓓ
2. Ⓐ Ⓑ Ⓒ Ⓓ	22. Ⓐ Ⓑ Ⓒ Ⓓ
3. Ⓐ Ⓑ Ⓒ Ⓓ	23. [_____]
4. Ⓐ Ⓑ Ⓒ Ⓓ	24. Ⓐ Ⓑ Ⓒ Ⓓ
5. Ⓐ Ⓑ Ⓒ Ⓓ	25. [_____]
6. Ⓐ Ⓑ Ⓒ Ⓓ	26. Ⓐ Ⓑ Ⓒ Ⓓ
7. Ⓐ Ⓑ Ⓒ Ⓓ	27. Ⓐ Ⓑ Ⓒ Ⓓ
8. [_____]	28. Ⓐ Ⓑ Ⓒ Ⓓ
9. Ⓐ Ⓑ Ⓒ Ⓓ	29. Ⓐ Ⓑ Ⓒ Ⓓ
10. Ⓐ Ⓑ Ⓒ Ⓓ	30. [_____]
11. [_____]	31. Ⓐ Ⓑ Ⓒ Ⓓ
12. [_____]	32. Ⓐ Ⓑ Ⓒ Ⓓ
13. Ⓐ Ⓑ Ⓒ Ⓓ	33. Ⓐ Ⓑ Ⓒ Ⓓ
14. Ⓐ Ⓑ Ⓒ Ⓓ	34. Ⓐ Ⓑ Ⓒ Ⓓ
15. Ⓐ Ⓑ Ⓒ Ⓓ	35. Ⓐ Ⓑ Ⓒ Ⓓ
16. Ⓐ Ⓑ Ⓒ Ⓓ	36. [_____]
17. Ⓐ Ⓑ Ⓒ Ⓓ	37. Ⓐ Ⓑ Ⓒ Ⓓ
18. Ⓐ Ⓑ Ⓒ Ⓓ	38. [_____]
19. Ⓐ Ⓑ Ⓒ Ⓓ	39. [_____]
20. Ⓐ Ⓑ Ⓒ Ⓓ	40. Ⓐ Ⓑ Ⓒ Ⓓ

Mathematics Formula Sheet

Area	
Square	$A = s^2$
Rectangle	$A = lw$
Parallelogram	$A = bh$
Triangle	$A = \frac{1}{2}bh$
Trapezoid	$A = \frac{(b_1 + b_2)}{2}h$
Circle	$A = \pi r^2$

Perimeter	
Square	$P = 4s$
Rectangle	$P = 2l + 2w$
Triangle	$P = s_1 + s_2 + s_3$
Circumference	$C = 2\pi r$ or $C = \pi d$, $\pi = 3.14$

Surface area and volume	Surface area	Volume
Rectangular prism	$SA = 2lw + 2lh + 2wh$	$V = lwh$
Right prism	$SA = ph + 2B$	$V = Bh$
Cylinder	$SA = 2\pi rh + 2\pi r^2$	$V = \pi r^2 h$
Pyramid	$SA = \frac{1}{2}ps + B$	$V = \frac{1}{3}Bh$
Cone	$SA = \pi rs + \pi r^2$	$V = \frac{1}{3}\pi r^2 h$
Sphere	$SA = 4\pi r^2$	$V = \frac{4}{3}\pi r^3$
(p = perimeter of base with area B; $\pi = 3.14$)		

Data	
Mean	Mean is the average.
Median	Median is the middle value in an odd number of ordered values of a data set or the average of the two middle values in an even number of ordered values in a data set.

Algebra	
Slope of a line	$m = \frac{y_2 - y_1}{x_2 - x_1}$
Slope-intercept form of the equation of a line	$y = mx + b$
Point-slope form of the equation of a line	$y - y_1 = m(x - x_1)$
Standard form of a quadratic equation	$y = ax^2 + bx + c$
Quadratic formula	$x = \frac{-b \pm \sqrt{b^2 - 4ac}}{2a}$
Pythagorean theorem	$a^2 + b^2 = c^2$
Simple interest	$I = Prt$ (I = interest, P = principal, r = rate, t = time)
Distance	$D = rt$ (D = distance, r = rate, t = time)
Total cost	total cost = (number of units) × (price per unit)

GED Mathematics Diagnostic Test

Time: 90 minutes for 40 questions

Directions: Choose the appropriate answer for each question. Mark your answers on the answer sheet provided by filling in the corresponding oval, writing your answer in the blank box, or marking your answer on the graph.

1. Georgina is making sale signs for the Super Summer Sale at Benny's Big Beautiful Bargain Bin. Sales tax in Georgina's state is 5%. She makes a series of signs:

   Sign A: $\frac{1}{2}$ off all merchandise

   Sign B: Buy one item, get the second item of equal value free

   Sign C: 50% off all merchandise

   Sign D: Ten times your sales tax back

   What would a shrewd consumer notice about the signs?

   (A) Sign A offers a better buy.

   (B) Sign C offers the worst deal.

   (C) Sign D offers the worst deal.

   (D) No sign offers a better deal.

2. Irving is framing a painting. He draws the following diagram to help him make it:

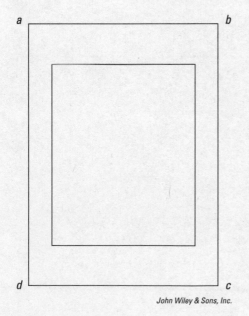

John Wiley & Sons, Inc.

   Which of the following is true about the diagram?

   (A) *ab* must be perpendicular to *ad*.

   (B) *ab* must be parallel to *bc*.

   (C) *ad* must be parallel to *ab*.

   (D) *ab* and *dc* must be perpendicular.

3. The Jackson family is building a deck behind their house. The deck is to be 20 feet long and 25 feet wide, and the decking material is priced at $47.50 a square yard. The cost of the decking material would be:

   (A) $23,750.00

   (B) $26,391.00

   (C) $2,660.00

   (D) $7,916.83

4. Margaret Manningford, the Chief Financial Officer of Aggravated Manufacturing Corporation, must deliver a presentation to the Board of Directors. She has been instructed to analyze the sales of each of the company's product lines as shown in the following graph, research each product's net profit per unit (sales price minus manufacturing cost), and recommend one product line to drop — the product line that generates the least amount of net revenue.

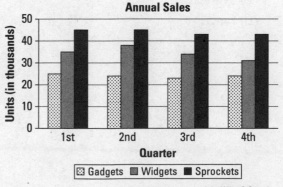

John Wiley & Sons, Inc.

Go on to next page ⇨

When researching manufacturing costs, Margaret discovered that net profit per gadget was twice that of sprockets and net profit per sprocket was half that of widgets. Which product line should Margaret recommend be dropped?

(A) gadgets

(B) widgets

(C) sprockets

(D) not enough information given

5. Eager to get admitted to the college of his choice, John is obsessive about his final grades and class standing. On John's final report, his grades were as follows:

Computer Studies: 97

English: 98

Mathematics: 99

Physical Education: 87

Science: 97

Social Studies: 94

Spanish: 86

The results for John's entire class were

Average: 93.27

Median: 96

Mode: 97

Range: 14

In considering John's average, median, mode, and range, and comparing them to the results of his class, which of these measures would be of most interest to the admissions office of a college?

(A) median

(B) mode

(C) average

(D) range

6. Mary was trying to explain how the length of time she could run each morning had improved each month since she started, except for the month she twisted her ankle. She drew the following graph to show her friends Josef and Kevin the average length of time (in minutes) she ran each day each month:

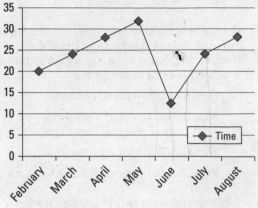

John Wiley & Sons, Inc.

Between which two months did Mary see the biggest improvement in her time?

(A) February to April

(B) March to May

(C) June to July

(D) July to August

Go on to next page

7. Gavin and Tina were comparing their report cards:

Gavin's Report Card

Subject	Grade (%)
Mathematics	82
Social Studies	86
Science	92
Language Arts	84
Physical Education	96

Tina's Report Card

Subject	Grade (%)
Mathematics	80
Social Studies	92
Science	77
Language Arts	87
Physical Education	84

The teacher told them that the ratio of their total grades was very close. What is the ratio of Gavin's to Tina's grades on these report cards?

(A) 10:11

(B) 21:22

(C) 11:10

(D) 22:21

8. In the series 4, 6, 10, 18, . . . , the first term that is a multiple of 11 is: [＿＿＿].

9. Sally follows the stock market very carefully. She has been following Dastardly Deeds Corporation the last few months, keeping track of her research in the following table:

Date	Closing Price (in U.S. Dollars)
August 7	14.03
August 17	16.12
September 1	14.73
September 9	14.01
September 16	14.94
September 20	15.06
September 23	15.19
September 24	15.19

Sally bought shares of the stock on September 24 and wants to make a 10% profit before selling it. She paid a 2.5% commission to her broker for buying and will pay the same for selling. What is the lowest price for which Sally can sell each of her shares to break even?

(A) $17.13

(B) $17.57

(C) $16.83

(D) $15.57

10. If $22.4 = \dfrac{56a}{5a+10}$, what is the value of a?

(A) 0

(B) –56

(C) 4

(D) –4

> *Question 11 refers to the following graph.*

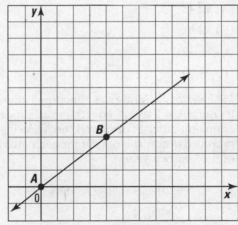

John Wiley & Sons, Inc.

11. Calculate the slope of the line AB. The slope of AB is: [＿＿＿].

12. Gilbert's Gadgets just hired 14 new employees. If the company's total number of employees is now 156, the newly hired employees represent how much of a percentage increase in employees? Round your answer to the nearest whole number: [＿＿＿].

Go on to next page

13. An assembly line packages 12-ounce jars of peanut butter with a tolerance of $\frac{1}{4}$ ounce. Jars not within the tolerance are recycled. Which of the following inequalities can be used to determine whether jars of peanut butter are recycled?

    p is the weight of peanut butter in each jar.

    (A) $|p-0.25| \leq 12$

    (B) $|p-0.25| \geq 12$

    (C) $|p-12| \leq 0.25$

    (D) $|p-12| \geq 0.25$

14. Rosa and Warren are shopping for carpets for their home and are looking for the best carpet at the best price. Carnie's Custom Carpet Emporium offers them a wool carpet for $26.75 per square yard. Flora's Fine Flooring says it will match that same carpet for only $2.45 per square foot, while Dora's Deep Discount Designs offers them an 8-by-12-foot rug of the same carpet material for $292.80. What is the lowest price per square foot offered to Rosa and Warren?

    (A) $2.45

    (B) $2.97

    (C) $2.19

    (D) $3.05

15. Miscellaneous Motors is concerned about its output at Plant A. For its annual report, company officials prepared the following graphs to show the output for each quarter of the last two years:

Output at Plant A – 2013

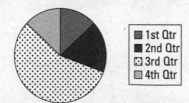

- 1st Qtr
- 2nd Qtr
- 3rd Qtr
- 4th Qtr

Output at Plant A – 2014

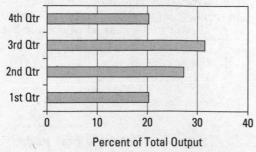

Percent of Total Output

Which quarter showed a dramatic decrease in production from 2013 to 2014?

(A) third quarter

(B) first quarter

(C) fourth quarter

(D) second quarter

16. Mr. and Mrs. Smith are looking to expand their two-story house and have calculated that they need at least another 750 square feet to live comfortably. They want to use the basement level for storage and the rest for living. A contractor quotes them $23.80 per square foot for the renovation without redecoration. A real estate agent tells them that they can increase the value of their home by about $26,000 by building the addition. They estimate there will be an additional $7,500 in expenses involved in selling the house and moving. If they want to add as much additional space as possible for the $26,000 they will recover and not take a loss on moving expenses, how much more space can they add if they can get the higher value for their home and keep their moving expenses within their budget?

    (A) 878 square feet

    (B) 778 square feet

    (C) 84 square yards

    (D) not enough information given

17. Lori is shopping for a new vehicle. She drives about 18,000 miles per year and expects gasoline to average $3.50 a gallon during the 5 years she plans to own the car. She has narrowed her choice to four vehicles she loves equally: the Goomba, the Moomba, the Toomba, and the Zoomba.

Vehicle	Price	Miles per Gallon
Goomba	$18,500	27
Moomba	$21,700	32
Toomba	$22,900	35
Zoomba	$27,300	29

Which car will cost the least over the 5 years Lori plans to own it?

(A) Goomba

(B) Moomba

(C) Toomba

(D) Zoomba

Go on to next page

18. Alicia has just received her midterm report card. Her grades are as follows:

Alicia's Report Card

Subject	Grade (%)
English	82
Geography	76
Mathematics	68
Physical Education	87
Physics	82

To get into the college of her choice, she needs an average of 80%. Physical Education is her best subject. By how many percentage points will she need to improve this mark, assuming all her other subjects stay the same, to get into college?

(A) 1

(B) 92

(C) 10

(D) 5

19. Peter has an amazing recipe for rice pilaf. For each 1 cup of rice, he adds 2 cups of vegetable soup and a quarter cup of lentils. This weekend, Peter is having a large dinner party and figures he needs to cook $3\frac{1}{2}$ cups of rice for his guests. How much of the other two ingredients should he use?

(A) 7 cups of soup and $\frac{7}{8}$ cup of lentils

(B) $3\frac{1}{2}$ cups of soup and $\frac{1}{2}$ cup of lentils

(C) 7 cups of soup and 1 cup of lentils

(D) 1 cup of soup and 7 cups of lentils

20. What is the probability of rolling 3 consecutive fives on a 6-sided die?

(A) 1 in 6

(B) 1 in 36

(C) 1 in 216

(D) 1 in 1,296

21. The Symons are redecorating a room in their house. They have some interesting ideas. They want to put a rug on the floor surrounded by a border of oak laminate. They are considering teak paneling halfway up each wall. In addition, they may cut away part of the ceiling to put in a skylight. This is a diagram of their room:

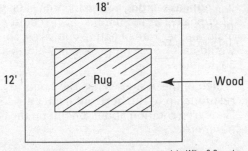

John Wiley & Sons, Inc.

The rug costs $8.95 a square foot, and oak laminate costs $17.59 a square yard. One rug they like is 16 feet by 10 feet, leaving just a little area around the rug for wood. At the store, however, they see another rug that is only 12 feet by 8 feet for $860.00, but it's just the right pattern and colors for their room. Which floor treatment is less expensive?

(A) both are the same cost

(B) the larger rug

(C) the smaller rug without the paneling

(D) the smaller rug

22. Brad is a secret shopper for Fred's Friendly Furniture store. His boss wants to start a new advertising campaign: "Fred's Friendly Furniture — always lower than the average price of our competitors." Brad's job is to shop several stores to make sure the claim is accurate. Brad's results are recorded in the following table:

Item	Store A	Store B	Store C	Store D	Fred's
Couch	$1,729	$1,749	$1,729	$1,699	$1,719
Dining room set	$4,999	$4,899	$5,019	$4,829	$4,899
Loveseat	$1,259	$1,199	$1,279	$1,149	$1,229
Coffee table	$459	$449	$479	$429	$449
Reclining chair	$759	$799	$739	$699	$739

Which item can't be advertised as "lower than the average price"?

(A) couch

(B) dining room set

(C) love seat

(D) coffee table

Go on to next page

23. In a cupcake-eating contest, Sarah eats 12 cupcakes in 18 minutes. If she could maintain her rate of eating cupcakes, she would eat [ ] cupcakes in 2 hours and 30 minutes.

24. Which of these shapes has the same relationship to the horizontal after a 90-degree rotation about a point on the perimeter?

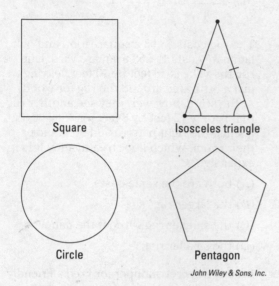

Square   Isosceles triangle

Circle   Pentagon

John Wiley & Sons, Inc.

(A) isosceles triangle

(B) circle

(C) pentagon

(D) not enough information given

25. In a large company, the top four positions are organized as follows:

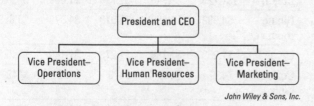

John Wiley & Sons, Inc.

Each department has the following budget:

Department	Budget ($ Millions)
Operations	16.8
Human Resources	2.1
Marketing	15.6

What is the ratio of the largest budget to the smallest budget? [ ]

26. A company has doubled its sales from the first to the third quarters. Which of the following graphs indicates this pattern?

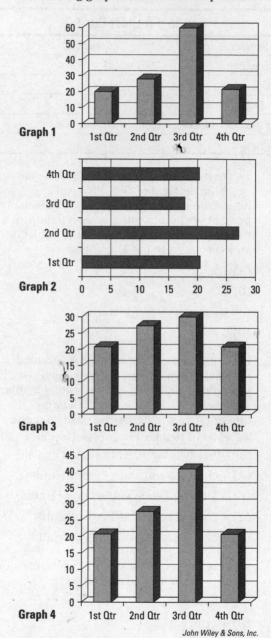

John Wiley & Sons, Inc.

(A) graph 1

(B) graph 2

(C) graph 3

(D) graph 4

Go on to next page

27. A 6-foot-tall forester standing 25 feet from a tree uses his digital range finder and calculates the distance between the top of his head and the top of the tree to be 36 feet. How tall is the tree?

    (A) $\sqrt{36} - \sqrt{25} + 6$

    (B) $\sqrt{671}$

    (C) 25

    (D) $6 + \sqrt{671}$

28. The equation that relates sound volume to amplifier settings for one particular amplifier is $V = S^2$, where V is the volume in decibels and S is the volume setting. If the volume is 144 decibels, what is the volume setting on the amplifier?

    (A) 9

    (B) 10

    (C) 11

    (D) 12

Questions 29–31 refer to this table.

Average Mileage and Annual Fuel Cost of Selected Vehicles

Vehicle	Mileage (Miles per Gallon) City	Mileage (Miles per Gallon) Highway	Annual Cost ($)*
A	23	28	840
B	21	29	875
C	19	25	1,000
D	18	24	1,050
E	17	22	1,105
F	16	22	1,167
G	15	21	1,235
H	14	19	1,314
I	13	18	1,400
J	12	16	1,823

Annual cost includes 15,000 miles driven annually; 55% of the miles in the city and 45% on the highway; standard price of fuel

29. If you were in the market for a car and really liked the styling and features of car F but your practical side said that you should buy the most economical car and dream about the others, how much could you save over a 3-year period by buying the most economical car over car F?

    (A) $981

    (B) $1,167

    (C) $1,968

    (D) $656

30. What is the difference in miles per gallon between the mean highway mileage and the median of the highway mileages for these vehicles? [ ]

31. What is the approximate price of fuel used to calculate the annual fuel cost for each of these vehicles?

    (A) $3.50/gallon

    (B) $2.50/gallon

    (C) $2.00/gallon

    (D) $1.50/gallon

32. To answer a question in her mathematics class, Mary had to solve the following set of equations:

$$2x + 3y = 10$$
$$5x + 6y = 13$$

    What is the correct value of y?

    (A) –8

    (B) –6

    (C) 6

    (D) 8

Go on to next page

33. An international survey found the following information about participation in adult education:

Percent of Population over Age 21 Participating in Adult Education in the Year 2013

Country	Total Participation Rate (%)
Denmark	62.3
Hungary	17.9
Norway	43.1
Portugal	15.5
United States	66.4

Assuming the adult population (over 21) of Denmark is 4 million, of Portugal is 6 million, of Hungary is 7 million, and of Norway is 3 million, which of those four countries has the fewest adults participating in adult education?

(A) Denmark

(B) Portugal

(C) Hungary

(D) Norway

34. Gina has the following six bills to pay this month:

Bill Payable To	Amount
Electricity	$123.00
Gas	$131.00
Internet	$65.00
Car payment	$113.00
Credit card	$114.00
Rent	$739.00

She has $789.65 in her checking account. If she deposits her paycheck of $754.37 and pays all her bills, what will her checking account balance be?

(A) $259.12

(B) $249.02

(C) $249.12

(D) $259.02

35. Daniel needs $165 to buy books for his Philosophy course. He goes online and finds a loan for up to $200 for one month at $20 interest. He decides to borrow $165 to buy the books and work extra hours to pay off the loan.

When Daniel applies for the loan, he reads the contract carefully and notices that after the initial one-month period, the interest rate climbs to 20% per month, and the calculation includes both the previous month's principal and the interest. If he earns $11.00 per hour, how many extra hours (rounded up to the nearest half-hour) would he have to work to pay off the entire loan, including interest, at the end of the second month?

(A) 20.5

(B) 20

(C) 21

(D) 24

36. What is the surface area of the following cone? ☐

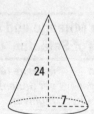

37. If Greg borrows $150 for 18 months and repays $165, including simple interest, what rate of interest was he charged?

(A) 6.7%

(B) 8.0%

(C) 4.0%

(D) 4.6%

Go on to next page

38. What is the area of the shaded portion of the following rectangle If all dimensions are given in inches? [   ] inches

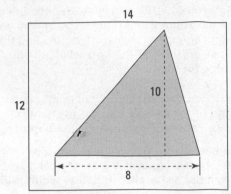

39. From the numbers listed, what number should go in the box?

    2, 5, 3, 11, 4, [   ], 38, . . .

40. A rectangle 7 units wide and 6 units high is represented on a graph. If three of the corners are placed at (–1, 3), (6, 3), and (6, –3), where should the fourth corner be placed?

    (A) (–1, –3)

    (B) (1, 3)

    (C) (–1, 3)

    (D) (1, –3)

STOP DO NOT TURN THE PAGE UNTIL TOLD TO DO SO.
DO NOT RETURN TO A PREVIOUS TEST.

Answers and Explanations

This section provides you with answers and explanations for the Mathematical Reasoning diagnostic test you just completed. The answers tell you whether you answered the questions right or wrong, but the explanations are even more important. They explain why your answers were right or wrong and give you some hints about the areas tested. Reading the explanations and checking the areas where your answers weren't the best will help you identify where you should spend more time preparing for the test.

1. **(D) No sign offers a better deal.** This problem tests your understanding of numbers and their equivalents (integers, fractions, decimals, and percents) in a real-world situation. Signs A, B, C, and D give customers 50% off. For more about percentages, see Chapter 5.

2. **(A) *ab* must be perpendicular to *ad*.** This problem involves measurement and geometry and tests your understanding of perpendicular and parallel lines in a geometrical figure. Frames are rectangles. Each pair of opposite sides must be parallel, and intersecting sides (*ab* and *ad*) must be perpendicular. See Chapter 7 for more about geometry.

3. **(C) $2,660.00.** This problem tests your knowledge and mastery of number operations and number sense. It also requires a conversion of units from square feet to square yards. Use a calculator because numerous conversions are involved, including the following:

   Area of the deck is $20 \times 25 = 500$ square feet

   9 square feet = 1 square yard

   500 square feet $\frac{500}{9} = 55.56$ square yards

   Because you have to buy building materials a full square yard at a time, you'd have to buy 56 square yards. One square yard of decking costs $47.50, and 56 square yards of decking (rounded to the nearest square yard) cost $56 \times \$47.50 = \$2,660.00$.

   If you got $23,750.00, you forgot to convert square feet to square yards. $7,916.83 would mean that you thought that there were 3 square feet in a square yard. $26,391.00 is a calculation error, as is any answer other than the correct one.

   When presented with a problem, read it carefully and make sure that the units are consistent. If you must convert units, be careful to do it correctly, and always double-check your calculations. See Chapter 6 for more about solving word problems and Chapter 7 for calculating area.

   If you are not familiar with all the conversions, such as feet to yards, now is the time to learn them. Enter "linear measurement conversions" into your favorite search engine and start making a list to memorize.

4. **(C) sprockets.** Compare gadgets to sprockets first. The graph shows that the company sells a little over half the number of gadgets as it sells sprockets, so if gadgets are twice as profitable as sprockets, the company earns more from the sales of gadgets than it does from the sales of sprockets, so the company would be wise to keep the gadgets product line. Now, compare sprockets to widgets. You can tell from the graph that the company sells about 10% to 30% more sprockets than it does widgets, but if sprockets are 50% less profitable, the company makes more money selling widgets than it does sprockets, so the company would be wise to keep widgets. If the company keeps gadgets and widgets, and one product must be dropped, that product must be sprockets. This is one of those questions that can be completed by a careful reading of the item. That would lead you to the same conclusion as doing the question using the graphs. See Chapter 7 for guidance on how to extract data from graphs and tables.

5. **(C) average.** This problem tests your skills in determining what a question wants you to answer. You're asked to consider the presented data to calculate the measures of John's performance and compare them to those of his classmates. However, the question doesn't ask you to do the calculations.

   If you really wanted to do the calculations, you would find the *average* by adding the marks and dividing by the total number of marks. The *median* is the middle value; in John's case, the middle value is the fourth value, which just happens to be equal to the fifth value. His average was 94, his median was 97, and the range of his marks was 13. The *mode* is the most frequent, or common, value in the list, and the *range* is the difference between the largest and smallest numbers. This question is a good example of why some familiarity with mathematical vocabulary is an asset but reading the problem carefully and considering the answers is far more important. You're not asked for the numerical values of any of these measures but an opinion as to which is most important to a college. The admissions department of a college would put the most weight on John's average because it's a reflection of how well he did in all his subjects. For more about mean, median, and mode, turn to Chapter 7.

6. **(C) June to July.** Mary has converted her story into a graph, and you're being asked to interpret the line graph in conjunction with her story. From February to April, Mary's time increased less than 10. No unit is mentioned, and the unit doesn't really matter, although it's probably minutes. From March to May, her time increased about the same — a little less than 10. From June to July, probably after she twisted her ankle, her time jumped slightly more than 10. And from July to August, her time increased by less than 5. Turn to Chapter 6 for guidance in solving word problems and Chapter 7 for more about reading and interpreting data in graphs.

7. **(D) 22:21.** Because Gavin and Tina have the same number of grades (5), you can compare their totals or their average grade to determine the ratio of their grades. Using the totals:

   The total of Gavin's marks is $82 + 86 + 92 + 84 + 96 = 440$.

   The total of Tina's marks is $80 + 92 + 77 + 87 + 84 = 420$.

   The ratio of Gavin's total to Tina's total is $\frac{440}{420} = \frac{22 \times 20}{21 \times 20} = \frac{22}{21}$

   To use their average grades, divide each of their totals by 5 grades:

   $440 \div 5 = 88$

   $420 \div 5 = 84$

   The ratio is then 88:84, which reduces to 22:21.

   Note that if one of the students had 6 grades and the other had 5, you'd have to use the ratio of the averages, not of the totals. See Chapter 6 for more about solving ratio and proportion problems.

8. **66.** This problem involves algebra, functions, and patterns. The numbers 4, 6, 10, and 18 form a *pattern* (also called a *series*). After looking carefully at the series, you see that the second term is formed by subtracting 1 from the first term and multiplying by 2. Try this on the third number: $(6-1) \times 2 = 10$. You've found your pattern. Continuing the series: 4, 6, 10, 18, 34, 66, . . . , the first term you come to that is a multiple of 11 is 66.

   You could also simply double the difference between the previous two numbers and add it to the second number to create the next one. For example, the difference between 4 and 6 is 2. Double that ($2 + 2 = 4$) and add it to the 6 ($4 + 6 = 10$) to get the next number. The difference between 6 and 10 is 4. Double that ($4 + 4 = 8$) and add it to the 10 ($8 + 10 = 18$) to get the next number. Continue with this pattern until you find the number you need. If you did not get this answer, either you have trouble with series or you miscalculated. In either case, you need more practice. Always remember that there are often more than two ways to answer such a question. Recognizing patterns requires a firm understanding of basic math, as presented in Chapter 5. Understanding functions (Chapter 9) is also helpful.

9. **(B) $17.57.** This problem involves data analysis and manipulation of numbers and is best done using a calculator. Most of the information given is irrelevant, except to decide that Simone may have bought at a high point. The important price to consider is $15.19. In addition to this price per share, Simone has to pay her broker 2.5% commission.

Therefore, her final price per share on September 24 is $15.19 + (0.025 \times \$15.19) = \$15.5697$. Because you're dealing with money, you have to round the number to two decimal places, making her final price per share $15.57. This amount of money came out of her bank account for each share she bought.

If Simone decides to sell the shares at this price, $15.57, she still has to pay her broker another 2.5% commission, or $0.025 \times \$15.57 = \$0.3893$. Rounded to two decimals, she has to pay a commission of $0.39 per share. She then receives the value of the shares, $15.57, minus the commission of $0.39, for a total of $15.18 per share — that is, for each share she sells, the broker deposits $15.18 into her account. Notice that this amount is less than the amount she paid for each share.

To make a 10% profit, Simone has to receive $15.57 per share plus $10\% = \$15.57 + 1.56 = \$17.13$ — after the commission. Set the equation up this way using x to represent the selling price:

$$1x - 0.025x = \$17.13$$
$$0.975x = \$17.13$$
$$x = \frac{\$17.13}{0.975} = \$17.57$$

This is a fairly complex question and needs careful reading, paying attention to what is written and what is asked. In addition, you have to do your calculations carefully to make sure that you get the correct answer. If you chose Choice (C) or any other answer besides Choice (B), you made a calculation error. Choosing Choice (A) means that you did not read carefully enough to add the commission, and selecting Choice (D) means that you neglected to figure in her profit. Read every question carefully, and because these are timed tests, try to increase your reading speed and accuracy to make sure you have time to answer all the questions without making careless mistakes. See Chapters 6 and 8 for more about solving word problems that involve algebra.

10. **(D) –4.** This question involves algebra. You have to solve a linear equation, as follows:

$$22.4 = \frac{56a}{5a + 10}$$

Cross-multiply and write this equation as $22.4(5a + 10) = 56a$. Then, getting rid of the parentheses, the equation looks like this: $112a + 224 = 56a$. Next, bring all the a's to the left and the numbers to the right, so you have $112a - 56a = -224$. Then, combine the a's to get $56a = -224$. Finally, divide both sides by 56 to get one a on the left: $a = -4$. Turn to Chapter 8 for additional guidance on solving linear equations.

11. $\frac{3}{4}$. The slope of a line is rise over run, so you can simply count the squares on the coordinate plane. Point A crosses the x and y axes at point (0, 0) and rises 3 squares up and runs 4 squares over to point B. Rise over run is 3 over 4, or $\frac{3}{4}$. For more complicated versions of problems like these, use this equation:

$$slope = \frac{y_2 - y_1}{x_2 - x_1}$$

In this example, you would use the coordinates that the line passes through. The coordinates for point A are (0, 0), meaning $x = 0$, $y = 0$. The coordinates for point B are (4, 3), meaning $x = 4$, $y = 3$. Because the line has a positive slope (is rising from left to right), you subtract the coordinates of the first point from those of the second:

$$slope = \frac{3-0}{4-0} = \frac{3}{4}$$

However, this is a timed test and not one to show off your ability with sophisticated solutions. If there's a simple way to do it, do it simply. See Chapter 9 for more about calculating a line's slope.

12. **10%.** If 14 new employees were hired, the company had $156 - 14 = 142$ employees before hiring the new people. To determine the percentage of change, divide the number of new employees by 142: $\frac{14}{142} = 0.0985$, which is 9.85%. Round that up to the nearest percent, and you have 10%. These computations are relatively simple, but take care that you get them correct. See Chapter 6 for more about solving percentage problems.

13. **(C)** $|p - 12| \leq 0.25$. The vertical lines around $p - 12$ ensure that $p - 12$ will be positive even if it's a negative value, so if $p - 12 = 7 - 12 = -5$, then $|7 - 12| = 5$. The weight of the jar minus the ideal jar weight must be within ±0.25 or it's recycled. Choice (C) is the correct answer. You can plug in 12.25 and 11.75 to check. See Chapter 6 for more about absolute value and Chapter 8 for more about inequalities.

14. **(A) $2.45.** Consider the price per square foot at each store:

Carnie's Custom Carpet Emporium: $26.75 per square yard is $26.75 \div 9 = $2.97 per square foot.

Flora's Fine Flooring: $2.45 per square foot.

Dora's Deep Discount Designs: The area of an 8-by-12-foot rug is $8 \times 12 = 96$ square feet. The cost for 96 square feet is $292.80, so the cost is $292.80 \div 96 = $3.05 per square foot.

Once again, you must convert to uniform units before performing calculations. Read carefully — the extra few seconds can pay dividends in correct answers. For guidance in solving word problems, turn to Chapter 6. See Chapter 7 to find out more about calculating area.

15. **(A) third quarter.** In this question, you're asked to analyze graphs to identify patterns in a workplace situation.

In the 2013 graph, the third quarter of 2013 produces over half of the output, whereas in 2014 it accounts for only slightly more than 30% of total output. The best answer for this question is the 3rd quarter.

Graphs have information everywhere, from the lines and bars to the titles, subtitles, and legends. Be sure to check the information written on the bottom and sides of the graph, as well as interpreting the graph itself.

See Chapter 7 to find out more about extracting data from graphs and tables.

16. **(B) 778 square feet.** This problem involves measurement, specifically area and money. Assuming that the estimate for renovation is accurate, the number of square feet of renovation that the Smiths can afford for $26,000 is $26,000 \div 23.80 = 1,092.44$ square feet. Round this number double to 1,093 square feet because you usually can't add part of a square foot. However, they estimate that they'll incur an additional $7,500 in expenses in moving. This means that the actual profit from the renovation would be $26,000 - $7,500 = $18,500. That allows them to add only $18,500 \div 23.80 = 777.31$, approximately 778 square feet when rounded up to the nearest square foot, which is just slightly more space than they wanted.

This is a problem involving calculations. If you read it carefully, you should have no problem figuring out the answer. There are some extra calculations provided at the beginning of the explanation to show you why omitting the moving costs will give you an incorrect answer.

Choice (B) is correct, and the other choices are incorrect because of calculation errors. Always double check your calculations.

Chapter 7 is the place to go to find out more about solving measurement problems.

17. **(A) Goomba.** Lori will own the car for 5 years, so you need to figure out which car is going to cost the least over those 5 years in terms of price plus fuel costs. Price is easy because it's given. To determine the fuel costs for each car over 5 years, use the following formula:

$$5 \text{ years} \times 18,000 \text{ miles} \times \frac{\$3.50}{\text{gallon}} \times \frac{1 \text{ gallon}}{x \text{ miles}} = \text{total cost}$$

Solve the equation for each vehicle by plugging in the number of miles per gallon for x:

$$\text{Goomba} = 5 \text{ years} \times 18,000 \text{ miles} \times \frac{\$3.50}{\text{gallon}} \times \frac{1 \text{ gallon}}{27 \text{ miles}} = \$11,666.66$$

$$\text{Moomba} = 5 \text{ years} \times 18,000 \text{ miles} \times \frac{\$3.50}{\text{gallon}} \times \frac{1 \text{ gallon}}{32 \text{ miles}} = \$9,843.75$$

$$\text{Toomba} = 5 \text{ years} \times 18,000 \text{ miles} \times \frac{\$3.50}{\text{gallon}} \times \frac{1 \text{ gallon}}{35 \text{ miles}} = \$9,000.00$$

$$\text{Zoomba} = 5 \text{ years} \times 18,000 \text{ miles} \times \frac{\$3.50}{\text{gallon}} \times \frac{1 \text{ gallon}}{29 \text{ miles}} = \$10,862.07$$

Now add the fuel cost for each car over the 5 years of ownership to the price of each car to find out which car is the better value:

Goomba = $11,666.66 + $18,500 = $30,166.66

Moomba = $9,843.75 + $21,700 = $31,543.75

Toomba = $9,000.00 + $22,900 = $31,900.00

Zoomba = $10,862.07 + $27,300 = $38,162.07

The Goomba would cost the least over the period of time. Remember to read the question carefully. Your answer should be to the question using the information presented to you in the problem. Head to Chapter 6 to find out more about solving rate and scale problems and Chapter 8 for additional guidance on solving algebra problems.

18. **(A) 1.** This question involves data analysis. You're asked to apply measures of central tendency (the average) and analyze the effect of changes in data on this measure. If Alicia's present average is 79% and she wants to get an average of 80%, she needs enough marks to get an additional 1% (80 – 79).

Because Alicia is taking 5 subjects, she requires 5 extra points for each percent increase. Thus, she requires $1 \times 5 = 5$ additional points. The problem says that Physical Education is her best subject, so she would need the 5 extra points in Physical Education, but that's not what the question asks.

This is a two-part problem. The first part requires you to find the average of her marks. This is a fairly simple arithmetic calculation. You total the numbers and divide by the number of numbers. Carefully reading the question and the table allows you to figure out both.

Choice (A) is the percentage increase needed and is what was asked. Choice (B) is the final mark required which was asked, and Choice (C) is the result of miscalculations. Remember that your answer has to be the best choice of answers to the question.

See Chapter 6 for additional guidance in solving such problems.

19. **(A) 7 cups of soup and $\frac{7}{8}$ cup of lentils.** This question tests your ability to figure out how a change in the amount of rice used results in changes to the amount of soup and lentils needed. Because each cup of rice requires 2 cups of soup, $3\frac{1}{2}$ cups of rice require $2 \times 3\frac{1}{2} = 7$ cups of soup. Because each cup of rice requires $\frac{1}{4}$ cup of lentils, $3\frac{1}{2}$ cups of rice require $3\frac{1}{2} \times \frac{1}{4} = \frac{7}{2} \times \frac{1}{4} = \frac{7}{8}$ cup of lentils.

The answer is the result of a series of calculations and requires careful reading of the problem. The tough part is calculating the amount of lentils. If you know how to convert a mixed number (a whole number and a fraction) into a fraction and how to multiply fractions (see Chapter 5), you should have no trouble coming up with the correct answer. Head to Chapter 6 for more about solving problems that involve proportions.

20. **(C) 1 in 216.** This is a probability question (see Chapter 7). To determine the probability of a sequence of events, multiply the probability of each event together. Each roll of the die is an event, so you have 3 events. The chance of rolling a 5 each time is $\frac{1}{6}$, so multiply $\frac{1}{6}$ 3 times: $\frac{1}{6} \times \frac{1}{6} \times \frac{1}{6} = \frac{1}{216}$.

    For additional guidance in solving probability questions, see Chapter 7.

21. **(D) the smaller rug.** You're asked to predict the impact of changes in the linear dimensions of the rug on the final cost of the floor treatment. Choice (C) seems logical, but the question never mentions the cost of the paneling or the skylight, so you can't consider it as an answer. Any choice must answer the question exactly.

    It will have a wood floor around it. You have to figure out how many square feet of wood and carpet you need for this floor treatment, as follows:

    The area of the room is $18 \times 12 = 216$ square feet.

    The larger rug will cover $16 \times 10 = 160$ square feet of the floor. This leaves 56 square feet $(216 - 160)$ to be covered with wood. The cost of the rug is $\$8.95 \times 160 = \$1,432.00$. The cost of the wood is $(\$17.59 \times 56) \div 9 = \$109.54$. The total cost is $\$1,432.00 + \$109.45 = \$1,541.45$.

    The smaller rug will cover $12 \times 8 = 96$ square feet of the floor. This leaves $216 - 96 = 120$ square feet to be covered with wood. The cost of the rug is $\$860.00$. The cost of the wood is $(\$17.59 \times 120) \div 9 = \$234.53$. The total cost is $\$860.00 + \$234.53 = \$1,094.53$. The larger rug will cost more for the entire floor treatment.

    Wood costs less per square foot than carpeting, so you know without doing any figuring that having more carpeting will result in higher costs. This is the type of problem where you can guess the answer, but if you have time, doing it step by step is safer. It's less frustrating at the end when you're checking your answers to have steps to check rather than try to recall the basis for your guess. On the other hand, guessing takes less time than calculating, and this problem involves a great deal of calculating.

    Whether you do the math or simply reason it out in your mind, remember to convert square yards to square feet. See Chapter 7 for more about solving measurement problems, including area.

22. **(C) love seat.** This question is an exercise in data analysis. You're asked to compare sets of data based on the mean (average) prices of 4 other stores. To find the answer, determine the average store price for each item listed. To determine the average, add up the prices for each item from stores A, B, C, and D and divide by 4. When you have a list of average prices, you can easily compare them to the prices at Fred's:

Item	Average Price	Fred's
Couch	$1,726.50	$1,719.00
Dining room set	$4,936.50	$4,899.00
Love seat	$1,221.50	$1,229.00
Coffee table	$454.00	$449.00
Reclining chair	$749.00	$739.00

You can see that the only item Fred's Friendly Furniture sells for over the average price is the love seat, which is the answer to the question. This question involves extracting information from tables and performing calculations on the numbers to reach a conclusion. If you make an error in this question, review your calculations, especially the finding of an average. (See Chapter 7 for more about evaluating data in graphs and tables.)

23. **100.** Sarah ate $\frac{12}{18} = \frac{2}{3}$ cupcakes per minute. In 2 hours and 30 minutes or 150 minutes, she could eat $150 \times \frac{2}{3} = 100$ cupcakes.

    This is a rate problem where you have to calculate cupcakes per minute. Be very careful how you set up the rate and perform the related calculations. See Chapter 6 for more about solving rate problems.

24. **(D) not enough information given.** This question tests your knowledge of measurement and geometry. You're asked to visualize and describe geometrical figures under a 90-degree rotation. Each of the figures is changed by the rotation. Try drawing each of these shapes, picking a point on the perimeter and rotating it 90 degrees. Because this is a timed test, try drawing one or two, noticing that they change quite a bit. Use your imagination to check the rest. After discovering that none of the four shapes has the same relationship to the horizontal after a 90-degree rotation about a point on its perimeter, you have your answer — not enough information given. Make sure that when you choose "not enough information given" that it really is the case. If enough information is given, then another choice would be correct. See Chapter 7 for more about answering geometry questions.

25. **8:1.** This question tests your data-analysis skills by asking you to interpret a chart and answer a question involving calculation.

    The largest budget is the Operations budget, while the smallest budget is Human Resources. The ratio between these two budgets is 16.8 to 2.1 or 8:1 (dividing both sides by 2.1). To find out more reading graphs, see Chapter 7. For additional guidance on working with ratios, turn to Chapter 6.

26. **(D) graph 4.** This question tests your knowledge of patterns by asking you to compare information from different types of graphs to extract information. Graph 4 has the first and third quarters in the required ratio and is the correct answer. This question asks you to interpret data from bar graphs. These bars give you relative information so that when you are asked about doubled production, you can make an informed guess from the length of the bars. If you got this question wrong, measure the lengths of the bars in each graph and compare the lengths. See Chapter 7 for more about reading graphs.

27. **(D) $6 + \sqrt{671}$.** If the forester is standing 25 feet from the tree, one leg of the triangle as measured straight from the top of his head to the tree is 25 feet. The hypotenuse of the triangle is 36 feet measured from the top of his head to the top of the tree. Use the Pythagorean theorem to calculate the other leg of the triangle measuring from 6 feet up the tree (due to the forester's height) to the top of the tree:

$$c^2 = a^2 + b^2$$
$$36^2 = 25^2 + b^2$$
$$1296 = 625 + b^2$$
$$1296 - 625 = b^2$$
$$671 = b^2$$
$$b = \sqrt{671}$$

Then, you must add 6 feet to account for the height of the forester to arrive at your final answer: $6 + \sqrt{671}$. Head to Chapter 7 to find out how to use the Pythagorean theorem to answer such questions.

28. **(D) 12.** This question tests your skills in algebra by asking you to solve equations. The equation given is $V = S^2$. $S^2 = 144$, then S is the square root of 144, or 12. Thus, the answer is 12. If you know the squares and square roots, this question is very simple. The square root of 144 is 12. If not, use a calculator. The on-screen calculator that's available when you take the test has a square root button. You simply key in the number and click the button that has the square root symbol on it.

Memorize the squares of numbers 2 through 12 and the square roots of those squares, so you won't have to use the calculator during the test. Having these numbers memorized will free up some precious time for answering other questions. See Chapter 5 for more about squares and square roots.

29. **(A) $981.** The most economical car would cost you $840 per year for fuel, but car F would cost you $1,167 per year for fuel. Car A would save you $1,167 – $840 = $327 per year, or $981 over the period of 3 years. If you picked Choice (B), that is just the fuel costs for car F, not the savings which you were asked for. Choice (C) compares the 3-year cost differential between car F and the most expensive car for gas, and Choice (D) does the same for one year. Read carefully and check calculations and you should get every question correct. See Chapter 7 for guidance on reading and extracting data from tables.

30. **0.4.** This question tests your ability to analyze data, using the mean and median to answer a question about the data given. The mean of the city mileages is the sum of the mileages divided by 10 (the number of entries):

$$(28 + 29 + 25 + 24 + 22 + 22 + 21 + 19 + 18 + 16) \div 10 = 22.4$$

The median of the mileages is the average of the two middle numbers because there are an even number of numbers, and both of those are 22, so their average is 22. See Chapter 7 for more about mean and median.

Then $22.4 - 22 = 0.4$

31. **(D) $1.50/gallon.** The table's footnote indicates that annual cost represents 15,000 miles driven annually with 55% of those miles in the city and 45% on the highway. Multiply 15,000 by 0.55 and by 0.45 to find out the actual number of miles driven in the city and on the highway:

$$0.55 \times 15,000 = 8,250 \text{ miles city}$$
$$0.45 \times 15,000 = 6,750 \text{ miles highway}$$

Now, pick a car and calculate the number of gallons required to drive that many miles in the city and on the highway. For example, vehicle C gets 25 miles per gallon on the highway and 19 in the city. That's the same as saying it uses one gallon to go 25 miles on the highway and one gallon to go 19 miles in the city. Multiply total miles by gallons per mile, and you get gallons:

Add the two and you find out that the car used about 704 gallons of fuel. To determine dollars per gallon, multiply annual cost in dollars by $\dfrac{1}{704 \text{ gallons}}$ and you get

$$\frac{\$1,000}{704 \text{ gallons}} = \$1.42 / \text{gallon}$$

Try the same calculations for the other cars, and you'll find that the cost per gallon of fuel is less than $1.50. See Chapter 6 for more about solving common word problems.

32. **(D) 8.** This question tests your skill in algebra by asking you to solve a system of linear equations:

$$2x + 3y = 10$$
$$5x + 6y = 13$$

A *linear equation* is one in which the powers of the variables are all equal to 1. To solve this system, you have to eliminate x by multiplying each equation by a number that allows you to subtract one from the other and end up with just y's. Multiply the first equation by 5 and the second equation by 2 (note that as long as you multiply both sides of each equation by the same number, the values on each side of the equal sign remain equal):

$$5(2x + 3y) = 10x + 15y = 50$$
$$2(5x + 6y) = 10x + 12y = 26$$

Subtract the second equation from the first, and you get $3y = 24$; $y = 8$. (Note that you can also multiply the first equation by –2 and add the two equations together. Either way gets you the same answer.) You could get the value of x by substituting for y in either equation and solving for x. You could check both answers by substituting for both x and y in one equation and making sure that the left side equals the right side. See Chapters 8 and 9 for more about solving linear equations.

33. **(B) Portugal.** Multiply the percentage in each country by the total adult population in each country and compare the numbers:

Denmark: $4 \times 0.623 = 2.49$ million

Portugal: $6 \times 0.155 = 0.93$ million

Hungary: $7 \times 0.179 = 1.25$ million

Norway: $3 \times 0.431 = 1.29$ million

Portugal has the fewest number of adults participating in adult education: 0.93 million. Always read the questions and answers carefully. You're asked for the fewest number of adults participating in adult education, not the lowest participation rate. See Chapter 7 for more about reading graphs and tables and Chapter 6 for additional guidance in solving word problems.

34. **(D) $259.02.** This problem is pretty simple. Add the amount Gina currently has in her checking account with what she's about to deposit: $789.65 + $754.37 = $1,544.02. Then, subtract her bills from that: $1,544.02 − $123 − $131 − $65 − $113 − $114 − $739 = $259.02. You need a firm grasp of the basics to solve this problem; if you're rusty, head to Chapter 5.

35. **(A) 20.5.** At the end of the first month, Daniel will owe $165 + $20 = $185. The second month's interest will be $185 × 0.20 = $37. At the end of the second month, he will owe $185 + $37 = $222. At $11 an hour, he would have to work an additional $222 ÷ 11 = 20.18 hours, which is closest to 20.5 hours when rounded up to the nearest half-hour. This problem is a lesson in life as well as one that tests your ability to calculate simple interest and see the difference it makes if you let interest accumulate. If you picked Choice (D), you probably based your calculation on Daniel having borrowed the entire $200 and not just the $165 he needed for books. See Chapter 6 for guidance in solving word problems.

36. **703.36.** The formula for the surface area of a cone is $SA = \pi rs + \pi r^2$, but the figure doesn't give a value for *s,* which stands for *side length,* the length measured down the slope of the cone. To determine the side length, you can use the Pythagorean theorem because the radius, height, and side length form a right triangle with the side length being the hypotenuse *(c):*

$$c^2 = a^2 + b^2$$
$$c^2 = 7^2 + 24^2$$
$$c^2 = 49 + 576 = 625$$
$$c = \sqrt{625} = 25$$

With the side length and radius, you can calculate the surface area of the cone:

In Chapter 7, you find out all you need to know about solving surface area problems.

37. **(A) 6.7%.** This question tests your ability to evaluate an answer by using a formula. This formula, $I = prt,$ isn't in the format you want because you want to calculate the rate, which means solving for *r.* You can change the equation to $r = \dfrac{I}{p \times t}$, which allows you to calculate the rate from the information given. *I* represents the total interest paid, *p* is the principal or the amount of money borrowed (in this case $150), and *t* is the length of time the money was borrowed (in this case 1.5 years). Substituting into this equation, you get

$r = \dfrac{{}^{1}\cancel{15}}{{}^{10}\cancel{150} \times 1.5} = \dfrac{1}{15} = 0.0666$, which rounds up to 6.7%.

See Chapter 6 for more about solving word problems.

38. **128.** Use the area of a rectangle and area of a triangle formulas to solve this problem. Calculate the area of the rectangle first and then subtract the area of the triangle. The area of the rectangle is $14 \times 12 = 168$, and the area of the triangle is $A = \frac{1}{2}bh = \frac{1}{2}(8 \times 10) = 40$. $168 - 40 = 128$. Find out more about calculating area in Chapter 7.

39. **19.** This question tests your knowledge of patterns by asking you to figure out the next number in a series. The pattern here is $2^2 + 1 = 5$, $3^2 + 2 = 11$, so the next number will be $4^2 + 3 = 19$. Be careful with your calculations. Do them on paper if you can. That way you can check your calculations if you need to. Recognizing patterns requires a firm understanding of basic math, as presented in Chapter 5. Understanding functions (Chapter 9) is also helpful.

40. **(A) (–1, –3).** This question tests your skills in geometry by asking you to visualize a graph of an object. Because the object is a rectangle, the opposite sides are equal in length and are parallel. The fourth corner will be 1 unit to the left of the *y*-axis, giving it an *x*-coordinate of –1, and 3 units below the *x*-axis, giving it a *y*-coordinate of –3. Therefore, the point would be (–1, –3).

Another way to solve the problem is to sketch it out like so:

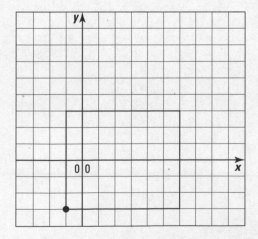

See Chapter 7 for more about solving geometry problems.

Chapter 4

Succeeding on the GED Mathematical Reasoning Test

....

In This Chapter

▶ Getting ready in the weeks and days leading up to the test

▶ Leveraging the power of the diagnostic and practice tests

▶ Bringing what you need to the test and making yourself comfortable

▶ Nailing down important test-taking strategies

▶ Staying calm and relaxed while you take the test

....

You may never have taken a standardized test before. Or if you have, you may wake up sweating in the middle of the night from nightmares about your past experiences.

Whether you've experienced the joys or sorrows of standardized tests, to succeed on the GED Mathematical Reasoning test, you must know how to perform well on this type of test, which consists mostly of multiple-choice questions.

The good news is, you've come to the right spot to find out more about this type of test. This chapter explains some important pointers on how to prepare on the days and nights before the test, what to do on the morning of the test, and what to do during the test to be successful. You also discover some important test-taking strategies to build your confidence.

Gearing Up for Test Time

Doing well on the GED Math test involves more than walking into the test site and answering the questions. You need to be prepared for the challenges on the test. To ensure that you're ready to tackle the test head-on, do the following leading up to the test:

✔ **Get enough sleep.** We're sorry if we sound like your parents, but it's true — you shouldn't take tests when you're approaching exhaustion. Plan your time so you can get a good night's sleep for several days before the test and avoid excess caffeine. If you prepare ahead of time, you'll be ready, and sleep will come easier.

✔ **Eat a good breakfast.** A healthy breakfast fuels your mind and body. You have to spend several hours taking the test, and you definitely don't want to falter during that time. Eat some protein, such as eggs, bacon, or sausage with toast for breakfast. Avoid sugars (donuts, jelly, and fruit) because they can cause you to tire easily. You don't want your empty stomach fighting with your full brain.

✔ **Take some deep breaths.** During your trip to the testing site, prepare yourself mentally for the test. Clear your head of all distractions, practice deep breathing, and imagine yourself acing the test. Don't panic.

✔ **Start at the beginning, not the end.** Remember that the day of the test is the end of a long journey of preparation and not the beginning. It takes time to build mental muscles.

✔ **Be on time.** Make sure you know what time the test begins and the exact location of your test site. Arrive early. If necessary, take a practice run to make sure you have enough time to get from your home or workplace to the testing center. You don't need the added pressure of worrying about whether you can make it to the test on time. In fact, this added pressure can create industrial-strength panic in the calmest of people.

Traffic congestion happens. No one can plan for it, but you can leave extra time to make sure it doesn't ruin your day. Plan your route and practice it. Then leave extra time in case a meteor crashes into the street and the crowd that gathers around it stalls your progress. Even though the GED test is now administered on a computer and not everyone has to start at the same time, test centers are open only for certain hours, and if they close before you finish, you won't get any sympathy. Check the times the test center is open. Examiners won't show you a lot of consideration if you show up too late to complete the test because you didn't check the times. They have even less sympathy if you show up on the wrong date.

Using the Diagnostic and Practice Tests to Your Advantage

Taking diagnostic and practice GED Math tests is important for a few reasons, including the following:

✔ **They help you prepare for the test.** Practice tests, the diagnostic test in particular, shed light on the knowledge and skills you need to focus on leading up to the actual test.

✔ **They give you an indication of how well you know the material.** One or two tests won't give you an accurate indication of how you'll do on the actual test, because you need to do four or five tests to cover all possible topics, but they do give you an indication of where you stand.

✔ **They confirm whether you know how to use the computer to answer the questions.** You don't get this by taking the practice tests in the book, but you can go online at www.gedtestingservice.com/educators/freepracticetest to take a computer-based practice test.

✔ **They familiarize you with the test format.** You can read about test questions, but you can't actually understand them until you've worked through several.

✔ **They can ease your stress.** A successful run-through on a practice test allows you to feel more comfortable and confident in your own abilities to take the GED test successfully and alleviate your overall anxiety.

Turn to Chapter 3 to take the diagnostic test or to Chapter 10 to take the practice test. These tests are an important part of any preparation program. They're the feedback mechanism that you may normally get from a private tutor. To get the most out of any practice test, be sure to check your answers after each test and read the answer explanations. If possible, take as many practice tests as you can before taking the actual GED test. You can find more practice tests at www.gedtestingservice.com/educators/freepracticetest and a few more sample questions at www.gedtestingservice.com/testers/sample-questions. Use your favorite Internet search engine to find more practice tests online. The GED Testing Service also offers GED Ready tests that you can purchase through authorized outlets.

Packing for Test Day

The GED test may be the most important exam you ever take. Treat it seriously and come prepared. Make sure you bring the following items with you on test day:

- ✔ **You:** The most important thing to bring to the GED test is obviously you. If you enroll to take the test, you have to show up; otherwise, you'll receive a big fat zero and lose your testing fee. If something unfortunate happens after you enroll, contact the test center and explain your situation to the test administrators. They may reschedule the test with no additional charge.

- ✔ **Correct identification:** Before test officials let you into the room to take the test, they want to make sure you're you. Bring the approved photo ID — your state GED office can tell you what's an approved form of photo ID. Have your ID in a place where you can reach it easily. And when asked to identify yourself, don't pull out a mirror and say, "Yep, that's me."

- ✔ **Registration receipt and any fees you still owe:** The same people don't run all test centers. With some, you may have to pay in advance, when booking the test. If so, bring your receipt to avoid any misunderstandings. Others may allow you to pay at the door. If so, find out whether you can use cash, check, debit card, or credit card. The amount of the GED test registration fee also varies from state to state. (Check with your local administrator to confirm when and where the fee has to be paid and how to pay it.) If you don't pay, you can't play.

  If needed, you may be able to get financial assistance to help with the testing fees. Further, if you do the test one section at a time, which we recommend, you can probably pay for each test section separately. Check with your state or local education authorities.

- ✔ **Registration confirmation:** The registration confirmation is your proof that you did register. If you're taking the test in an area where everybody knows you and everything you do, you may not need the confirmation, but we suggest you take it anyway. It's light and doesn't take up much room in your pocket.

- ✔ **Other miscellaneous items:** In the instructions you receive after you register for the test, you get a list of what you need to bring with you. Besides yourself and the items we listed previously, other items you want to bring or wear include the following:

  - • **Comfortable clothes and shoes:** When you're taking the test, you want to be as relaxed as possible. Uncomfortable clothes and shoes may distract you from doing your best. You're taking the GED test, not modeling the most recent fashions. Consider dressing in layers; you don't want to be too hot or too cold.

  - • **A bottle of water or some coffee:** Check with the administrators before the test whether drinks are allowed. Computers and liquids don't mix, so they may not allow you to take drinks in with you. Mints and gum may be an alternative, but consider taking them in a transparent plastic bag so that no one can question whether you're carrying written material into the test. In general, food and beverages count as "personal medical items" and can only be brought to the test with prior documentation from a physician. Find specifics at `https://gedtestingservice.com/uploads/files/4b9d3cfb159f888a2386929d85de9dfb.pdf`

  - • **Reading glasses:** If you need glasses to read a computer monitor, don't forget to bring them to the test. Bring a spare pair, if you have one. You can't do the test if you can't read the screen.

The rules about what enters the testing room are strict. Don't take any chances. If something isn't on the list of acceptable items and isn't normal clothing, leave it at home. Laptops, cellphones, and other electronic devices will most likely be banned from the testing area. Leave them at home or locked in your car. The last place on earth to discuss whether you can bring something into the test site is at the door on test day. If you have questions, contact the test center in advance. Check out `www.gedtestingservice.com` to start the registration process and find a list of sites close to your home with their addresses and phone numbers. You can also call 877-EXAM-GED to have real people answer your questions.

Whatever you do, be sure *not* to bring the following with you to the GED testing center:

- ✔ Books
- ✔ Notes or scratch paper
- ✔ MP3 players or tablets
- ✔ Cellphone (leave it at home or in your car)
- ✔ Anything valuable, like a laptop computer that you don't feel comfortable leaving outside the room while you take the test

You're provided with an on-screen calculator. You can bring your own hand-held calculator, but it must be a specific make and model. Visit www.gedtestingservice.com/testers/ calculator to find out more about the on-screen calculator and which hand-held make and model you're allowed to bring.

Getting Comfortable Before the Test Begins

You usually take the GED Math test in an examination room with at least one official (sometimes called a *proctor* or *examiner*) who's in charge of administering the test. Some locations have smaller test centers that have space for no more than 15 test-takers at a time. In either case, the test is the same.

As soon as you sit down to take the GED Math test, spend a few moments, before the test actually starts, to relax and get comfortable. You're going to be in the chair for quite some time, so settle in. Keep these few tips in mind before you begin:

- ✔ **Make sure that the screen is at a comfortable height and adjust your chair to a height that suits you.** Unlike a pencil-and-paper test, you'll be working with a monitor and keyboard. You can adjust the monitor's color scheme to make it more comfortable. Although you can shift the keyboard around and maybe adjust the angle of the monitor, generally you're stuck in that position for the duration of the test. If you need to make any adjustments, make them before you start. You want to feel as physically comfortable as possible.

- ✔ **Find out whether you can have something to drink at your computer station.** You may depend on that second cup of coffee to keep you upright and thinking. Even a bottle of water may make your life easier. However, see the information earlier in the chapter about bringing beverages to the test.

- ✔ **Go to the bathroom before you start.** This may sound like a silly suggestion, but it all contributes to being comfortable. You don't need distractions. Even if bathroom breaks are permitted during the test, you don't want to take away time from the test.

The proctor reads the test instructions to you and lets you log in to the computer to start the test. Listen carefully to these instructions so you know how much time you have to take the test as well as any other important information.

Brushing Up on Test-Taking Strategies

You can increase your score by mastering a few smart test-taking strategies. To help you do so, we give you some tips in these sections on how to

- ✔ Plan your time.
- ✔ Determine the question type.
- ✔ Figure out how to answer the different types of questions.
- ✔ Guess intelligently.
- ✔ Review your work.

Watching the clock: Using your time wisely

When you start the computerized version of the GED Math test, you may feel pressed for time and have the urge to rush through the questions. We strongly advise that you don't. You have sufficient time to do the test at a reasonable pace. You have only a certain amount of time for each section in the GED exam, so time management is an important part of succeeding on the test. You need to plan ahead and use your time wisely. Don't spend a great deal of time on a question you don't understand. Leave it until the end and try it again. Never sacrifice an easy question for a difficult one.

During the test, the computer keeps you constantly aware of the time with a clock in the upper right-hand corner. Pay attention to the clock. When the test begins, check that time, and be sure to monitor how much time you have left as you work your way through the test. The GED Math test is 115 minutes long and is given in two sections. The first five questions are to be done without a calculator and the last 41 to 45 questions allow the use of a calculator. As we mention earlier, you may bring a specific hand-held calculator to the test, but if you do, you must place it in a secure location before the test and retrieve it after the first five questions are completed. You will get a short break of some kind to retrieve your calculator. Ask yourself if all this trouble is worth using your own calculator instead of using the one on the screen. Questions are presented in two parts:

| Part 1 | 5 questions | No calculator allowed |
| Part 2 | 41 to 45 questions | Calculator allowed |

Although these two parts are timed separately, you must submit your answers to the Part 1 questions before moving on to the questions in Part 2. There is a three-minute break between these two parts.

Budget your time carefully so you don't run out of time before you have a chance to answer all the questions. To budget your time, divide the amount of time you have by the number of questions. For the Math test, you have 115 minutes to answer 46 questions, so $115/46 = 2.5$ minutes per question. As you progress, repeat the calculation, dividing the remaining time by the remaining number of questions, to see how you're doing. Remember, too, that you can do questions in any order, except for submitting your first five answers before moving on to the rest. Do the easiest questions first. If you get stuck on a question, leave it and come back to it later, if you have time. Keeping to that schedule and answering as many questions as possible are essential.

If you don't monitor the time for each question, you won't have time to answer all the questions on the test. Keep in mind the following general time-management tips to help you complete each exam on time:

- ✔ **Tackle questions in groups.** For example, calculate how much time you have for each item on each test. Multiply the answer by 5 to give you a time slot for any five test items. Then try to answer each group of five items within the time you calculated. Doing so helps you complete all the questions and leaves you several minutes for review.

✔ **Keep calm and don't panic.** The time you spend panicking could be better spent answering questions.

✔ **Practice using the sample tests in this book.** The more you practice timed sample test questions, the easier managing a timed test becomes. You can get used to doing something in a limited amount of time if you practice. Refer to the earlier section "Using the Diagnostic and Practice Tests to Your Advantage" for more information.

When time is up, immediately stop and breathe a sigh of relief. When the test ends, the examiner will give you a log-off procedure. Listen for instructions on what to do or where to go next.

Evaluating the different questions

Although you don't have to know much about how the test questions, or items, were developed to answer them correctly, you do need some understanding of how they're constructed. Knowing the types of items you're dealing with can make answering them easier — and you'll face fewer surprises.

To evaluate the types of questions that you have to answer, keep these tips in mind:

✔ **As soon as the computer signals that the test is running, start by skimming the questions.** Don't spend a lot of time doing so — just enough to spot the questions you absolutely know and the ones you know you'll need more time to answer.

✔ **Rely on the Previous and Next buttons on the bottom of the screen to scroll through the questions.** After you finish skimming, answer all the questions you know first; that way, you leave yourself much more time for the difficult questions. Check out the next section, "Addressing and answering questions," for tips on how to answer questions.

✔ **Answer the easiest questions first.** You don't have to answer questions in order. Nobody except you will ever know, or care, in which order you answer the questions, so do the easiest questions first. You'll be able to answer them fastest, leaving more time for the other, harder questions. Don't forget to come back to the skipped questions before finishing.

Addressing and answering questions

When you start the test, you want to have a game plan in place for how to answer the questions. Keep the following tips in mind to help you address each question:

✔ **Whenever you read a question, ask yourself, "What am I being asked?"** Doing so helps you stay focused on what you need to find out to answer the question. You may even want to decide quickly what skills are required to answer the question (see the preceding section for more on these skills). Decide whether you need a formula to answer the question and whether all the measurements are in the same units. Then try to answer it.

✔ **Try to eliminate some answers.** Even if you don't really know the answer, guessing can help. When you're offered four answer choices, some will be obviously wrong. Eliminate those choices, and you've already improved your odds of guessing a correct answer.

✔ **Don't overthink.** Because all the questions are straightforward, don't look for hidden or sneaky questions. The questions ask for an answer based on the information given. If you don't have enough information to answer the question, one of the answer choices will say so.

✔ **Find the answer choice you think is best and quickly verify that it answers the question.** If it does, click on that choice, and move on. If it doesn't, leave it and come back to it after you answer all the other questions, if you have time. *Remember:* You need to pick the *most* correct answer, not necessarily the perfect answer, from the choices offered.

Guess for success: Using intelligent guessing

The multiple-choice questions, regardless of the on-screen format, provide you with four possible answers. You get between 1 and 3 points for every correct answer. Nothing is subtracted for incorrect answers. That means you can guess on the items you don't know for sure without fear that you'll lose points if your guess is incorrect. Make educated guesses by eliminating as many obviously wrong choices as possible and choosing from just one or two remaining choices.

When the question gives you four possible answers and you randomly choose one, you have a 25 percent chance of guessing the correct answer without even reading the question. Of course, we don't recommend using this method during the test but thought we would sneak in a bit of probability theory.

If you know that one of the answers is definitely wrong, you now have just three answers to choose from and have a 33 percent chance (1 in 3) of choosing the correct answer. If you know that two of the answers are wrong, you leave yourself only two possible answers to choose from, giving you a 50 percent (1 in 2) chance of guessing right — much better than 25 percent! Removing two or three choices you know are wrong makes choosing the correct answer much easier.

If you don't know the answer to a particular question, try to spot the wrong choices by following these tips:

✔ **Make sure your answer really answers the question.** Wrong choices usually don't answer the question — that is, they may sound good, but they answer a different question than the one the test asks.

✔ **When two answers seem very close, consider both answers carefully because they both can't be right — but they both *can* be wrong.** Some answer choices may be very close, and all seem correct, but there's a fine line between completely correct and nearly correct. Be careful. These answer choices are sometimes given to see whether you have really read and understand the material.

✔ **Look for opposite answers in the hopes that you can eliminate one.** If two answers contradict each other, both can't be right, but both can be wrong.

✔ **Trust your instincts.** Some wrong choices may just strike you as wrong when you first read them. If you spend time preparing for these exams, you probably know more than you think.

Leaving time for review

Having a few minutes at the end of a test to check your work is a great way to set your mind at ease. These few minutes give you a chance to look at any questions that may be troubling. If you've chosen an answer for every question, enjoy the last few minutes before time is called — without any panic. Keep the following tips in mind as you review your answers:

✔ **After you know how much time you have per item, try to answer each item in a little less than that time.** The extra seconds you don't use the first time through the test add up to time at the end of the test for review. Some questions require more thought and decision making than others. Use your extra seconds to answer those questions.

✔ **Don't try to change a lot of answers at the last minute.** Second-guessing yourself can lead to trouble. Often, second-guessing leads you to changing correct answers to incorrect ones. If you've prepared well and worked numerous sample questions, then you're likely to get the correct answers the first time. Ignoring all your preparation and knowledge to play a hunch isn't a good idea, either at the racetrack or on a test.

Sharpening Your Mental Focus

To succeed in taking the GED Math test, you need to be prepared. In addition to studying the content and honing the skills required, you also want to be mentally prepared. Although you may be nervous, you can't let your nerves get the best of you. Stay calm and take a deep breath. Here are a few pointers to help you stay focused on the task at hand:

✔ **Take time to rest and relax.** Rest and relaxation are restorative, revitalizing your body and providing your brain with the downtime it needs to digest all the information you've been feeding it.

✔ **Make sure you know the rules of the room before you begin.** If you have questions about using the bathroom during the test or what to do if you finish early, ask the proctor before you begin. If you don't want to ask these questions in public, call the GED office in your area before test day and ask your questions over the phone. For general GED questions, call 877-EXAM-GED, but be patient. This number is an automated service with a myriad of answers to more than a myriad of questions. It is a bit faster to check out www.gedtestingservice.com. This site has many pages, but the FAQ page is always a good place to start. You can also send a question to help@gedtestingservice.com and they will answer within a couple of business days.

✔ **Keep your eyes on your computer screen.** Everybody knows not to look at other people's work during the test, but, to be on the safe side, don't stretch, roll your eyes, or do anything else that may be mistaken for looking at another test. Most of the tests will be different on the various computers, so looking around is futile, but doing so can get you into a lot of trouble.

✔ **Stay calm.** Your nerves can use up a lot of energy needed for the test. Concentrate on the job at hand. You can always be nervous or panicky some other time.

Because taking standardized tests probably isn't a usual situation for you, you may feel nervous. This is perfectly normal. Just try to focus on answering one question at a time, and push any other thoughts to the back of your mind. Sometimes taking a few deep breaths can clear your mind; just don't spend a lot of time focusing on your breath. After all, your main job is to pass this test.

Part II
Honing Your Math Skills

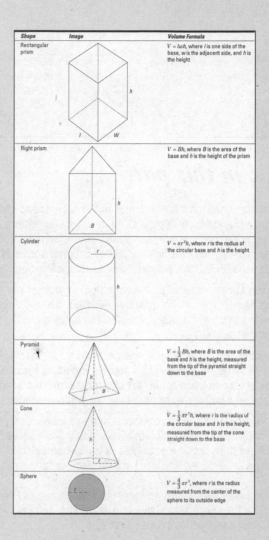

Shape	Image	Volume Formula
Rectangular prism		$V = lwh$, where l is one side of the base, w is the adjacent side, and h is the height
Right prism		$V = Bh$, where B is the area of the base and h is the height of the prism
Cylinder		$V = \pi r^2 h$, where r is the radius of the circular base and h is the height
Pyramid		$V = \frac{1}{3} Bh$, where B is the area of the base and h is the height, measured from the tip of the pyramid straight down to the base
Cone		$V = \frac{1}{3} \pi r^2 h$, where r is the radius of the circular base and h is the height, measured from the tip of the cone straight down to the base
Sphere		$V = \frac{4}{3} \pi r^3$, where r is the radius measured from the center of the sphere to its outside edge

In this part . . .

- ✔ Brush up on the most fundamental math concepts and skills, including factoring, multiples, absolute values, exponents, fractions, decimals, percentages, operations (addition, subtraction, multiplication, and division), and the all-important order of operations (PEMDAS). Master these to build a firm foundation.

- ✔ Reason out quantitative problems to figure out what you don't know based on what you do know — details that the question provides, such as finding a rate of speed when given the time and distance traveled.

- ✔ Calculate perimeter, circumference, and area of flat shapes and volume and surface area of 3D objects, including pyramids, cylinders, cones, and spheres; extract data from tables and graphs; and calculate the probability of random events.

- ✔ Discover how to solve expressions and equations, deal with polynomials and quadratic equations, and solve real-world problems that involve inequalities. If you're befuddled by equations such as $ax^2 + bx + c = 0$, turn here for clarification.

- ✔ Find out how to interpret and present data graphically on number lines, on the coordinate plane, and on graphs, and get to know functions, perhaps for the very first time.

Chapter 5

Brushing Up on the Basics

To score well on the GED Mathematical Reasoning test, you need quick and clear recall of all your basic math skills. Before you can step up to algebra, geometry, and other higher levels of math, you need to acquire some fundamental math knowledge and master a few core skills.

In this chapter, you take a short refresher course in the most essential math you learned in school. You discover what rational numbers are, if you don't already know; find out how to perform basic mathematical operations in the right sequence; get up to speed on adding, subtracting, multiplying, and dividing fractions; discover how to deal with decimals; and get the inside scoop on calculating percentages.

By the end of this chapter, you should be able to tackle at least a third of the questions on the GED Mathematical Reasoning test.

Getting to Know Rational Numbers

A *rational number* is any number that can be expressed as $\frac{a}{b}$, where a and b are *whole numbers* (the numbers you use to count, such as 1, 2, 3, and so on). Another way of looking at rational numbers is that they are fractions where neither a nor b can be 0. Any number that doesn't fit this definition is called an *irrational number* — not to imply that irrational numbers are unreasonable, only that their values can't be pinned down.

Rational numbers are everywhere, all the time, and never given a second thought, but that's a mistake. Take the opportunity now to give them a second thought.

If homeowners want to buy a carpet that measures 6 feet by 9 feet and costs $7 a square foot, they can calculate its cost using rational numbers. The area of the rug is $6 \times 9 = 54$ square feet, and the cost is $7 per square foot, which is $54 \times \$7 = \$378$. That was all done using rational numbers. Most problems on the test involve rational numbers, but beware: You may encounter some trick numbers, such as $\sqrt{2}$, that can't be expressed as a fraction and are thus *irrational numbers,* as explained in the nearby sidebar.

Rational numbers come in several forms, all of which you'll meet on the test, so spend some time getting to know all of them in the following sections.

What makes a number irrational?

An *irrational number* is any number that can't be expressed in the form of one rational number over another. Admittedly, we already said that a couple times, and it's getting old, so to get a better idea of what irrational numbers are, take a look at a couple examples. One common example is the ratio π — a circle's circumference divided by its diameter, which is always 3.141592653589793238. . . . The . . . at the end indicates that the number goes on forever, making the number irrational. It can't be expressed as 3 followed by a fraction.

Another common example is $\sqrt{2}$, which is 1.414213562373095. . . . Again, the . . . at the end shows that the number goes on forever. It can't be represented as 1 followed by a fraction. As you can see, irrational numbers are somewhat unreasonable and difficult to deal with.

Meeting integers

Integers are the basic building blocks of mathematics — the numbers that enable people to count and tell people how old they are and how well they did on the GED tests. You probably recognize them as 1, 2, 3, and so on. Progress along this wondrous voyage through mathematics will show just how useful integers are and how they help solve mathematical problems.

Recognizing fractions and decimals

How do you recognize your best friend? How do you tell a banana from an orange? Of course, by their appearance. Fractions look like $\frac{a}{b}$, where *a* and *b* are whole numbers. *a* is called the *numerator,* and *b* is called the *denominator.* The denominator is the number of equal portions a whole is divided into. The numerator is the number of equal portions represented by the fraction. Fractions are useful in solving problems. If 6 friends decided to share a pie equally, how much of the pie would each person get? If the portion each person would get is represented by 1 and the number of pieces is represented by 6, each person would get $\frac{1}{6}$ of the pie. Obviously, this is a simple example. We present it only to show the basic idea of a fraction. This is so basic, it would never appear on a test for high school students. However, this leads to more complex questions.

Sam, Larry, and Howard have contracted to paint a large room in a house. After calculating all the material costs, which are to be paid by the homeowner, they decide that $270 would be a fair price for the 16 hours it will take to prepare, paint, and clean up. Each of the men decides that $15.00 an hour is a fair wage for the job. If three-quarters of the work will be done by Larry, how much will Larry be paid for his work on the job?

(A) $90

(B) $225

(C) $180

(D) $125

Approaching any problem requires reading both the question and the possible answers carefully. A proper math problem is like a short story. In this case, Larry is going to do most of the work ($\frac{3}{4}$). If the total amount of work would take 16 hours, then $\frac{3}{4}$ of the work would be

$$\frac{3}{4} \times 16 = \frac{48}{4} = 12 \text{ hours}$$

Larry is to be paid $15 an hour, so he would receive $12 \times \$15 = \$180$ for his work, which is Choice (C).

Locating rational numbers on a number line

Number lines can be a great help in mathematics. Examine a standard ruler carefully. It has a series of increasing numbers going from left to right. Basically, this is a positive number line. If a ruler had equally spaced sequential numbers increasing from right to left, it would be the equivalent of a negative number line. Putting the two together with the zeros one on top of the other would produce a traditional number line, as shown in Figure 5-1. Positive numbers appear to the right of zero (0), and negative numbers appear to the left. The farther right you go, the bigger the number. The farther left you go, the smaller the number.

To indicate the position of 12 on this number line, first decide whether the number is positive or negative. If the number were positive, it would go 12 hash marks to the right of zero, because all positive numbers are placed to the right of zero. To mark –12, you'd go 12 hash marks to the left of zero.

Figure 5-1:
A typical
number line.

John Wiley & Sons, Inc.

Circle the hash mark that indicates –12 on the following number line:

–12 would be 12 hash marks to the left of zero.

Number lines come in handy for demonstrating the relationship among numbers and for performing addition and subtraction. For example, to tell the difference in value between –15 and 12, count the spaces between the two numbers, and you discover that the difference between the two is 27. If you were to add the two numbers, you'd count 12 hash marks to the right of zero and then go back 15 hash marks and land on –3, the total of $12 + (-15)$. We explain the reasoning behind this in the next section on absolute value. Try these simple exercises to make sure that you understand number lines.

Mark the following points on the number line:

(A) 18

(B) –4

(C) –17

(D) 2

Check your number line against the following number line.

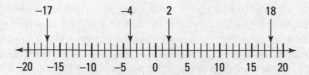

Calculate the distance between A and C. The distance is _____.

Calculate the distance between C and D. The distance is _____.

The distance from A to C is $18 + 17 = 35$. The distance from C to D is $17 + 2 = 19$.

Grasping the concept of absolute value

The *absolute value* of a number is its distance from zero, regardless of direction. For example, +34 and −34 are the same distance from zero on the number line; the only difference is that one is to the left of zero and the other is to the right of zero. Although you're well aware of the fact that +34 is a whole lot more than −34, they are equal in terms of their absolute value. This is a useful concept in theoretical mathematics. Just don't try using it to establish a budget!

Math has a very specific way to represent the absolute value of a number; it encloses the number between two perpendicular lines, like so: $|-34|$ and $|34|$. Each of these values equals 34.

Which of the following numbers has the greatest value?

(A) 18

(B) −22

(C) $|-18|$

(D) $|-22|$

If you picked Choice (D), you are correct. The absolute value of −22 is 22, which is obviously greater than 18, −22, and the absolute value of −18, which just happens to be 18. Choices (A) and (C) present two numbers with the same value.

Factoring a number

Factors are numbers that are multiplied to form another number, called a *product*. For example, in the equation $3 \times 5 = 15$, 3 and 5 are factors, and 15 is the product. To factor a number, you break it down into the smallest numbers that, multiplied together, reproduce the number you started with. For example, to factor 30, you can break it down into 3×10 and break it down further into $3 \times 2 \times 5$. You can't break it down any further than that without getting into some higher math.

Sounds simple so far, but to get really good at factoring, here are some rules that enable you to identify the factors of a product just by looking at it:

✔ **Every even number can be divided evenly by 2.** $144 = 2 \times 64$, and $3,286 = 2 \times 1,643$. You know that even numbers end in 0, 2, 4, 6, and 8, which means that any number ending in one of these digits can be divided by 2. In other words, 2 is a factor of all such numbers.

✔ **Every number that ends in 5 or 0 can be divided evenly by 5.** For example, $30 = 5 \times 6$, and $65 = 5 \times 13$. Even a number as large as $1,935 = 5 \times 387$. Every number that ends in 5 or 0 has 5 as one of its factors.

✔ **If the individual digits in a number add up to a multiple of 3, then that number can be divided evenly by 3.** For example, consider the number 1,647. Add up its digits: $1 + 6 + 4 + 7 = 18$, and $1 + 8 = 9$, and 9 can be divided by 3, so you know that 1,647 can be divided by 3: $1,647 = 3 \times 549$. You can keep doing this. $549 = 5 + 4 + 9 = 18$, and $1 + 8 = 9$, so 549 can be divided by 3: $3 \times 183 = 549$. Now take 183: $1 + 8 + 3 = 12$, which can be divided by 3: $3 \times 61 = 183$. Now you're stuck. 61 can't be divided by 3 or any other number. So factoring 1,647 gives you $61 \times 3 \times 3 \times 3$.

✔ **If a two-digit number has the same two digits, 11 is one of its factors.** Check it out: 11, 22, 33, 44, 55, 66, 77, 88, and 99 all have 11 as a factor. $2 \times 11 = 22$, $3 \times 11 = 33$, $4 \times 11 = 44$, and so on. You can continue into three-digit numbers, but it becomes more difficult: $10 \times 11 = 110$, $11 \times 11 = 121$, $12 \times 11 = 132$, and so on.

Consider the number 144. Because it ends in 4, you can divide it by 2: $144 \div 2 = 72$. 72 ends in 2 and can be divided by 2 again: $72 \div 2 = 36$. 36 ends in an even number, 6, so $36 \div 2 = 18$, which again ends in an even number, and $18 \div 2 = 9$, and $9 \div 3 = 3$. Putting it all together, $144 = 2 \times 2 \times 2 \times 2 \times 3 \times 3$. With a little practice, you can factor a number in a long sequence instead of doing it in a series of smaller steps.

Factor the following numbers. Check your answers by multiplying the factors together to make sure the product is the number you started with.

63 _____

106 _____

178 _____

111 _____

85 _____

170 _____

44 _____

45 _____

75 _____

76 _____

166 _____

99 _____

148 _____

136 _____

One or more questions on the test may refer to a common factor. A *common factor* is simply any factor that two numbers have in common. For example, a common factor of 6 and 9 is 3. A common factor of 15 and 45 is 5. The *greatest common factor* is the largest number that can be divided into both numbers evenly. For example, the greatest common factor of 30 and 45 is 15:

$$30 \div 15 = 2$$
$$45 \div 15 = 3$$

Recognizing a prime number

A *prime number* is any number that can only be factored by itself and 1. For example, 13 has no factors other than 1 and 13. Here's a list of prime numbers between 1 and 1,000:

1 2 3 5 7 11 13 17 19 23 29 31 37 41 43 47 53 59 61 67 71 73 79 83 89 97 101 103 107 109 113 127 131 137 139 149 151 157 163 167 173 179 181 191 193 197 199 211 223 227 229 233 239 241 251 257 263 269 271 277 281 283 293 307 311 313 317 331 337 347 349 353 359 367 373 379 383 389 397 401 409 419 421 431 433 439 443 449 457 461 463 467 479 487 491 499 503 509 521 523 541 547 557 563 569 571 577 587 593 599 601 607 613 617 619 631 641 643 647 653 659 661 673 677 683 691 701 709 719 727 733 739 743 751 757 761 769 773 787 797 809 811 821 823 827 829 839 853 857 859 863 877 881 883 887 907 911 919 929 937 941 947 953 967 971 977 983 991 997

If you had nothing better to do, you could memorize all these, and if you're really bored, you can dig up even longer lists on the Web, but the purpose of this workbook is to prepare you to successfully pass the GED exams. Memorizing large lists of numbers may seem like an interesting conversation starter in certain circles, but it will do little to help you achieve your goal.

Go at this from the opposite direction. A quick test for smaller numbers is to divide them by 2, 3, 5, and 7. If none of those works, chances are the number is a prime. If you can't find a factor using your experience and the rules presented in the preceding section, you're probably looking at a prime number.

Exploring multiples

A *multiple* is the product of any quantity and an integer. Here are a few examples:

Number and Its Multiples

4   4, 8, 12, 16, 20, 24, 28, . . .
5   5, 10, 15, 20, 25, 30, 35, . . .
6   6, 12, 18, 24, 30, 36, 42, . . .

The *least common multiple* (LCM) is the smallest integer that's divisible by both numbers. In the previous examples, the LCM of 4 and 5 is 20. Aside from some mental exercise, LCMs do have a utilitarian purpose in mathematics. Before adding and subtracting fractions with different denominators, you must convert the fractions so that their denominators are the same, and you use the LCM in that conversion process. See the later section, "Adding and subtracting fractions," for details.

To determine the LCM of two numbers, here's what you do:

1. **Factor the numbers, as explained in the preceding section.**

   For example, to find the LCM of 30 and 45, factor the two numbers as follows:

$$30 = 2 \times 3 \times 5$$
$$45 = 3 \times 3 \times 5$$

2. **Multiply each factor by the greatest number of times it occurs in either number.**

   In this example, 2 appears once as a factor of 30, 3 appears twice as a factor of 45, and 5 appears once in both, so:

   $$2 \times 3 \times 3 \times 5 = 90$$

3. **Check your work by dividing your answer by each number you started with.**

   The result in each case must be an integer:

   $$90 \div 30 = 3$$
   $$90 \div 45 = 2$$

Find the least common multiple of the following pairs of numbers:

1. 63 and 99   _____

2. 136 and 96   _____

3. 38, 85, and 102 _____

4. 85 and 166   _____

5. 75 and 147   _____

Here are the answers, along with an explanation for each:

1. $63 = 3 \times 3 \times 7$ and $99 = 3 \times 3 \times 11$. 3 appears twice as a factor for each number, 7 appears once, and 11 appears once, so $3 \times 3 \times 7 \times 11 = 693$.

2. $136 = 2 \times 2 \times 2 \times 17$ and $96 = 2 \times 2 \times 2 \times 2 \times 2 \times 3$. 2 appears five times in the second number and three times in the first, 17 appears once, and 3 appears once, so $2 \times 2 \times 2 \times 2 \times 2 \times 17 \times 3 = 1,632$.

3. $38 = 2 \times 19$, $85 = 5 \times 17$, and $102 = 2 \times 3 \times 17$. All three numbers have no common factor, so the LCM is $2 \times 19 \times 5 \times 17 \times 3 = 9,690$.

4. $85 = 5 \times 17$ and $166 = 2 \times 83$. Again, these two numbers have no common factors, so multiply all the factors together: $5 \times 17 \times 2 \times 83 = 14,110$.

5. $75 = 3 \times 5 \times 5$ and $147 = 3 \times 7 \times 7$. The only common factor is 3, and the LCM is $3 \times 5 \times 5 \times 7 \times 7 = 3,675$.

Mastering Basic Mathematical Operations

You're probably familiar with the four basic mathematical operations: addition, subtraction, multiplication, and division. So most of this section will serve as a refresher course for you and provide some practice to warm up your brain cells. But this section also covers a couple topics you may be less familiar with — exponents, such as 3^2 (the 2 is the exponent), and the order of operations. (We don't want to spoil the ending; you find out more about these concepts later in this section.)

Although you may know most of this stuff already, we encourage you to read through this section and perform the exercises. These basic mathematical operations and the order in which you perform them in an equation form the foundation for every other math skill required on the test.

Addition

Addition combines two or more quantities to determine the total quantity. For example, $14 + 23 = 37$. Adding relatively small numbers, as in this example, is easy, but addition becomes more difficult when you're challenged to add several larger numbers, such as 1,385, 458, and 2,196. To add these numbers, you need to know a little about the different *places* — the value of each digit based on where it appears in a number. Each place in a number has a value of 10 times the value of the place to its right, so in the number 2,196, the 6 is 6, the 9 is 90, the 1 is 100, and the 2 is 2,000. Writing 2,196 is the same as writing $2,000 + 100 + 90 + 6$. Figure 5-2 illustrates places out to a million.

Figure 5-2:
The value of a digit depends on its place in the number.

7,654,321

John Wiley & Sons, Inc.

If you need to add two or more large numbers and you can't do it confidently in your head, stack the numbers on top of one another so their ones places are lined up, and add each column of numbers, like so:

$$
\begin{array}{r}
\overset{1\,2\,1}{1,385} \\
458 \\
+2,196 \\
\hline
4,039
\end{array}
$$

Notice the tiny numbers at the top. If you total the digits in the ones column, you end up with 19, which is $10 + 9$. You put the 9 in the ones place at the bottom and carry the 10, as a 1, to the top of the tens column. When you add the digits in the tens column, be sure to add in that tiny 1 at the top. When you do, you get 23, but since that 23 is in the tens column, it's actually 230, or $200 + 30$. Put the 3 in the tens place at the bottom and carry the 2 over to the top of the hundreds place. When you add the digits in the hundreds place, you get 10, which represents 10 hundreds, or 1,000. Put the zero in the hundreds place at the bottom and carry the 1 to the top of the thousands place. Add the digits in the thousands place and you get 4 with nothing to carry. Place the 4 at the bottom, and you have your answer: 4,039.

Practice adding some large numbers. You can use a calculator to check your answers, but do the math on paper first. Try the stacking method, and be sure to line up your numbers properly along the ones place; otherwise, you're certain to get the wrong answer.

1. $7,921,492 + 4,228 + 9,293,161 + 1,031,385 =$ _____

2. $2,076,023 + 3,714,224 + 8,823,291 + 9,900,306 =$ _____

3. $608,283 + 687,482 + 505,299 + 837,529 =$ _____

4. $164,089 + 748,698 + 310,189 + 128,978 =$ _____

5. $249,618 + 624,759 + 783,026 + 374,250 =$ _____

Here are the answers:

1.
$$\begin{array}{r} \scriptstyle 1\ \ 111\ 21 \\ 7,921,492 \\ 4,228 \\ 9,293,161 \\ \underline{1,031,385} \\ 18,250,266 \end{array}$$

2.
$$\begin{array}{r} \scriptstyle 2\ 11\ \ \ 11 \\ 2,076,023 \\ 3,714,224 \\ 8,823,291 \\ \underline{9,900,306} \\ 24,513,844 \end{array}$$

3.
$$\begin{array}{r} \scriptstyle 1\ 2\ 1\ 2\ 2 \\ 608,283 \\ 687,482 \\ 505,299 \\ \underline{837,529} \\ 2,638,593 \end{array}$$

4.
$$\begin{array}{r} \scriptstyle 1\ 2\ 1\ 3\ 3 \\ 164,089 \\ 748,698 \\ 310,189 \\ \underline{128,978} \\ 1,351,954 \end{array}$$

5.
$$\begin{array}{r} \scriptstyle 2\ 2\ 1\ 1\ 2 \\ 249,618 \\ 624,759 \\ 783,026 \\ \underline{374,250} \\ 2,031,653 \end{array}$$

Subtraction

Subtraction removes one quantity from the other, making it the opposite of addition. You can usually subtract small numbers in your head. For example, you probably have no trouble figuring out that $23 - 7 = 16$. When confronted with larger numbers, however, the operation becomes a little more challenging. Unless you're a math whiz, for example, you'd probably have a tough time figuring out this one: $753,874 - 394,826 = ?$

To subtract larger numbers, take a similar approach to the approach described in the preceding section on addition. Only this time, instead of carrying over numbers to the tens, hundreds, and thousands places, you may need to borrow from those places. Here's an example:

$$\begin{array}{r} \overset{2}{3}\overset{15}{6}\overset{1}{2} \\ -189 \\ \hline 173 \end{array}$$

Keep in mind what you learned in the preceding section about places. 362 is actually $300+60+2$, and 189 is $100+80+9$. You can't subtract 9 from the 2 above it, so you borrow 10 from the 60 to give yourself 12. $12-9=3$, which is what you put at the bottom in the ones place. Borrowing 10 from 60 makes the 6 at the top a 5. You can't subtract 8 from 5, so you have to borrow 100 from the 300. That gives you 15 where the 6 was. $15-8=7$, so put that in the tens place at the bottom. You now have $2-1$ in the hundreds place. $2-1=1$, so put the 1 down at the bottom in the hundreds place, and you have your answer: 173.

Try your hand at the following subtraction problems:

1. $237-159 = $ _____

2. $123-84 = $ _____

3. $92-29 = $ _____

4. $743-574 = $ _____

5. $327-132 = $ _____

Check your work against the following answers, not only to make sure you got the answer right but also to see whether you did the math correctly:

1.
$$\begin{array}{r} \overset{1}{2}\overset{12}{3}\overset{1}{7} \\ -159 \\ \hline 78 \end{array}$$

2.
$$\begin{array}{r} \overset{0}{1}\overset{11}{2}\overset{1}{3} \\ -84 \\ \hline 39 \end{array}$$

3.
$$\begin{array}{r} \overset{8}{9}\overset{1}{2} \\ -29 \\ \hline 63 \end{array}$$

4.
$$\begin{array}{r} \overset{6}{7}\overset{13}{4}\overset{1}{3} \\ -574 \\ \hline 169 \end{array}$$

5.
$$\begin{array}{r} \overset{2}{3}\overset{1}{2}7 \\ -132 \\ \hline 195 \end{array}$$

On the GED Math test, you have to do some basic arithmetic without a calculator, so be sure you do understand this work. If you're weak in subtraction or need additional practice, check out `http://www.math-aids.com/Subtraction/` or search for "subtraction worksheets" online for lots of examples for you to work on.

Multiplication

Multiplication is a shortcut for adding a number to itself a specified number of times; for example, $8 \times 3 = 8 + 8 + 8$. At some point in your life, you probably had to learn your multiplication tables from 1 to 12, as shown in Figure 5-3. If you haven't, now's a good time to practice. Being able to multiply numbers in your head will save you time on the test and probably help you answer one or more of the first five questions you have to tackle without a calculator.

x	1	2	3	4	5	6	7	8	9	10	11	12
1	1	2	3	4	5	6	7	8	9	10	11	12
2	2	4	6	8	10	12	14	16	18	20	22	24
3	3	6	9	12	15	18	21	24	27	30	33	36
4	4	8	12	16	20	24	28	32	36	40	44	48
5	5	10	15	20	25	30	35	40	45	50	55	60
6	6	12	18	24	30	36	42	48	54	60	66	72
7	7	14	21	28	35	42	49	56	63	70	77	84
8	8	16	24	32	40	48	56	64	72	80	88	96
9	9	18	27	36	45	54	63	72	81	90	99	108
10	10	20	30	40	50	60	70	80	90	100	110	120
11	11	22	33	44	55	66	77	88	99	110	121	132
12	12	24	36	48	60	72	84	96	108	120	132	144

Figure 5-3: Multiplication table.

John Wiley & Sons, Inc.

When challenged to multiply longer numbers, you have two options. The first option is to multiply the larger number by the smaller number in steps and add the results; for example:

$$214 \times 34 = 214 \times 4 + 214 \times 30 = 856 + 6,420 = 7,276$$

Another option is to stack the numbers with the smaller number on the bottom and use long multiplication, as follows:

1. **Write the smaller number below the larger number so their ones places align.**

$$\begin{array}{r} 214 \\ \times 34 \\ \hline \end{array}$$

2. **Multiply the number in the top row by the ones place number in the bottom row and write your answer below the line.**

   $4 \times 4 = 16$, so write a 6 below the line and carry the 1, so it appears over the 1 in 214. Then, multiply $4 \times 1 = 4$, add the 1 you carried to get 5, and then write that below the line to the left of the 6. Now multiply $4 \times 2 = 8$ and write that to the left of the 5.

$$\begin{array}{r} \overset{1}{2}14 \\ \times 34 \\ \hline 856 \end{array}$$

3. **Place a 0 below the ones place in the first answer you arrived at, because the next number you'll be multiplying is in the tens place, which will not produce any values in the ones place.**

   In this example, the 0 goes below the 6 in 856.

$$\begin{array}{r} 2\overset{1}{1}4 \\ \times 34 \\ \hline 856 \\ 0 \end{array}$$

4. **Multiply the number in the top row by the tens place number in the bottom row and write your answer at the bottom.**

   $3 \times 4 = 12$, so write a 2 below the 5 in 856 and carry the 1, so it appears over the 1 in 214. Then, multiply $3 \times 1 = 3$, add the 1 you carried to get 4, and then write that below the 8. Now multiply $3 \times 2 = 6$ and write that to the left of the 4.

$$\begin{array}{r} 2\overset{1}{1}4 \\ \times 34 \\ \hline 856 \\ 6,420 \end{array}$$

5. **Add the two numbers below the line and you have your answer.**

$$\begin{array}{r} 214 \\ \times 34 \\ \hline \overset{1}{8}56 \\ 6,420 \\ \hline 7,276 \end{array}$$

Try your hand at the following multiplication problems:

1. $13 \times 7 =$ _____

2. $21 \times 42 =$ _____

3. $57 \times 2 =$ _____

4. $743 \times 574 =$ _____

5. $327 \times 79 =$ _____

Check your work against the following answers, not only to make sure you got the answer right but also to see whether you did the math correctly:

1. This one's easy: $13 \times 7 = 10 \times 7 + 3 \times 7 = 70 + 21 = 91$.

2. $$\begin{array}{r} 21 \\ \times 42 \\ \hline 42 \\ 840 \\ \hline 882 \end{array}$$

3. This is another easy one: $57 \times 2 = 50 \times 2 + 7 \times 2 = 100 + 14 = 114$.

4. This is a tough one. Hope you didn't forget to put your zeros in the bottom rows. Add one zero when multiplying by the tens place and two zeros when multiplying by the hundreds place.

$$
\begin{array}{r}
743 \\
\times 574 \\
\hline
2{,}972 \\
52{,}010 \\
371{,}500 \\
\hline
426{,}482
\end{array}
$$

5. This one would rank as moderately difficult:

$$
\begin{array}{r}
327 \\
\times 79 \\
\hline
2{,}943 \\
22{,}890 \\
\hline
25{,}833
\end{array}
$$

Division

Division splits a quantity into equal parts. For example, divide a pizza by 8 and you end up with 8 equal slices. A division problem is usually written in the form $a \div b$, where a is the *dividend* and b is the *divisor,* or as $b\overline{)a}$. The answer is called the *quotient.*

 If you know your multiplication tables, you should have no problem dividing small numbers. If you need practice, eat more pizza or visit www.math-drills.com/division.shtml. To divide larger numbers, you need to use *long division,* as in the following steps.

1. **Write the two numbers in standard long-division format with the dividend inside and divisor outside the long division symbol.**

   For example, $925 \div 25$ would look like this:

   $$25\overline{)925}$$

2. **Figure out how many times the divisor can go into the left-most digit(s) of the dividend and write that number above the line.**

   In this case, 25 goes into 9 zero times, but it goes into 92 three times.

   $$\begin{array}{r}03 \\ 25\overline{)925}\end{array}$$

3. **Multiply the top number by the divisor and write it below the digit(s) of the dividend you just divided.**

   So, $3 \times 25 = 75$ goes below the 92.

   $$\begin{array}{r}03 \\ 25\overline{)925} \\ 75\end{array}$$

4. **Subtract the product you just wrote below the dividend from the digits above it:**
   $92 - 75 = 17$.

$$\begin{array}{r} 03 \\ 25\overline{)925} \\ 75 \\ \hline 17 \end{array}$$

5. **Drop the next digit in the divisor down to the number you just calculated.**

In this example, you drop down the 5 at the end of 925: $25\overline{)925}$ $\dfrac{03}{}$.

$$\begin{array}{r} 75 \\ \hline 175 \end{array}$$

6. **Figure out how many times the divisor goes into the number you arrived at in Step 5 and write that number above the line to the right of the previous number you wrote above the line:** $175 \div 25 = 7$, **so write 7 to the right of the 3.**

$$\begin{array}{r} 037 \\ 25\overline{)925} \\ 75 \\ \hline 175 \end{array}$$

To check your work, multiply your answer by the divisor: $37 \times 25 = 925$.

Of course, the answer may not be so neat and tidy. If you end up with a number at the end that can't be evenly divided by the divisor, then that number is the *remainder*. You note it at the top by writing *r* followed by the remainder, as in the following example:

$$\begin{array}{r} 15\,r4 \\ 5\overline{)79} \\ 5 \\ \hline 29 \\ 25 \\ \hline 4 \end{array}$$

Place the remainder over the divisor to create a fraction, so the quotient in this example would be written as $15\frac{4}{5}$. If you wanted to end up with a decimal answer, you could change the fraction to a decimal $15\frac{4}{5} = 15.8$

Practice your division skills on the following problems:

1. $208 \div 13 =$ _____

2. $357 \div 17 =$ _____

3. $56 \div 7 =$ _____

4. $462 \div 33 =$ _____

5. $127 \div 8 =$ _____

Check your work:

1. The answer is 16.

$$
\begin{array}{r}
016 \\
13\overline{)208} \\
\underline{13} \\
78 \\
\underline{78} \\
0
\end{array}
$$

2. The answer is 21.

$$
\begin{array}{r}
021 \\
17\overline{)357} \\
\underline{34} \\
17 \\
\underline{17} \\
0
\end{array}
$$

3. If you know your multiplication tables, this one's a snap. $7 \times 8 = 56$, so the answer is 8.

4. The answer is 14.

$$
\begin{array}{r}
014 \\
33\overline{)462} \\
\underline{33} \\
132 \\
\underline{132} \\
0
\end{array}
$$

5. The answer is 15 remainder 7, or $15\frac{7}{8}$, or 15.875.

$$
\begin{array}{r}
015\,r7 \\
8\overline{)127} \\
\underline{8} \\
47 \\
\underline{40} \\
7
\end{array}
$$

 Long division is difficult for many people who rely on calculators. It's actually quite easy, so look for some practice worksheets online. One good site is www.dadsworksheets.com. The worksheets show you how to do the math, give you lots of practice, and even provide the answers and explanations.

Exponents

Exponents are a shorthand method of indicating the repeated multiplication of the same number. For example, 2^4, which is read "two to the fourth," equals 16. In this case, the 2 is referred to as the *base,* and the 4 is the *exponent* or *power.* Following are some simple rules that must be followed with exponents:

- Any number raised to the power of 0 equals 1, so 1^0 and $127{,}895^0$ both equal 1.

    Tip: Next time you owe someone money, offer to pay the person what you owe to the zero power. If the person says yes, your debt will be forgiven for $1.00.

- Any number raised to the power of 1 equals itself, so $16^1 = 16$.

- To multiply numbers with exponents where the base is the same, simply keep the one base and add the exponents. For example, $35^4 \times 35^2 \times 35^5 = 35^{11}$.

- To divide exponents with the same base, keep the base and subtract the exponents. For example, $35^5 \div 35^3 = 35^2$.

A negative exponent is the inverse of the number, written as a fraction consisting of 1 over the base. For example, 25^{-2} means 1 over 25 squared, or $\frac{1}{25^2}$, which works out to $\frac{1}{625}$.

For the test, you should be able to determine common squares for numbers 1 through 12 forward and backward. By "backward," we mean if you know that the square of 9 is 81, you should recognize that the square root of 81 is 9. Here are the squares for the numbers 1 through 12:

Number	Squared
1	1
2	4
3	9
4	16
5	25
6	36
7	49
8	64
9	81
10	100
11	121
12	144

Many calculators will calculate powers and roots for you, but a quicker way of doing simple powers is to repeatedly multiply the base the number of times indicated by the power.

To get some practice with exponents, try your hand at answering the following questions:

1. What is the value of $(9^x)^y$ if $x = 2$ and $y = 3$?

   (A) 9^5

   (B) 9^6

   (C) 527,144

   (D) 54

2. Simplify the following equation: $(12^3 + 9^2 + 7^4)^0$

   (A) 4,210

   (B) 0

   (C) 1

   (D) 28^{10}

3. Simplify the following equation: $x^2 \times x^5 \times x^3$

   (A) $10x$

   (B) x^{21}

   (C) x^{10}

   (D) cannot be determined

4. Find $8^9 \div 8^7$

   (A) 1

   (B) 64

   (C) 128

   (D) 32

5. Find $27^{\frac{1}{3}}$

   (A) 9

   (B) 81

   (C) 3

   (D) 27

Check your answers:

1. Plug in the numbers for x and y and you get $(9^2)^3$. Knowing the rule "when an exponent has an exponent, keep the base and multiply the exponents together," you keep the 9 and multiply the exponents to get 9^6, which is Choice (B).

2. We hope you didn't do all that math inside the parentheses! Any number raised to the 0 power is 1, so the answer is Choice (C).

3. When you multiply values with the same base and different exponents, you keep the base and add the exponents, so $x^2 \times x^5 \times x^3 = x^{2+5+3} = x^{10}$, which is Choice (C).

4. To divide numbers that have the same base, subtract the exponents, so $8^9 \div 8^7 = 8^{9-7} = 8^2 = 64$, or Choice (B).

5. What is the cube root of 27? The answer is 3: $3 \times 3 \times 3 = 27$, answer Choice (D).

Honoring the order of operations (PEMDAS)

When you're solving mathematical equations, you must perform the operations in the correct sequence to arrive at the correct answer. The sequence, known as PEMDAS, goes like this:

Parentheses

Exponents

Multiplication

Division

Addition

Subtraction

or "Please Excuse My Dear Aunt Sally"

Perform the operations in the wrong order and you get the wrong answer. For example, $54 + 10 \div 2$ can produce two different answers. If you add 54 and 10 and then divide by 2, you get 64 divided by 2 equals 32. If you divide 10 by 2 first and then add 54, you get $54 + 5 = 59$.

Some folks refer to the order of operations as BEMDAS, where the B stands for **B**rackets, a synonym for parentheses.

Note: There is an exception concerning the priority of order when multiplication and division are both present and/or when addition and subtraction are both present. When D for division comes before M for multiplication, these operations have the same priority, so the math computations should be completed in the order they occur from left to right. The same is also true when S for subtraction occurs before A for addition.

Here are a few practice problems:

1. $4^3 \div 2 \times 8 =$ _____

2. $(123 - 43) \times 3 =$ _____

3. $1,000 - (12 - 6)^3 =$ _____

4. $12 - 9 \div 3 \times (5 + 2) =$ _____

5. $128 \div 8^{-3} \times 4 =$ _____

Check your answers:

1. No parentheses in this one, so do your exponent first: $4^3 = 64$. Working left to right, division is next, so $8 \div 2 = 4$. Finally, $64 \div 4 = 16$.

2. Parentheses first, so $123 - 43 = 80$. $80 \times 3 = 240$.

3. Parentheses first gives you $12 - 6 = 6$. Exponent next, so $6^3 = 216$. Subtract that from 1,000 and you get 784.

4. Parentheses first gives you $5 + 2 = 7$. Going left to right, division comes next, so $9 \div 3 = 3$. Multiply $3 \times 7 = 21$. Wrap up with subtraction: $63 - 21 = 42$.

5. Exponent first; the cube root of 8 is 2. Working left to right, next up is division: $128 \div 2 = 64$. Finally, multiply: $64 \times 4 = 256$.

Now try it on a real-world problem:

Joe and Sandy are planning to move in to a new apartment and want to spend some of their tax refund redecorating and buying new furniture. After hours of shopping and research, they decide to purchase the following items:

    1 sofa at $1,250

    1 chair at $350

    2 table lamps at $28 each

    1 side table at $5

Unfortunately, their living room floor is in terrible shape. They find an interesting pattern of broadloom carpeting at $17 per square yard. If the room is square and measures 18 feet across, how much money would they need to buy everything?

(A) $7,259

(B) $2,335

(C) $2,363

(D) $2,057

For the purposes of this example, look at the operations needed to answer the question. The first thing you should notice is that the broadloom is priced in square yards, while the room was measured in feet. You must convert the dimensions of the room from feet to yards (or the price of the carpet from dollars per square yard to dollars per square foot) to begin working on the question. Because a yard is 3 feet and the room dimension given is a multiple of 3, converting the room dimensions from square feet to square yards is easier. If the room is square and 18 feet across, it's 6 yards across, so you need 6^2 square yards of carpet to cover the floor, and your equation looks like this:

Note: To convert square feet into square yards, you divide by 9. To convert square yards to square feet, you multiply by 9.

$$\$1,250 + \$350 + (2 \times \$28) + 6^2 \times \$17$$

Parentheses first gives you

$$\$1,250 + \$350 + \$56 + 6^2 \times \$17$$

Exponents next gives you

$$\$1,250 + \$350 + \$56 + 36 \times \$17$$

Multiplication gives you

$$\$1,250 + \$350 + \$56 + \$612$$

Do the addition and you get your answer

$$
\begin{array}{r}
1,250 \\
350 \\
56 \\
+612 \\
\hline
2,268 \\
\end{array}
$$

Fiddling with Fractions

Fractions are mathematical shorthand for representing division. For example, $\frac{32}{56}$ is the same as $32 \div 56$. Normally, fractions aren't likely to cause a lot of aggravation, but when you need to add, subtract, multiply, or divide fractions, they can become cumbersome. You need to know the rules that govern these operations. In this section, we explain the rules and show you how to put them into practice.

In a fraction, the top number is called the *numerator,* and the bottom number is called the *denominator.* The denominator tells you how many parts the whole is divided into, and the numerator shows you how many parts are left. You probably won't be asked to identify a numerator or denominator in a police lineup or on the test, but these names come in handy when we discuss fractions in this section.

Reducing fractions to their lowest terms

Before you get into the nitty-gritty of doing math with fractions, take some time to simplify your life by simplifying the fractions you're working with. Simplifying fractions — converting them to their lowest terms — gives you smaller numbers to work with.

To convert a fraction to its lowest terms, factor the numerator and denominator, cross out any and all common factors, and then multiply any remaining factors in the numerator and denominator separately. You have to admit that finding $\frac{4}{5}$ of 80 is a lot easier than finding $\frac{12}{15}$ of 80!

To reduce quickly, divide by the greatest common factor. (See the earlier section, "Factoring a number," for more info.) Or, just use numbers you're certain divide both the numerator and denominator, and repeat until no common factors remain.

When you're looking at your answer choices, remember that the choices are probably in simplest form, so make sure your answer is too.

Adding and subtracting fractions

To add or subtract fractions, they must have a common denominator. Imagine the nightmare of figuring out how much pie you have left after a party if one was cut into six pieces and the other was cut into eight! So, the first order of adding and subtracting fractions is to make sure they all have a common denominator. When they do, adding and subtracting is a snap. All you do is add or subtract the numerators, like so:

$$\frac{3}{12} + \frac{4}{12} = \frac{7}{12}$$

The tricky part is getting those denominators to match. The easiest way is to simply multiply the denominators; for example, if your denominators are 4 and 5, you multiply them to get 20. However, very importantly, you must also multiply the numerator by the same number you used to change the denominator to avoid changing the actual value of the fraction. Here's an example:

$$\frac{3}{4} + \frac{4}{5} = \left(\frac{3}{4} \times \frac{5}{5}\right) + \left(\frac{4}{5} \times \frac{4}{4}\right) = \frac{15}{20} + \frac{16}{20} = \frac{31}{20}$$

Always multiply the numerator and the denominator by the same number to avoid changing the actual value of the fraction. When you multiply any number by a fraction that has the same numerator and denominator, you're multiplying the number by 1 and not changing its value. All these fractions are equal to 1:

$$\frac{2}{2}, \frac{3}{3}, \frac{15}{15}, \frac{270}{270} = \frac{1}{1} = 1$$

As long as the denominators match, you're good to go, but aim for finding the least common denominator (LCD), so you're working with smaller numbers. In the case of $\frac{3}{4}$ and $\frac{4}{5}$, the LCD is the product of the two denominators: $4 \times 5 = 20$. However, that's not always the case. For example, if you're looking at $\frac{3}{4}$ and $\frac{2}{8}$, the LCD is 4: $\frac{2}{8} = \frac{1}{4}$. To find the LCD of two fractions, you need to find the least common multiple (LCM) of the two denominators. (See the earlier section, "Exploring multiples," for instructions.)

Try reducing the fractions before hunting for their LCDs. (See the preceding section, "Reducing fractions to their lowest terms.") Sometimes, the common denominator is actually *smaller* than either of the two denominators provided in the question. Just be sure to divide the numerator by the same factor used to reduce the denominator, so you're not changing the value of the fraction.

Here are a few sample problems that challenge your ability to add and subtract fractions:

1. $\frac{9}{27} - \frac{2}{18} =$ _____

2. $\frac{8}{25} + \frac{4}{16} =$ _____

3. $\frac{3}{7} + \frac{2}{3} + \frac{9}{10} =$ _____

4. $\frac{7}{8} + \frac{2}{5} - \frac{3}{5} = \left(\frac{7}{8} \times \frac{5}{5}\right) + \left(\frac{2}{5} \times \frac{8}{8}\right) - \left(\frac{3}{5} \times \frac{8}{8}\right) = \frac{35}{40} + \frac{16}{40} - \frac{24}{40} = \frac{27}{40} =$ _____

Check your answers:

1. Divide the numerator and the denominator in the first fraction by 3 and divide the numerator and denominator in the second fraction by 2 to make this a very easy problem:

$$\frac{9}{27} - \frac{2}{18} = \frac{3}{9} - \frac{1}{9} = \frac{2}{9}$$

2. The first order of business is to reduce $\frac{4}{16}$ to $\frac{1}{4}$. The resulting numerator has no common factors with the other numerator, so you need to multiply them: $4 \times 25 = 100$. Here's the math:

$$\frac{8}{25} + \frac{1}{4} = \left(\frac{8}{25} \times \frac{4}{4}\right) + \left(\frac{1}{4} \times \frac{25}{25}\right) = \frac{32}{100} + \frac{25}{100} = \frac{57}{100}$$

3. The numerators have no common factor, so you must multiply the numerators: $7 \times 3 \times 10 = 210$. Now, multiply each factor by a form of 1 that makes each denominator 210 and do the math:

$$\frac{3}{7} + \frac{2}{3} + \frac{9}{10} = \frac{(3x30) + (2x70) + (9x21)}{210} = \frac{90 + 140 + 189}{210} = \frac{419}{210}$$

4. The first order of business is to leave the second fraction as $\frac{2}{3}$. You can then multiply the denominators 7, 3, and 10 to get the least common denominator of 210 and do the math.

Multiplying fractions

To multiply one fraction by another, simply multiply the numerators by the denominators; for example:

$$\frac{a}{b} \times \frac{c}{d} = \frac{ac}{bd}$$

To multiply a series of fractions, just continue the process. Remember that you should simplify the resultant fraction by dividing the numerator and denominator by the least common multiple. (See the earlier section, "Exploring multiples," for instructions.)

When multiplying fractions, look for opportunities to reduce the numerator in one fraction and the denominator in the other fraction by a common factor. Here's an example:

$$\frac{^{3}\cancel{51}}{^{12}\cancel{144}} \times \frac{^{1}\cancel{12}}{^{1}\cancel{17}} = \frac{3}{12} = \frac{1}{4}$$

$51 = 17 \times 3$ is the numerator of the first fraction and 17 is the denominator of the second, so you can divide both by 17 to reduce 51 to 3 and 17 to 1. Likewise, both the denominator of the first fraction and the numerator of the second are divisible by 12, so that reduces 144 to 12 and 12 to 1. These simplifications make the fractions much smaller and easier to manage.

Here are a couple sample problems:

1. $\frac{7}{12} \times \frac{3}{4} =$ _____

2. $\frac{2}{3} \times \frac{3}{5} \times \frac{7}{8} =$ _____

Check your work:

1.

$$\frac{7}{^{4}\cancel{12}} \times \frac{^{1}\cancel{3}}{4} = \frac{7}{16}$$

2.

$$\frac{^{1}\cancel{2}}{^{1}\cancel{3}} \times \frac{^{1}\cancel{3}}{5} \times \frac{7}{^{4}\cancel{8}} = \frac{7}{20}$$

Dividing fractions

To divide a fraction by a fraction, invert the fraction you're dividing by and multiply; for example:

$$\frac{a}{b} \div \frac{c}{d} = \frac{a}{b} \times \frac{d}{c} = \frac{ad}{bc}$$

Always remember to simplify by dividing the numerator and denominator by the same common factors.

Work a couple sample problems to get the hang of it:

1. $\dfrac{9}{17} \div \dfrac{3}{4} =$ _____

2. $\dfrac{8}{24} \div \dfrac{24}{48} =$ _____

Check your work:

1. Invert the second fraction, convert the division sign to a multiplication sign, simplify if possible, and do the math:

$$\frac{\overset{3}{\cancel{9}}}{17} \times \frac{4}{\cancel{3}_{1}} = \frac{12}{17}$$

2. This one's mind-numbingly easy if you simplify the two fractions after inverting the second one:

$$\frac{\overset{1}{\cancel{8}}}{\cancel{24}_{1}} \times \frac{\overset{2}{\cancel{48}}}{\cancel{24}_{3}} = \frac{2}{3}$$

Working with mixed numbers

A *mixed number* is a combination of a whole number and a fraction; for example, $8\frac{1}{2}$.

If you need to use a mixed number as a fraction to solve a problem, multiply the whole number by the denominator and add it to the numerator. In this case it would produce

$$\frac{8 \times 2 + 1}{2} = \frac{16 + 1}{2} = \frac{17}{2}$$

From this point on, you can use the mixed number as a fraction.

Dealing with Decimals

A *decimal* represents a fraction whose denominator is a multiple of 10. You use decimals all the time whenever you buy something or compare prices. $.53, for example, is really the fraction $\frac{53}{100}$, where the 100 represents the number of cents in a dollar.

The number system used in math is a base 10 system, as was explained earlier in this chapter in the discussion of number places. Just as a number can have a tens place, a hundreds place, and a thousands place to the left of a decimal, it can have a tenths place, a hundredths place, and a thousandths place to the right of a decimal:

.1 is one-tenth

.01 is one one-hundredth

.001 is one one-thousandth

In the following sections, we cover the basics of adding, subtracting, multiplying, and dividing decimals, explain how to round decimals, and touch on the inner workings of scientific notation, which depends heavily on the base 10 system.

Adding and subtracting decimals

You add and subtract decimals the same way you add and subtract other numbers. The only tricky part is making sure your column of numbers is aligned along the decimal points, as in the following example:

$$
\begin{array}{r}
\overset{1\ 1\ 1\ \ 1\ 1}{3.87} \\
33.918 \\
+83.082 \\
\hline
120.870
\end{array}
$$

Multiplying decimals

Multiplying decimals is a three-step process:

1. **Ignore the decimals and multiply the numbers as you normally do.**

2. **Count the number of decimal places.**

3. **Move the decimal point at the end of the number to the left the number of decimal places you counted in Step 2.**

For example, suppose you're called on to multiply 4.03 and 7.83. Here's what you do:

1. **Ignore the decimals and multiply the numbers as you normally do:**

$$
\begin{array}{r}
403 \\
\times 783 \\
\hline
1,209 \\
32,240 \\
282,100 \\
\hline
315,549
\end{array}
$$

2. **Count the number of decimal places.**

   4.03 has two decimal places, plus the two decimal places in 7.83 equals four total.

3. **Move the decimal point at the end of the number four decimal places to the left to get your answer: 31.5549.**

Dividing decimals

To divide decimals or divide a larger number into a smaller number to produce a decimal, take the following steps:

1. **If both the dividend and the divisor contain decimal points, move the decimal point to the right the same number of places in both numbers to simplify things.**

   For example, suppose you have $1.44 \div 1.2$. Move the decimal point one place to the right in each number to get $14.4 \div 12$.

2. **Write the division problem in long-division format, as explained in the earlier section, "Division."**

   Continuing the example from Step 1, you should have the following:

$$12\overline{)14.4}$$

3. **Place your decimal point on the top line, above the existing decimal point in the dividend if one is present or above the space to the left of the dividend if the dividend has no decimal point.**

$$12\overline{)14.\overset{\cdot}{4}}$$

4. **Do the math.**

$$\begin{array}{r} 1.2 \\ 12\overline{)14.4} \\ \underline{12} \\ 24 \end{array}$$

When performing long division to produce an answer with a decimal in it, you can add zeros to the end of the dividend without changing its value. For example, $4.23 = 4.230 = 4.2300$. This comes in handy when you run out of numbers to drop down during the division process.

Here are a few practice problems:

1. $0.1 \div 5 =$ _____

2. $3 \div 7 =$ _____

3. $24 \div 36 =$ _____

Check your work:

1. You can't move the decimal point in either number, so you need to divide 5 into 0.1. Be sure to place your decimal point above the line and above the decimal point in the dividend. Because 5 goes into 0 zero times, write 0 to the left of the decimal point. Because 5 goes into 1 zero times, write 0 to the right of the decimal point. Add 0 to the end of the dividend to give yourself more numbers to work with. Now, 5 goes into 10 twice, so write a 2 in the hundredths place, and you have your answer: 0.02.

$$\begin{array}{r} 0.02 \\ 5\overline{)0.10} \end{array}$$

2. Use long division and remember to place your decimal point:

$$\begin{array}{r} 0.428 \\ 7\overline{)3.000} \\ \underline{28} \\ 20 \\ \underline{14} \\ 60 \\ \underline{56} \\ 4 \end{array}$$

3. Start by writing this problem as a fraction and reducing it:

$$\frac{24}{36} = \frac{2}{3}$$

Now divide 2 by 3:

$$
\begin{array}{r}
0.66 \\
3{\overline{\smash{\big)}\,2.00}} \\
\underline{18} \\
20 \\
\underline{18} \\
2
\end{array}
$$

Rounding decimals

Many decimals are very long, and with each additional digit comes less accuracy. If you went into a store and saw a price listed as $26.78294830, you would start to wonder. There is no currency less than one cent, which means that any numbers after the .78 are so small as to be meaningless. To get around this issue, you may have to "round" decimals to the nearest digit. After you decide on the digit you want to end with, look at the digit to the right of it. If it's 5 or greater, add 1 to the digit in question. If not, just let it be.

In the price example, the price would be $26.78 rounded to two decimal points.

Test your skills at rounding up and down:

1. Round 0.2395 to the nearest hundredth place: _____

2. Round 756.646 to the nearest hundredth place: _____

3. Round 10.097 to the nearest thousandths place: _____

Check your answers:

1. Nearest hundredths is two decimal places. The 3 is followed by a 9, so you round the 3 up to 4. Answer: 0.24.

2. The 4 is followed by a 6, so you round the 4 up to 5. Answer: 756.65.

3. Trick question. It's already rounded to the thousandths place.

Understanding scientific notation

Scientific notation is a system that scientists use to simplify the expression of really big or really small numbers. For example, instead of describing a particle as 0.000000000000000381 centimeters in diameter, a scientist would probably write 3.81×10^{-16}.

If the 10 is raised to a negative power, move the decimal point to the left the same number of spaces as the exponent's value; for example, if the number is 2.47×10^{-7}, move the decimal place seven spaces to the left, and insert a zero in each space that doesn't already have a number, so $2.47 \times 10^{-7} = 0.000000247$. If the 10 is raised to a positive power, move the decimal point to the right and insert a zero in each space that doesn't have a number. The initial integer must be a number which is greater than or equal to 1 or less than 10.

Handling Percentages

A *percentage* is a fraction of 100. 50% is $\frac{50}{100}$ or $\frac{1}{2}$ or 0.5. You're likely to bump into a few percentage problems on the GED Math test, especially in the form of word problems. As you'll see in this section, percentages are close cousins with decimals and fractions. Test takers often get tripped up by percentage problems, however, because they're not accustomed to seeing them. Don't make that mistake.

Percentages can be manipulated like any other number. If Store A offered you a 17% discount and Store B offered to double it, Store B would be offering you a discount of $2 \times 17\% = 34\%$.

Converting among percentages, decimals, and fractions

You can easily transform percentages into decimal equivalents or fractions and vice versa to simplify calculations. In some cases, for example, you may find it easier to multiply a value by $\frac{1}{2}$ than by 50% or .50. Here are the standard operating procedures for performing the conversions.

To Convert	Do This
Percent to decimal	Move the decimal two places to the left and drop the percent sign
Percent to fraction	Write the percent over 100 and simplify
Decimal to fraction	Write the decimal over 1 and multiply the top and bottom by 10 for every number to the right of the decimal point
Decimal to percent	Move the decimal point to the left two places and add a percent sign
Fraction to decimal	Do the math — long division — or use a calculator
Fraction to percent	Divide the top number by the bottom number, multiply the result by 100, and add the percent sign

Think in terms of dollars and cents. Twenty-five cents is a quarter because it's a quarter of a dollar. One quarter $= \frac{25}{100}$ or 25% or 0.25.

Practice performing a few conversions. Test your skills at rounding up and down:

1. Convert 72% to a fraction and simplify: _____

2. Convert $\frac{5}{6}$ to a decimal rounded to the nearest hundredth: _____

3. Convert 0.63 to a percent: _____

Check your answers:

    1. 72% is $\frac{72}{100}$, which reduces to $\frac{18}{25}$.

2. Divide 5 by 6 to get 0.833, which rounds to 0.83.

$$
\begin{array}{r}
0.833 \\
6\overline{)5.000} \\
\underline{48} \\
20 \\
\underline{18} \\
20 \\
\underline{18} \\
2
\end{array}
$$

3. Easy: Move the decimal point two steps to the right and add a percent sign to get 63%.

Finding the percent of change

You may be asked to calculate the percentage of change between two quantities. For example, a manufacturer decides, due to rising material prices, to reduce the size of a box of its product instead of increasing its price. If the original size was 16 ounces and the new size is 14 ounces, what is the percentage change?

To solve this problem, you would first calculate the difference in size of the two packages: $16 - 14 = 2$.

Then divide the change by the original size, $2 \div 16 = 0.125$, and multiply by 100: $0.125 \times 100 = 12.5\%$. The new box is 12.5% smaller than the original box.

Practice Session

You'll probably never meet questions on the GED Math test that require the use of only one basic math skill. So here we provide a few questions that require a combination of skills to find the answer. In addition, we provide answers and explanations. If you answer a question incorrectly, definitely go over the explanation to make sure that you can answer similar questions correctly on test day.

1. George is trying very hard to get a scholarship to his local city college. He is told that with the severe competition this year, he'll need a minimum average of 93% in his best five subjects. In his final two semesters, George earns the following grades:

Mathematics	93%
English:	87%
History:	95%
Geography:	94%
Chemistry:	98%
Physics:	91%
Biology:	89%
Physical Education:	81%

    Would George qualify for a scholarship? _____.

2. Superior Detergent Company is planning to offer a special holiday package of detergent containing 25 ounces instead of the usual 16. What percentage more detergent does the special package offer?

    (A) 36%

    (B) 57%

    (C) 56.25%

    (D) 36.54%

3. Jean and Sally are playing bingo. The bingo cards are numbered 1 through 75. Fascinated with mathematics, they wonder how many of those numbers are prime numbers?

    (A) 22

    (B) 21

    (C) 23

    (D) 75

4. Jose and Fern are decorating their apartment. Because they do not want to make an irreversible change, they decide to buy an area rug. They see two interesting area rugs, one 9 feet by 12 feet and another 8 feet by 14 feet. Both will fit into the space. The 9-by-12 rug sells for $12.50 per square yard, and the 8-by-14 rug sells for $13.00 per square yard. Fern notices a small stain on the 8-by-14 rug, and the embarrassed salesperson offers them a 5% discount if they take it as is. What's the cost of the more expensive rug?

    (A) $1,350

    (B) $150.12

    (C) $1,456

    (D) $153.44

5. Jim is anxious to get home to celebrate Christmas with his family. He leaves his dorm at 6 in the morning with no plans to stop during the 300 miles to his parents' house. If he can average 55 miles per hour on the trip, what time will he arrive?

(A) 11:27 a.m.

(B) 12:45 a.m.

(C) 1:00 p.m.

(D) 1:27 p.m.

Check your answers:

1. Yes. George's 5 best subjects are Mathematics (93%), History (95%), Chemistry (98%), Geography (94%), and Physics (91%). Total the scores and divide by the number of scores to determine their average:

$$(93 + 95 + 98 + 94 + 91) / 5 = 471 / 5 = 94.2$$

George needed to average 93%, so yes, he qualifies for the scholarship.

2. (C) Subtract 16 from 25 to determine how much more detergent is being offered, and you get 9. Divide 9 by the original amount of detergent, which is 16 ounces, and you get 0.5625. Move the decimal point to the right two spaces and add a percent sign and you have your answer: 56.25%, Choice (C).

3. (B) The bingo cards contain the numbers from 1 to 75, and the prime numbers greater than 1 and less than 75 are: 2, 3, 5, 7, 11, 13, 17, 19, 23, 29, 31, 37, 41, 43, 47, 53, 59, 61, 67, 71, and 73. Choice (B) is the correct answer. If you're unsure, try factoring each of the numbers listed. Choice (A) probably includes 1, which is not a prime number, and Choices (C) and (D) are incorrect, probably through counting or assuming all 75 numbers are primes. When faced with a question where the skill required is counting a set of objects, make sure each object is rightly in the set and that you count carefully.

4. (D) The rug dimensions are expressed in feet, while the prices are given in square yards, so the first order of business is to convert feet to yards, or vice versa. Because the dimensions of the second rug don't easily convert to square yards, convert the prices to square feet by dividing each price by 9 (a square yard is 9 square feet):

   - For the 9-by-12-foot rug, the price per square foot is $12.50 \div 9 = \$1.39$ (actually $1.388, but you need to round up to the nearest penny).

   - For the 8-by-14-foot rug, the price is $13.00 \div 9 = \$1.44$ (rounded up to the nearest penny). A 5% discount would be $\$1.44 \times 0.05 = \$0.07$ (rounded down to the nearest penny). So, the actual cost is $\$1.44 - \$0.07 = \$1.37$.

   The cost of the 9-by-12 rug is $9 \times 12 \times \$1.39 = \$150.12$.

   The cost of the 8-by-14 rug is $8 \times 14 \times \$1.37 = \$153.44$, making it the higher-priced rug. Choice (D) is the correct answer. Choices (A) and (C) are calculated without converting the units, and Choice (B) doesn't answer the question.

5. (A) If Jim travels at a constant 55 mph, it will take him 5 hours and 27 minutes for the trip, because $300 \div 55 = 5.45$ hours, and 0.45 hours in minutes is $0.45 \text{ hours} \times \dfrac{60 \text{ minutes}}{1 \text{ hour}} = 27$ minutes. If he left the dorm at 6 and traveled for 5 hours and 27 minutes, he would arrive at 11:27 a.m.

Chapter 6

Solving Quantitative Problems with Rational Numbers

In This Chapter
▶ Making sense of word problems
▶ Solving math problems that require comparing quantities
▶ Squaring and cubing numbers and calculating their square and cube roots
▶ Tackling problems that involve rates and scales
▶ Calculating ratios, proportions, and percentages
▶ Practicing your skills on a variety of problems

Quantitative problems are questions that ask you to determine an amount or compare amounts in some way. The quantities may be purely numerical, such as 2 or $\sqrt{245}$, or a value combined with a unit, such as 255 marbles, 12 hours, or $125.87. Every one of these problems is, to some degree, a word problem, so you need to read the question, fully understand what it's asking you to figure out, assign a letter (such as x or y) to the unknown value you're asked to find, translate the words into an equation, and solve the equation. This doesn't just sound complicated and challenging — it is. Even if you're very good at math, word problems can twist things around in your brain, and with the added pressure of a time limit, it's easy to get flustered.

To successfully answer quantitative problems, you really have to know what you're doing. You need to know how to approach each type of problem, and you need to practice to the point at which you feel comfortable and confident. In this chapter, we help you gain the knowledge and skills you need to solve quantitative problems and provide plenty of practice to build your confidence.

You can't answer any math problem until you've mastered the basics. If you're having trouble understanding any of the concepts referenced in this chapter, flip back to Chapter 5 to refresh your memory.

Note: In some questions, metric measures are used because the metric system is a common system of measurement in science and in math. Because the questions do not ask you to convert from one system to another, you can use the numbers and attach the names, such as meters.

Tackling Word Problems

Making sense of word problems is a little like translating Spanish into English. Before you can do the math, you need to convert the problem, as described in the question, into a mathematical equation or at least figure out what the question is asking you to do in terms of mathematics. In addition, word problems typically require you to perform two or more steps to arrive at the answer.

When you encounter a word problem on the GED Mathematical Reasoning test (and most are word problems), remember the three Ds — Decipher, Decide, and Do:

1. **Decipher:** Read the problem and the answers carefully and write down what you know and need to figure out.

2. **Decide:** Figure out what you need to do or what steps you need to take to find the answer.

3. **Do:** Do the math and identify the correct answer.

Step 1: Decipher

The first step in solving a word problem is to figure out what the question instructs you to do. Is it asking you to determine a difference, an average, or a total? Do you need to determine a total time, a rate of speed, or a percentage? And what information does the question provide to help you figure out the answer? During this first step, you're sizing up the question, so you can decide how to proceed.

Read the question and the answer choices carefully. Both give clues as to what the answer looks like and help you envision your goal. Misreading a question is far too easy. For example, the following questions are similar but call for very different answers:

- Michael and Jenny sold their Halloween candy to earn some money. Jenny earned $35, and Michael earned $25. How much more money did Jenny earn than Michael?

- Michael and Jenny sold their Halloween candy to earn some money. Jenny earned $35, and Michael earned $25. They pooled their money and bought a used camera for $37.50. How much money did they have left?

- Michael and Jenny sold their Halloween candy to earn some money. Jenny earned $35, and Michael earned $25. They bought three garden gnomes and had $8.25 left. What is the average price they paid for each gnome?

When a question presents more details than you can keep in mind at one time, jot down notes on the scratchpad provided to list the knowns and the unknowns. Notes for the third example presented in the previous list may look something like this:

Jenny: $35

Michael: $25

J & M total = ?

Number of gnomes: 3

Cost of gnomes = ?

Average price = ?

Change: $8.25

With notes such as these, you now have a pretty good idea of what you need to figure out (your goal) and the information you have to get you there.

Step 2: Decide

You sized up the question and identified what you know and what the question is asking you to find out. At this point, you must decide how to use what you know to find out what you don't know. We can't provide you with step-by-step instructions that work for solving every problem, because every problem is different, but one approach is to write an equation using an unknown to represent the answer:

1. **Write what the question asks you to find, followed by the equal sign.**

   For example, if you're trying to determine the average price of the garden gnome in the last example in the previous section, you may want to use *g* to represent the average price of a garden gnome and start your equation like this:

   $g =$

2. **Using what you know, write your equation to the right of the equal sign.**

   For example, you know that the price of all three gnomes is the total amount of money Michael and Jenny earned minus what they have left. You also know that they bought three garden gnomes, and you know from math class that to determine the average, you have to divide the total cost by the number of items. So your equation looks like this:

   $g = (\$35 + \$25 - \$8.25)/3$

The other option is to do some of the math before writing your equation. This is more of a step-by-step approach, solving the problem in stages. (You're actually alternating between deciding *and* doing.) To solve the garden gnome problem using this approach, you'd take the following steps:

1. **Calculate the total that Jenny and Michael earned.**

   You can do this in your head: $\$35 + \$25 = \$60$.

2. **Calculate the cost of the garden gnomes by subtracting what they have left from their total: $\$60 - \$8.25 = \$51.75$.**

   Maybe you can do this in your head. If not, you can use the on-screen calculator provided by the testing service.

3. **Write your equation.**

   You know from math class that the average is the total cost divided by the number of items, so your equation is:

   $$g = \frac{\$51.75}{3}$$

Step 3: Do

Assuming you deciphered the question correctly and decided on the correct steps for solving the problem, it's crunch time — time to crunch the numbers and find the answer. If the math is straightforward and you're working with small, round numbers, you may be able to do the math in your head. If not, you can use the calculator or scribble your work on the scratchpad that's provided. To wrap up the garden gnome example, here's what this step looks like:

$$(\$35 + \$25 - \$8.25)/3 = (\$60 - \$8.25)/3 = \$51.75/3 = \$17.25$$

or

$$\frac{\$51.75}{3} = \$17.25$$

Now, all you need to do is cross your fingers and hope your answer matches one of the answer choices. If it does, you select the matching answer choice and move on to the next question. If it doesn't match, you need to step back through the process you took to figure out where you went wrong, correct the error, and redo the math.

TIP

If the quantities in the answer choices differ widely, you can often estimate to pick the correct answer and save yourself some time doing the math. For example, you can round the $8.25 in the example down to $8.00. Subtracting that from $60 gives you $52, and $52/3 is a little more than $17. Without determining the average precisely, you can easily pick the correct answer from choices like this:

(A) $20.25

(B) $19.75

(C) $17.25

(D) $15.25

Calculating and Comparing Quantities

The GED Math test contains very few of what we consider to be "true math" questions, such as "Factor 85" or "Determine the common factors of 9 and 21." You can find plenty of such questions in Chapter 5. Most problems involve both math and reason and take multiple steps to solve. However, a few problems focus more narrowly on working with and comparing numeric values. These questions rely heavily on the knowledge and skills presented in Chapter 5.

In the following sections, we describe types of questions that challenge you to calculate and compare quantities and present examples, so you know what to expect on the test.

Placing fractions and decimals in order

Certain math questions may instruct you to arrange fractions and decimals in order from lowest to highest value, indicate their positions on a number line, or compare a fraction and a decimal and determine which is greater. To answer these questions, you need to be able to convert fractions into decimal equivalents, and vice versa, as explained in Chapter 5. Here's an example:

EXAMPLE

After a party, the three hosts divide one gallon of leftover punch. Mary takes $\frac{3}{10}$ of it, Cindy takes $\frac{1}{2}$, and Jerry gets the rest. Plot the points on the following number line to represent the amount of punch each person took.

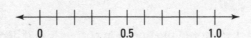

To answer this question, you first need to figure out how much punch Jerry took. If Mary took $\frac{3}{10}$, she has 0.3 gallon. Cindy took half, or 0.5 gallon. Doing some basic addition and subtraction, you discover that Jerry leaves with 0.2 gallon. Now all you have to do is plot the points:

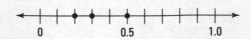

Arrange the following values from lowest to highest:

$$23.69$$

$$23\frac{4}{5}$$

$$23\frac{5}{7}$$

$$23\frac{3}{4}$$

1. _____ (lowest)

2. _____

3. _____

4. _____ (highest)

Because all the numbers start with 23, you can ignore that number for now. Convert the fractions to decimal equivalents: $\frac{4}{5} = \frac{8}{10} = 0.80$. Use your calculator to figure that $\frac{5}{7}$ is approximately 0.71. And $\frac{3}{4} = 75\%$ or 0.75 (you either know this from experience or can use your calculator). Add the 23 back in to each number, arrange the numbers, and you have

1. <u>23.69</u>

2. <u>23.71</u>

3. <u>23.75</u>

4. <u>23.80</u>

Solving problems with factors and multiples

You may encounter one or more questions on the Math test that require the ability to factor or determine multiples of two or more numbers. In Chapter 5, we explain factors, factoring, and multiples in greater detail, but questions aren't likely to ask you so directly to factor a number or determine its multiples. In fact, they may not even mention factors or multiples.

Simplify the following expression, leaving the answer in radical form: [　　　].

$$\sqrt{21} \cdot \sqrt{14}$$

To multiply square roots, you multiply the numbers inside the radicals and then simplify, but because these two numbers have obvious common factors, factoring the numbers before multiplying simplifies the process:

$$\sqrt{21} \cdot \sqrt{14} = \sqrt{3 \cdot 7 \cdot 2 \cdot 7} = \sqrt{3 \cdot 2 \cdot 7^2} = 7\sqrt{6}$$

Questions that require you to determine common multiples may be trickier.

Every 3 days, we feed our anaconda. Every 14 days, we clean his cage. Today, we cleaned his cage and fed him. How many days from today will we feed him and clean his cage on the same day?

(A) 28

(B) 42

(C) 26

(D) 35

You can find the answer in either of two ways:

✔ Write the multiples of each number and find the first match:

3, 6, 9, 12, 15, 18, 21, 24, 27, 30, 33, 36, 39, **42**

14, 28, **42**

✔ Factor the numbers and multiply each factor by the greatest number of times it occurs in either number:

$2 \times 3 \times 7 = 42$

Solving problems with rational exponents and scientific notation

Some questions on the test involve rational exponents and scientific notation, numbers such as 6^3, 27^2, and 10^{-4}. Chapter 5 provides detailed guidance on how to handle such numbers, but you need to practice questions that demand these skills. Here's an example.

Angels are known to be 3×10^{-5} millimeters wide. The head of a pin is 1.5 millimeters wide.

How many angels will fit on the head of a pin?

(A) 5×10^4

(B) 0.53×10^{-4}

(C) 5×10^5

(D) 2×10^4

To find the answer, you divide the width of the pinhead by the width of an angel:

$$\frac{1.5}{3 \times 10^{-5}} = \frac{0.5}{10^{-5}} = \frac{5 \times 10^{-1}}{10^{-5}} = 5 \times 10^4$$

From Chapter 5, you know that $0.5 = 5 \times 10^{-1}$ and that to divide exponents with the same base, you subtract exponents, so $10^{-1} \div 10^{-5} = 10^{-1-(-5)} = 10^4$, so the answer is 5×10^4.

Here's another word problem that challenges your ability to write and solve a mathematical expression that contains exponents.

A particle travels through space at 7^5 miles per hour. How many miles does it travel in 7^{12} hours?

(A) 7^{60}

(B) 7^7

(C) 7^{17}

(D) 7^{15}

To find out how far the particle travels, you multiply rate × time:

$$7^5 \times 7^{12} = 7^{5+12} = 7^{17}$$

Solving problems with absolute values

Absolute value is the magnitude of a number, which is its distance from zero on a number line, regardless of whether it's negative or positive, so the absolute value of 9 and –9 are the same. (See Chapter 5 for more about absolute value.) You may encounter one or two problems on the Math test that involve absolute values. The problem probably won't mention the term "absolute value," but the answer choices may bracket values or expressions between vertical lines, indicating that the value is an absolute. Here's an example:

An assembly line packages 16-ounce boxes of cereal with a tolerance of plus or minus $\frac{1}{2}$ ounce. Boxes not within the tolerance are discarded. Which of the following inequalities can be used to determine whether boxes of cereal are discarded?

(A) $|w - 0.5| \leq 16$

(B) $|w - 0.5| \geq 16$

(C) $|w - 16| \leq 0.5$

(D) $|w - 16| \geq 0.5$

The weight of the box minus the ideal box weight must be within ±0.5 or it is discarded. Choice (D) is the correct answer. You can plug in 16.6 and 15.4 to check.

Here's another problem related to absolute value:

Leslie's checking account balance is $150. She writes checks for a pair of boots costing $120 and an outfit costing $45. How much money must she deposit into her checking account to bring the balance up to $25? [   ]

Solving this problem is easy because it requires only addition and subtraction, as long as you don't get confused by the negative number. Leslie buys $165 in merchandise but has only $150 in her account. Unless she deposits more money, the account balance will be –$15. To bring the balance up to $25, she needs to deposit $25 + |-$15| = $40. Or you can think of it this way: Leslie needs to deposit $15 to bring the balance to zero, plus another $25 for a total of $40.

Answering Questions with Squares, Cubes, and Roots

Certain problems on the Math test require that you know how to determine a value's square or square root, or its cube or cube root. In the following sections, we briefly explain these terms, demonstrate the skills you need to answer questions on the test, and provide some practice problems to build your confidence.

Squaring and cubing numbers

The *square* of a number is the number multiplied by itself; for example, $6^2 = 6 \times 6 = 36$.
A number *cubed* is multiplied by itself twice; for example, $6^3 = 6 \times 6 \times 6 = 216$.

Solve the following problems to make sure you understand the concept:

1. 6^4

2. 23^3

3. $9^2 + 4^3$

4. $34^2 - 14^3$

5. $(27^2 - 11^3) - 33^2$

Check your work:

1. $6^4 = 6 \times 6 \times 6 \times 6 = 1,296$

2. $23^3 = 23 \times 23 \times 23 = 12,167$

3. $9^2 + 4^3 = 9 \times 9 + 4 \times 4 \times 4 = 81 + 64 = 145$

4. $34^2 - 14^3 = 34 \times 34 - 14 \times 14 \times 14 = 1,156 - 2,744 = -1,588$

5. $(27^2 - 11^3) - 33^2 = (27 \times 27 - 11 \times 11 \times 11) - 33 \times 33 = (729 - 1,331) - 1,089 =$
   $(-602) - 1,089 = -1,691$

If you arrived at an incorrect answer for any of the problems, check your math. If you calculated an incorrect answer for the fifth problem, you may have performed the operations in the wrong order. Remember that you must perform multiplication before addition or subtraction. (See Chapter 5 for more about the order of operations.)

On the test, you're not likely to encounter problems involving squares and cubes in the form presented in the previous examples. Those were just to get you warmed up. Instead, the test presents word problems, such as the following.

1. George is framing several square pictures, two of which measure 8 inches by 8 inches and the third of which measures 7 inches by 7 inches. How many square inches of glass would he need to exactly cover the pictures before putting them in frames?

    (A) 128

    (B) 177

    (C) 49

    (D) 113

2. Jenny and Ricco are redecorating their living room and want a circular rug to put in the middle of the room. After measuring, they find that a rug with a diameter of 14 feet would just fit perfectly. If circular rugs would cost them $9.89 per square yard, a rug with a diameter of 14 feet would cost them $ ☐.

3. Donna is in charge of filling the dunk tank at the local fair. The tank is a large cube, one side of which measures 8 feet. Given the fact that there are approximately 7.5 gallons in a cubic foot, how many gallons will it take to fill the tank? ☐

Check your work:

1. (B) Two of the pictures measure 8 inches by 8 inches, so they would require $2 \times (8 \times 8) = 128$ square inches of glass. The third one would require $7 \times 7 = 49$ square inches of glass. In total, George would need $128 + 49 = 177$ square inches of glass.

2. The formula for the area of a circle is $A = \pi r^2$, but the diameter and not the radius is given. To find the radius, divide the diameter by 2: $14 \div 2 = 7$. You know that $\pi = 3.14$, so the area is $3.14 \times 7 \times 7 = 153.86$ square feet. If the rug cost $9.89 per square yard, it would cost $9.89 \div 9 = \$1.10$ per square foot (rounded to the nearest penny). Total cost would be $153.86 \times \$1.10 = \$169.25$ (rounded to the nearest penny).

3. The volume of the tank is length times width times height. Because it's a cube, all three dimensions are the same: 8 feet. So the volume of the tank is 8^3 feet, or $8 \times 8 \times 8 = 512$ cubic feet. If 7.5 gallons is required for each cubic foot, then $512 \times 7.5 = 3,840$ gallons would be required to fill the tank.

Calculating square roots and cube roots

The *square root* of a number is a value that, multiplied by itself, produces the number; for example, the square root of 25 is 5, because $5 \times 5 = 25$. The *square root symbol* (or *radical sign*) is commonly used to indicate the square root of a number; for example, $\sqrt{25}$. Square root may also be represented as the number raised to the power of $\frac{1}{2}$, as in $25^{\frac{1}{2}}$.

The *cube root* of a number is a value that, multiplied by itself twice, produces the number; for example, the cube root of 64 is 4, because $4 \times 4 \times 4 = 64$. A number's cube root may be represented using the cube root symbol $\sqrt[3]{64}$ or by raising the number to the $\frac{1}{3}$ power, as in $64^{\frac{1}{3}}$.

To determine a square root of a number, factor the number inside the radical sign and look for any repeating factors. Any factors that appear twice can be moved outside the radical sign, as in this example:

$$\sqrt{540} = \sqrt{3 \cdot 3 \cdot 3 \cdot 2 \cdot 2 \cdot 5} = 6\sqrt{15}$$

To determine a cube root of a number, factor the number inside the radical sign and look for any factors that appear three times. Any factors that appear three times can be moved outside the radical sign, as in this example:

$$\sqrt[3]{540} = \sqrt[3]{3 \cdot 3 \cdot 3 \cdot 2 \cdot 2 \cdot 5} = 3\sqrt[3]{20}$$

Questions on the test typically instruct you to reduce the radical to its simplest form, which you do by factoring. If you need to simplify further, you can do so by using the calculator provided to compute the value inside the radical sign and then multiply that by the number outside the radical sign. For example, $\sqrt[3]{20}$ in the previous example rounded to the nearest hundredth is 2.71, so $3 \times 2.17 = 8.13$, which is approximately the cube root of 540.

To test your understanding of square roots and cube roots, solve the following expressions:

1. $\sqrt{144}$

2. $\sqrt[3]{216}$

3. $315^{\frac{1}{2}}$

4. $\sqrt[3]{945}$

Check your answers:

1. $\sqrt{144} = \sqrt{12 \cdot 12} = 12$

2. $\sqrt[3]{216} = \sqrt[3]{6 \cdot 6 \cdot 6} = 6$

3. $315^{\frac{1}{2}} = \sqrt{315} = \sqrt{3 \cdot 3 \cdot 5 \cdot 7} = 3\sqrt{5 \cdot 7} = 3\sqrt{35}$

4. $\sqrt[3]{945} = \sqrt[3]{3 \cdot 3 \cdot 3 \cdot 5 \cdot 7} = 3\sqrt[3]{5 \cdot 7} = 3\sqrt[3]{35}$

Of course, the test won't pepper you with these "easy" problems. It tries to confuse you by muddling the math with a word problem. Here are a couple examples.

1. The Birdock family built a square deck with an area of 85 square yards. The length of one side of the deck is between which pair of values?

   (A) 8 and 9

   (B) $\sqrt{81}$ and $\sqrt{100}$

   (C) $\sqrt{64}$ and $\sqrt{81}$

   (D) 10 and 11

2. A cubic box holds 4,320 jelly beans. If there are 20 jelly beans per cubic centimeter, what is the length of one side of the box?

   (A) 5.0

   (B) 5.5

   (C) 6.0

   (D) 6.5

   Check your answers:

   1. **(B)** If the area of a square deck is 85 square yards, one side of the deck is $\sqrt{85}$. You should recognize that this number is very close to the square root of 81, which is 9. The square of the next higher whole number, 10, is 100, so the correct answer is Choice (B).

   2. **(C)** First divide the total number of jelly beans in the box by 20 jelly beans per cubic centimeter to determine the volume of the box in cubic centimeters, which comes to 216. One side of the cube is $\sqrt[3]{216} = 6$. Choice (C) is the correct answer.

Solving Rate and Scale Problems

Rate and scale problems typically challenge your mastery of fractions and units. In the following sections, we introduce each type of problem, explain how to solve a typical problem of each type, and present a few problems for you to practice on.

If you have trouble working rate and scale problems, you may need a refresher on working with fractions. For more about fractions, see Chapter 5.

Working on unit rates

A *unit rate* is a quantity of something as measured against *one* of another something, such as miles per hour or pounds per square inch. Mathematically, unit rates are expressed as fractions, as in the following example:

$$\frac{75 \text{ miles}}{1 \text{ hour}}$$

When working a unit rate problem, you must make sure that the number on the bottom (the *denominator*) is 1. To perform the conversion, you divide the *numerator* (on top) by the denominator (on bottom). For example if a car travels 100 miles in 2 hours, its unit rate would be:

$$\frac{100 \text{ miles}}{2 \text{ hours}} = \frac{50 \text{ miles}}{1 \text{ hour}}$$

If a school with 84 students goes on a field trip and hires buses that seat 42 students each, how many buses would be needed? Because the ratio of students to buses is 42 to 1, the trip would require $84 \div 42 = 2$ buses.

Unit rate problems vary, so we can't give you step-by-step instructions that apply to every problem, but solving most of these problems requires converting a general rate into a unit rate, as in the following case:

Gary drives 120 miles in 3 hours. How many miles will he drive in 7 hours?

To solve this problem, first calculate Gary's speed in miles per hour: $120 \div 3 = 40$. Traveling 40 miles per hour in 7 hours, Gary would travel $40 \times 7 = 280$ miles.

Units provide valuable clues for solving all sorts of math problems. As with numbers in a fraction, you can cancel units in the numerator and denominator when multiplying fractions in order to simplify. So, you know that if the question instructs you to calculate the number of miles and gives you the number of hours driven, you must calculate miles per hour times hours spent traveling to get miles:

$$\frac{\text{miles}}{\cancel{\text{hour}}} \times \frac{\cancel{\text{hour}}}{1}$$

Try your hand at these more challenging sample questions.

1. Karen was in a hurry to get home from school. She lived 560 miles from home and could take the entire trip on the highway except for 12 miles. The speed limit on the highway was 70 miles per hour, but she knew that she could safely exceed it by 10%. How long would it take her to complete the highway portion of her trip home?

(A) 7 hours and 49 minutes

(B) 7 hours

(C) 7 hours and 34 minutes

(D) 7 hours and 7 minutes

2. Billy was working hard on his sample GED Mathematical Reasoning test but was having trouble finishing it on time. He knew that he would need to answer 90 questions in 115 minutes and was told by his instructor in class that he should leave 10 minutes at the end for review and corrections. How many minutes should he spend on each question to finish the test and have time for review?

(A) 2

(B) 1.30

(C) 1.17

(D) 0.86

3. Sheran was studying for her exams and knew that she could read, review, and makes notes on 23 pages of her textbook in 25 minutes. If her textbook was 480 pages long and she could study for 3 hours at a time, could she finish her studying in two sessions? ☐

4. Gordo and Michael decide to try out for their school's gymnastics team and are concerned about the coach's weight restrictions. Gordo is 7 pounds over the limit for his height, and Michael is 3 pounds under. Coach tells them to eat 3,500 more calories per pound they want to gain, or 3,500 fewer calories per pound they want to lose. Gymnastics team tryouts are

7 weeks away. How many calories would Gordo have to cut from his diet each day to lose the 7 pounds 1 week before tryouts?

(A) 500

(B) 492

(C) 583

(D) 24,500

Check your work:

1. (D) If the non-highway portion of Karen's trip home was 12 miles, then she traveled $560 - 12 = 548$ miles on the highway. Assuming that she chose to drive at 10% over the speed limit and was able to do so the entire trip, it would take her $548 \div 77 = 7.12$ hours, or 7 hours and $0.12 \times 60 = 7$ minutes (rounded to the nearest minute). She could complete the highway portion of her trip in 7 hours and 7 minutes.

2. (C) If there are 90 questions to be completed in 115 minutes but it was suggested that Billy leave 10 minutes at the end, he would have 105 minutes to complete 90 questions, or $105 \div 90 = 1.17$ minutes (rounded to two decimal points). For extra credit, convert 0.17 minutes into seconds: $0.17 \times 60 = 10.2$ seconds.

3. No. If it took Sheran 25 minutes to complete 23 pages of her book, that would represent $25 \div 23 = 1.08$, or about 1 minute per page. Her 480-page book would take her about 480 minutes to complete, or about $480 \div 60 = 8$ hours. If she was able to study for 3 hours at a time, it would take her more than 2 study sessions to complete her studying of the book. The answer is no.

4. (C) If tryouts are 7 weeks away and Gordo wants to be at the preferred weight 1 week in advance, he would only have 6 weeks to arrive at the preferred weight. If he would have to consume 3,500 calories for each pound he wants to lose, he would have to reduce his caloric intake by $3,500 \times 7 = 24,500$ during those 6 weeks. Because a week has 7 days, he needs to reduce his daily caloric intake by $24,500 \div (7 \times 6) = 24,500 \div 42 = 583$ calories/day (rounded to the nearest calorie).

Using scale factors

A *scale factor* is a number that multiplies a certain quantity. Suppose you want to represent 10 miles on a map. Obviously, the map can't be 10 miles wide. You need a way to represent the 10 miles. Scale to the rescue! With a scale, you can show that 1 inch on the map equals 10 miles. Using the scale, someone can figure out the distance between any two points on the map. If two locations are $\frac{1}{2}$ inch apart on the map, they're 5 miles apart in reality.

Scales are typically represented as fractions or ratios in the form of $\frac{10}{1}$ or 10:1. To solve a scale problem, you need to first form the fraction or ratio that represents the scale factor and then use it to determine the answer. Here's an example:

On a map, the scale shows that 25 miles equals 10 inches. How far apart would two locations be in real life if they are 2 inches apart on the map?

Because you're trying to figure out how many miles 2 inches represents on the map, you first need to figure out how many miles is represented by 1 inch:

$$\frac{25 \text{ miles}}{10 \text{ inches}} = 2.5 \text{ miles} / \text{inch}$$

So locations that are 2 inches apart on the map are $2 \times 2.5 = 5$ miles apart in real life.

Try solving this scale unit problem on your own.

Beatrice is in design school and has been given the assignment of designing a tile floor for a commercial building. The architect wants a very specify look consisting of the following elements:

- A circle with diameter 14 feet in the center of the area
- A triangle with sides 4 feet in the center of the circle
- A border 3 feet wide all around the perimeter of the area
- A carpeted area 26 feet long by 6 feet wide along the side wall leading from the front doors to the elevator entrances

If Beatrice is creating a drawing with a scale of $\frac{1}{4}$ inch : 1 foot , what would be the dimension of each element on her drawing? Complete the following table with your answers.

Element	Actual Dimension	Scale Dimension
Circle		
Triangle		
Border		
Carpet		

Check your work:

Element	Actual Dimension	Scale Dimension
Circle	Diameter = 14 feet	$14 \times \frac{1}{4} = 3\frac{1}{2}$ inches
Triangle	Each side – 4 feet	$4 \times \frac{1}{4} - 1$ inch
Border	Width = 3 feet	$3 \times \frac{1}{4} = \frac{3}{4}$ inch
Carpet	26×6 square feet	$\left(26 \times \frac{1}{4}\right) \times \left(6 \times \frac{1}{4}\right) = 6\frac{1}{2} \times 1\frac{1}{2}$

Figuring Out Ratio, Proportion, and Percentage Word Problems

Ratios, percentages, and proportions are three ways of comparing quantities. You're likely to encounter a couple questions on the test that ask you to determine a ratio, proportion, or percentage when given two quantities or to determine an unknown quantity when the ratio, proportion, or percentage is provided along with one of the quantities.

In the following sections, we cover each of these types of problems in turn and present examples and sample problems for you to practice on.

Ratios

A *ratio* is a relationship of two numbers of the same kind. For example, if a class has 16 men and 24 women, the ratio of men to women would be 16:24, which can be simplified to 2:3 (divide each number by 8).

Questions may ask you to determine a ratio when given two quantities or to find an unknown quantity when given a ratio and another quantity, as in the following example:

The bakers at Acme Bakery can make 138 muffins in 10 hours. How many muffins can they bake in 20 hours? [   ]

To solve a question such as this, create your ratio and reduce it to determine the number of muffins the bakers can make in 1 hour:

$$\frac{138\ \text{muffins}}{10\ \text{hours}} = 13.8\ \text{muffins} / \text{hour}$$

In 20 hours, the bakers can make $13.8 \times 20 = 276$ muffins.

1. Many landscape photographs measure 8 inches in length by 10 inches in width. What is the ratio of the length to the width?

    (A) 8:10

    (B) 4:5

    (C) 16:20

    (D) all of the above

2. The speed limit in most cities is 30 miles per hour, and it's 70 miles an hour on most highways. What is the simplified ratio of the highway speed to the city speed limit?

    (A) 30:70

    (B) 10:3

    (C) 50:15

    (D) none of the above

3. Jeremy measured the heights of the pupils on his basketball team. The heights were 6 feet, 5 feet 11 inches, 6 feet 1 inch, 5 feet 10 inches, and 5 feet 8 inches. The ratio of the tallest to the shortest would be: [   ]

4. Karen's class was highly competitive, always striving to have the highest average marks in the school. On a test with 20 one mark questions, the ratio of the average mark in Karen's class to the lowest average in the school was 19:16. What was the average mark in Karen's class?

    (A) 95

    (B) 85

    (C) 80

    (D) 75

Check your work:

1. (D) The ratio would be 8:10, which can also be written as 4:5 or even 16:20 because the question doesn't specify whether the ratio should be simplified.

2. (B) The ratio would be 70:30, or 7:3 simplified. The ratio is in this order because the question asks for the ratio of the highway speed limit to the city speed limit. Choice (A) is incorrect because the ratio has the city speed limit first. Always double-check for a correct answer as one of the choices whenever you see "none of the above."

3. In order to form a ratio, the units must be the same — in this case, inches. The heights would then be:

   - 6 feet = 72 inches

   - 5 feet 11 inches = 71 inches

   - 6 feet 1 inch = 73 inches

   - 5 feet 10 inches = 70 inches

   - 5 feet 8 inches = 68 inches

   The tallest member of the team is 73 inches tall, and the shortest member is 68 inches tall, which means the ratio would be 73:68. Because 73 is a prime number, the two numbers have no common factors other than 1, so you can't simplify the ratio.

4. (A) If the ratio of the average marks was 19:16, then to compare averages, both numbers should be out of 100%. Because 19 is $\frac{95}{100}$ and 16 is $\frac{80}{100}$, then Karen's class had an average of 95%.

Proportions

A *proportion* is a representation of two equal ratios. Here's an example of a proportion written in two different forms:

$$\frac{1}{3} = \frac{7}{21} \text{ or } 1:3 = 7:21$$

On the test, proportion problems typically provide you with three of the values you need to calculate the fourth, unknown value. To calculate a missing number in a proportion, assign a variable to the missing number and create a proportion. If you use n as the variable, the proportion is $8:16 = n:64$. Now set up the proportion using fractions and cross-multiply to solve for the variable:

$$\frac{8}{16} = \frac{n}{64}, \text{ so } 16n = 8 \times 64 = 512, \text{ and } n = \frac{512}{16} = 32$$

Of course, you can probably solve this particular problem on sight. If you notice that $\frac{8}{16} = \frac{1}{2}$, you quickly see that n must be half of 64, which is 32.

If Leon ate 8 ounces of jelly beans out of a 16-ounce bag, and the whole bag contained 112 jelly beans, how many jelly beans did Leon eat?

If you use J to represents the number of jelly beans Leon ate, then $8:16 = J:112$. Set up your proportion as fractions and solve for J:

$$\frac{8}{16} = \frac{J}{112}, \text{ so } 16J = 8 \times 112 = 896, \text{ and } J = \frac{896}{16} = 56$$

Practice solving the following proportion problems.

1. One day at Fern's school, 3 out of the 27 students wore school sweaters. If the same proportion of the 918 students in the school were wearing school sweaters, how many school sweaters were being worn that day?

   (A) 102

   (B) 9

   (C) 109

   (D) 27

2. Deb knows she can average 66 miles per hour when driving to visit her boyfriend. If he lives 121 miles from Deb's home, how long would it take her to arrive at his home? ☐ hour(s) and ☐ minutes.

3. Warren is cooking a beef stew for company. He knows that the ratio of beef to potatoes and vegetables should be 1:3 when he is preparing 1 pound of beef stew for himself and his friend Helen. If he invites 5 people to join them for dinner and makes his almost famous beef stew, how much beef should he buy to prepare the same recipe?

   (A) 2 pounds

   (B) 1 pound and 17 ounces

   (C) 1 pound and 6 ounces

   (D) 1 pound and 3 ounces

Check your work:

1. (A) If 3 out of 27 students wore school sweaters, then $\frac{3}{27}$ or $\frac{1}{9}$ of Fern's class was wearing school sweaters. If you represent the number of students that were wearing school sweaters that day in school by b, then $1:9 = b:918$, and b is

$$\frac{1}{9} = \frac{b}{918}$$
$$9b = 918$$
$$b = \frac{918}{9}$$
$$b = 102$$

2. The answer is 1 hour and 49.8 minutes. If Deb can complete the entire trip at an average speed of 66 miles per hour, then the ratio of her speed to time would be 66:1. If t represents the time required for the trip of 121 miles, then the ratio of time to distance is t:121. The proportion is $66:1 = 121:t$ or $66t = 121$. Divide both sides by 66, and you get $t = 1.83$ hours (rounded to two decimal places), or 1 hour and 49.8 minutes.

3. (D) Represent the amount of beef required by B. The ratio of beef to vegetables can be represented by $\frac{1}{3}$ pound for Warren's usual recipe. The proportion for the amount needed for Warren, Helen, and 5 guests, a total of 7 people, would be $2:\frac{1}{3} = 7:B$ or $2B = \frac{1}{3} \times 7$, then $B = \left(\frac{1}{3} \times 7\right) \div 2 = 1.17$ (rounded to two decimal places), or 1 pound and 3 ounces of beef (rounded to the nearest ounce).

Percentages

Percentage is another way of saying "per hundred." 27% is 27 per 100, and 68% is 68 per 100. Questions on the Math test are likely to provide you with a quantity and a percentage and ask you to use the two values to determine an unknown quantity.

To simplify the math, convert the percentage to its decimal equivalent by dropping the percent sign and moving the decimal two spaces to the left. For example, 27% = 0.27, and 68% = 0.68. For more about percentages, check out Chapter 5.

Here's an example of a question involving percentage.

If George answered 88% of the questions on a test correctly and the test contained 200 questions, how many questions did George answer incorrectly?

If he answered 88% of the questions correctly, he answered $0.88 \times 200 = 176$ questions correctly. But the question asks how many he answered *incorrectly,* so the answer would be $200 - 176 = 24$.

Always read the question carefully, as explained earlier in this chapter, to be sure you're answering the question that was actually asked and not one that you think was asked.

Try your hand at the following percentage question.

Kelly was offered a discount of 25% off a sofa priced at $1,250 if she would arrange for her own delivery. How much would she pay for the sofa by arranging to have it delivered herself?

(A) $250.00

(B) $937.50

(C) $312.50

(D) not enough information given

Choice (B) is the correct answer. If the sofa originally cost $1,250 and she was offered a 25% discount, then she would save $0.25 \times \$1,250 = \$312.50$. But that's not what the question asks. It asks how much she would pay for the couch if she received that discount, so you need to subtract that amount from the sticker price of the couch: $\$1,250 - \$312.50 = \$937.50$. On some items, you'll see an option of "not enough information given." Before you consider it, make sure that you really don't have enough information to answer the question. This question provides sufficient information to answer the question. Remember to read both the question and the answers carefully.

Practice Session

One of the skills required to answer word problems is the ability to figure out which type of problem you're dealing with. Here we provide a variety of problems to help you sharpen this skill. Follow the Decipher, Decide, and Do approach to solving word problems, as explained earlier in this chapter.

Round all answers to the second decimal place with the exception of weights (round to the nearest ounce) and currency (round to the nearest penny).

1. Henry is shopping for winter clothes. He needs 3 shirts, 2 pairs of slacks, and a winter jacket to complete his wardrobe. While shopping at Wonderful Warren's Almost Wholesale Clothing Emporium, he notices a special sale section with a sign that reads:

   Shirts: 2 for 1 (same price only)

   Slacks: 35% off

   Winter Jackets: 49% off with purchase of shirts or slacks

If the shirts are priced at $29.99, $30.99, and $35.99, and he preferred the most expensive ones, slacks are priced at $89.99, and winter jackets are priced at $179.99 to $249.99, how much would he save on his entire purchase if he bought the lowest-priced winter jacket and took advantage of the 2 for 1 sale on shirts?

(A) $178.18

(B) $117.17

(C) $335.96

(D) $187.18

2. Shirley always wanted to dress like a princess for her tenth birthday. Finally, her parents agree and take her to a costume shop to outfit her for the occasion. They find a princess gown they can rent for $29.00 for 2 days and a cape they can rent for $19.00 for 2 days, but they still need a tiara, gloves, shoes, special princess stockings, and costume jewelry. Shirley wants to invite 15 of her friends and serve them a special princess cake, sandwiches, and fruit punch. The prices for the items they need to purchase are as follows:

Tiara: $12.95

Gloves: $15.49

Shoes: $35.99

Princess stockings: $4.99

Costume jewelry: $23.00

Princess cake: $45.00

Sandwiches (per person): $4.99

Fruit punch: $25.00

The total cost for the party would be:

(A) $290.26

(B) $209.26

(C) $149.46

(D) $167.32

3. The Krocjit family is building a square deck behind their house. One side of the deck is to be 20 feet long, and the decking material is priced at $45.00 a square yard. What is the cost in dollars of the decking material?

(A) $18,900

(B) $981

(C) $2,000

(D) $1,218

4. Manuel needs some money to buy some extra reference books for his Civics course. If he borrows a total of $140 over one year and three months and repays the loan with monthly payments of $10.80 over the same period, what rate of interest was he charged?

(A) 12.6%

(B) 8.0%

(C) 14.0%

(D) 15.75%

5. Michelle is an avid coin collector and just bought a collection of old pennies, hoping to find a valuable few among the others. If she bought 1,472 pennies and was able to examine 384 in one day, it would take her ☐ days to examine the entire collection if she worked at the same rate.

6. At Consolidated Canning Corporation, the top three positions are organized as follows with the following budgets:

   Operations: $11.1 million

   Human Resources: $3.7 million

   Marketing $6.5 million

   What is the ratio of the smallest budget to the largest budget?

   (A) 7:1

   (B) 1:2

   (C) 1:3

   (D) 3:1

7. Alan is in charge of the swimming pool at the local recreation center. The pool is 120 feet long and 24 feet wide and holds 12,902 cubic feet of water. Alan knows that he can heat 250 cubic yards of water to an acceptable temperature in 1 hour. How many hours would it take him to bring the water up to an acceptable temperature?

   (A) 4.73

   (B) 5.73

   (C) 6.73

   (D) 7.73

8. Simplify the following expression, leaving the answer in radical form: ☐.

   $$\sqrt[3]{108} \cdot \sqrt[3]{64}$$

9. Every 5 days, a plane passes over our house heading to Tucson. On every 12th day, a plane passes over our house heading to Boston. Today, both planes passed over our house. In how many days from today will both planes pass over our house on the same day again?

   (A) 30

   (B) 60

   (C) 90

   (D) 120

10. Acme manufactures bottle caps that are 25 millimeters in diameter. Any bottle caps not within a tolerance of 0.05 millimeter are rejected. Which of the following inequalities can be used to determine whether bottle caps are accepted?

    (A) $|d - 0.05| \le 25$

    (B) $|d - 0.05| \ge 25$

    (C) $|d - 25| \le 0.05$

    (D) $|d - 25| \ge 0.05$

Check your work:

1. **(D)** If Henry bought 2 shirts priced at \$35.99, he would pay \$35.99 and save \$35.99. The third shirt would be at regular price and he would save nothing on that purchase. If he bought 2 pairs of slacks at \$89.99, the total price before discount would be \$179.98 and the discount would be \$179.98 $\times 0.35 = \$62.99$. Having fulfilled the sale requirements and purchasing the least expensive winter jacket, his total savings would be \$35.99 + \$62.99 + \$89.99 = \$188.97.

2. **(A)** The costs for the party would be:

Princess gown rental for 2 days	***\$29.00***
Cape (rental) for 2 days	\$19.00
Tiara	\$12.95
Gloves	\$15.49
Shoes	\$35.99
Princess stockings	\$4.99
Costume jewelry	\$23.00
Princess cake	\$45.00
Sandwiches (16 times \$4.99/person, including Shirley)	\$79.84
Fruit punch	\$25.00
Total	**\$290.26**

3. **(C)** The cost of the materials is quoted at \$45.00 per square yard, but all other measurements are in feet. To convert square yards to square feet, divide by 9, \$45 $\div 9 = \$5.00$ per square foot. The square deck has an area of $20^2 = 400$ square feet and the cost is $400 \times \$5.00 = \$2,000$.

4. **(A)** Manuel has borrowed \$140 from his parents for 1 year and 3 months, or $12 + 3 = 15$ months. If he repays \$10.80 per month including interest, in 15 months he would have repaid $15 \times \$10.80 = \$162.00$, which includes \$22.00 in interest. Over the term of the loan, he would have paid $\$22 \div 15 = \$1.47$ in interest, which is equal to \$17.64 per year. The annual interest rate would be $\$17.64 \div \$140.00 \times 100 = 12.6\%$.

5. Michelle is able to examine 384 pennies in a day. At that rate, she could examine $1,472 \div 384 = 3.83$, or rounded to the nearest day, 4 days.

6. **(C)** The ratio of the smallest budget to the largest is 3.7:11.1, or 1:3. Always remember to read the question carefully to ensure that you answer the question that is asked and not one you assumed was asked.

7. **(B)** Because the pool holds 12,902 cubic feet of water and the rate of heating the water is given in cubic yards per hour, you have to convert the rate to cubic feet per hour. 12,902 cubic feet equals $12,902 \div 9 = 1,433.56$ cubic yards. 250 cubic yards would take 1 hour to bring to an acceptable temperature, so $1,433.56 \div 250 = 5.73$ hours.

8. Factor the numbers inside a single radical sign and then pull any factors appearing three times outside of the radical sign: $\sqrt[3]{3 \cdot 3 \cdot 3 \cdot 4 \cdot 4 \cdot 4 \cdot 4} = 3 \cdot 4\sqrt[3]{4} = 12\sqrt[3]{4}$.

9. **(B)** To answer the question, you need to find the least common multiple of 5 and 12. Factor both numbers first. 5 is prime, so its only factors are 1 and 5. 12 factors into $2 \times 2 \times 3$. They have no common factors, so multiply all their factors together to get the answer: $5 \times 2 \times 2 \times 3 = 60$.

10. **(C)** The bottle caps must be within ± 0.05 of 25 millimeters to be accepted. Choice (C) is the correct answer. If you plug in 25.04 and 24.96, you see that both of these caps would be acceptable. Choice (D) would be correct if you needed an expression to determine whether to *reject* bottle caps that are outside the tolerance, but that's not what the question asks.

Chapter 7

Solving Measurement Problems

. . . .

In This Chapter

▶ Figuring a shape's perimeter and area

▶ Finding the length of one side of a right triangle

▶ Calculating the volume and surface area of 3D objects

▶ Working with data in graphs and tables

▶ Determining averages, probabilities, and more

▶ Practicing measurement problems

. . . .

Y ou started this journey by reviewing basic arithmetic, and now you get to more interesting stuff. This chapter looks at real objects that you can see and dream about. It considers the perimeter and area of such objects as rugs and challenges you to figure out how to compare prices should you want to buy one. You find out how to calculate the length of one side of a right triangle, which enables you to compare the real sizes of TV sets and computer monitors, whose sizes are always quoted as the diagonal measurement. You review how to calculate the volume of a 3D object such as a box, enabling you to figure out whether all your stuff will fit into a suitcase. You get more practice in working with graphs and tables, and suddenly, the financial section of the newspaper begins to make more sense. Perhaps best of all, you begin to understand how probability is calculated so you'll be able to make an educated guess regarding your chances of drawing an ace when playing poker. All this fun in just one chapter, and all you have to do is read the material carefully, do the exercises, and prepare to take the GED Mathematical Reasoning test.

 On the actual test, you can click an icon on the screen to bring up a list of formulas. Visit `http://www.gedtestingservice.com/uploads/files/0756c16704434ff71e43c81 17a5fa738.pdf` to see the official page of formulas, or turn to Chapter 3 or 10 to view a copy of the formula sheet in this book.

Shaping Up Perimeter and Area

To answer several questions on the Math test, you need to know how to calculate measurements of two-dimensional objects, including rectangles, triangles, and circles. Using formulas on the formula sheet, you should be able to calculate the perimeter (distance around) of a two-dimensional object and its area (the measurement of its surface). You should also be able to work backward to determine the length of a side of a two-dimensional object when given its perimeter or area. In the following sections, we show you how.

Calculating the perimeter of a rectangle or square

Perimeter is the distance around an object. The perimeter of a rectangle is $P = 2l + 2w$, where P represents the perimeter, l represents the length, and w represents the width. As long as each measurement is in the same units and you remember PEMDAS (from Chapter 5), you won't have trouble answering perimeter questions on the test. That formula works for determining the area of a square as well, or you can use the formula $P = 4s$, were s represents one side of the square. Here's an example:

Janice builds a square deck. One side of the deck is 16 feet long. What is its perimeter?

(A) 256

(B) 32

(C) 64

(D) 65,536

The correct answer is Choice (C): $P = 4 \times 16 = 64$.

Computing the area of a rectangle or square

Area is a measure of the surface of any shape in square units. Regular shapes have formulas to calculate the surface area. The simplest shape is the rectangle, and the formula for the area is $A = lw$, where A is the area in square units, l is the length in linear units, and w is the width in linear units. To calculate the area of a square, simply square the length of one side using the formula $A = s^2$.

The lengths of the sides must be in the same units. So, for example, if a question specifies the length in inches and the width in feet, you need to convert inches to feet or vice versa before plugging the numbers into the formula. If the question asks for the answer in square inches, you convert feet to inches. If the question asks for the answer in square feet, you convert inches to feet. Here's an example:

Phil needs a ribbon 6 inches wide by 14 feet long. What is the area of the ribbon?

(A) 1,008 square inches

(B) 84 square inches

(C) 40 square feet

(D) 84 square feet

The correct answer is Choice (A): Convert 14 feet to inches by multiplying 14 feet by 12 inches per foot, and you get 168 inches. Multiply 168 by 6 and you get 1,008 square inches.

Finding the length of a side when given area or perimeter

When it comes to perimeter and area, the Math test can be tricky. Instead of giving you the length of two sides of a rectangle and asking for the perimeter, it may give you the perimeter and the length of one side and ask for the length of the other side. To solve problems such as these, simply plug the numbers into your equation and solve for the unknown, as in the following example:

The playground is a rectangular area covering 1,200 square meters. If one side of the playground area is 30 meters long, what is the length of the other side?

Plug your numbers into the equation for the area of a rectangle and solve for the missing dimension:

$$A = lw$$
$$1200 = 30w$$
$$w = \frac{1200}{30} = 40$$

Try it yourself:

The area of a square postage stamp is 400 square millimeters. Its perimeter is: [   ].

This is a twist on the problem, but to determine the perimeter, you must first calculate the length of one side of the postage stamp. The area of a square is $A = s^2$, so $A = 400 = 20^2$ shows that one side of the square is 20, because the square root of 400 is 20. Plug 20 into the perimeter equation for a square: $P = 4s = 4 \times 20 = 80$.

Finding the perimeter and area of a triangle

A *triangle* is a three-sided figure. The perimeter of a triangle is simply the distance around it. Add the length of the three sides. Here's the official formula: $P = s_1 + s_2 + s_3$.

To calculate the area of a triangle, multiply half the length of its base times its height (see Figure 7-1). The equation looks like this: $A = \frac{1}{2}bh$. This works for any triangle. For example, the area of a triangle with a base of 4 inches and a height of 5 inches is $A = \frac{1}{2}bh = \frac{1}{2}(4 \times 5) = \frac{20}{2} = 10$ square inches.

Figure 7-1:
The area of any triangle is half its base times its height.

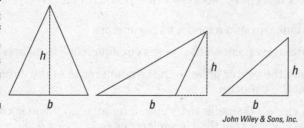

John Wiley & Sons, Inc.

Figuring the area of trapezoids and parallelograms

On the test, you may also be challenged to find the area of a trapezoid or parallelogram. A *trapezoid* is a quadrilateral (a four-sided shape) with only two sides that are parallel (see Figure 7-2). A *parallelogram* is a quadrilateral with opposite sides parallel. Use the following formulas to calculate the area of a trapezoid or parallelogram:

Area of a trapezoid $A = \frac{1}{2}h(b_1 + b_2)$

Area of a parallelogram $A = bh$

Trapezoid

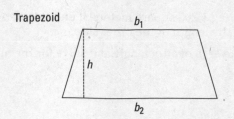

Parallelogram

Figure 7-2:
A trapezoid
and a paral-
lelogram.

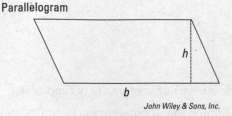

John Wiley & Sons, Inc.

Here's a simple sample problem:

The base of a parallelogram with an area of 180 square feet is 12. What is its height?

Plug the numbers you're given into the parallelogram equation and do the math to solve for the unknown value:

$$180 = 12h$$
$$h = \frac{180}{12} = 15$$

Finding your way around a circle

A *circle* is a perfectly round, flat shape. To work any math problem involving a circle, you first need to recognize the parts of a circle and a few other pertinent facts (see Figure 7-3):

- **Circumference** is the distance around a circle, its perimeter.
- **Diameter** is the distance from any point on the circle's circumference to its opposite point.
- **Radius** is the distance from the center point to the circumference of the circle. The radius is half the length of the diameter.
- **π or 3.14** is the ratio of a circle's diameter to its circumference, so if you know that the diameter of a circle is 2, you know that the circumference is $2 \times 3.14 = 6.28$.

On the test, you're likely to encounter at least one question that challenges you to find the circumference, radius, diameter, or area of a circle. In the following sections, we help you acquire the knowledge and skills to answer such questions.

Pinning down the value of pi

π is an irrational number that can't be accurately pre-sented as 3.14 or $\frac{22}{7}$. Its decimal equivalent actually extends out to infinity without repeating. Here's π to 100 decimal places: 3.1415926535897932384626433832795028841971693993751058209749445923078164062862089986280348253421170679 and it keeps going. To spare you the agony of entering all those numbers and more, the developers of the GED test allow you to round π to 3.14 unless otherwise specified in a question.

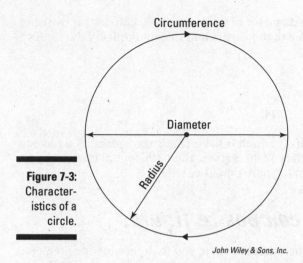

Figure 7-3: Character- istics of a circle.

John Wiley & Sons, Inc.

Computing the area of a circle

The area of a circle is the measure of what's inside it. To calculate a circle's area, use the formula $A = \pi r^2$, where A is the area of the circle in square units, r is the radius, and $\pi = 3.14$ *or* $\frac{22}{7}$, whichever is more convenient to use unless you're directed to use one or the other in the question. Try it:

A perfectly round pizza is 16 inches across. If you ate a third of the pizza, how many square inches of pizza would you have eaten? Round your answer to the nearest square inch: [   ] square inches.

If the pizza is 16 inches across, its radius is half that, or 8 inches. To determine the total area of the pizza in square inches, plug the numbers into the area of a circle equation and do the math: $A = \pi r^2 = \pi \times 8^2 = 3.14 \times 64 = 200.96$. Now, you have to divide the total by 3 to figure out how much of the pizza you ate and round to the nearest hundredth of a square inch: $200.96 \div 3 = 66.986$, which rounds up to 67 square inches.

Calculating a circle's circumference

To calculate the circumference of a circle, use the formula $C = 2\pi r$ or $C = \pi d$, where C is the circumference, r is the radius, d is the diameter, and $\pi = 3.14$. Try it:

The diameter of the earth is approximately 7,918 miles. What is its approximate circumfer- ence? Round your answer up to the nearest mile: [   ] miles.

To solve this problem, use the diameter version of the circumference formula: $C = \pi d = \pi \times 7,918 = 3.14 \times 7,918 = 24,862.52$. Round up to the nearest mile, and you have 24,863.

Finding the radius and diameter

To test your ability to reason, the GED Math test may try to see if you're paying attention by giving you the circumference or area of a circle and asking you to use that information to calculate the radius or diameter. Or, you may be given the circumference and be asked to find the area or given the area and asked to find the circumference. Whatever the case, you need to pick the right formula, plug in what you know, and solve the equation to find the unknown. Here's an example:

Cecie wants a round area rug for a square room that's 18 feet across. She notices an adver- tisement for a rug that is 132 square feet, but the ad doesn't include any other dimensions. Will that rug fit inside the room without hitting the walls? Yes or No: [   ].

To solve this problem, you need to find the diameter of the carpet. You can do this by using the area formula first to determine the radius of the carpet and then multiplying the radius by 2. First, use the area formula:

$$132 = \pi r^2$$
$$\frac{132}{\pi} = r^2 = \frac{132}{3.14} = 42.04$$

Round to $r^2 = 42$ and take the square root of 42, which is 6.48. That's the radius. You have to multiply 6.48 by 2 to get the diameter, which is 12.96. So, yes, the 12.96-foot-diameter rug will fit in the 18-foot square room with room to spare on either side.

Calculating the area of composite figures

Don't be surprised if you encounter a question that instructs you to determine the area of a composite figure. To answer these questions, divide the image into shapes, calculate the area of each shape, and go from there. Here are a couple examples:

Calculate the area of the following figure: ⬚.

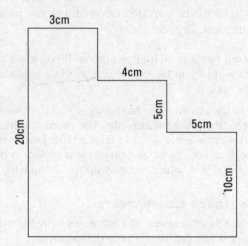

To solve this problem, divide the shape into three rectangles, calculate the area of each, and add up the three areas. The equation would look like this:

$A = (3 \times 20) + (4 \times 16) + (5 \times 10) = 60 + 64 + 50 = 174$ square centimeters.

What is the area of the shaded portion of the box: ⬚.

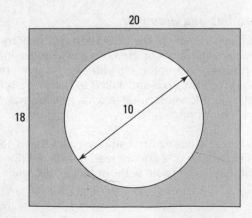

To solve this problem, calculate the area of the circle and rectangle and then subtract the area of the circle from the area of the rectangle. The area of the rectangle is $20 \times 18 = 360$, and the area of the circle is $\pi r^2 = 3.14 \times 5^2 = 3.14 \times 25 = 78.5$. Now subtract: $360 - 78.5 = 281.5$.

Exploring the Unique Properties of Right Triangles

A *right triangle* is a three-sided shape that contains one 90-degree angle, like the corner of a room (see Figure 7-4). The triangle contains two short sides and one long side, commonly referred to as the *hypotenuse*. The little box that appears in the right angle is common notation that the angle is a right angle equal to 90 degrees.

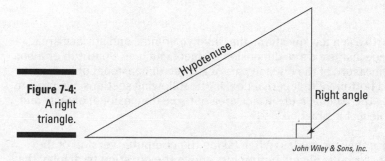

Figure 7-4: A right triangle.

Hypotenuse

Right angle

John Wiley & Sons, Inc.

A Greek mathematician named Pythagoras discovered some unique relationships among the sides of such triangles. The Pythagorean theorem states that the square of the hypotenuse of a right-angled triangle is equal to the sum of the squares of the other two sides. As a formula, the Pythagorean theorem looks like this: $c^2 = a^2 + b^2$, where c represents the length of the hypotenuse and a and b represent the lengths of the two shorter sides. By modifying the equation, you can find the length of any side as long as you're given the length of the other two sides:

Use	To Find
$a^2 + b^2 = c^2$	Length of side c, the hypotenuse
$a^2 = c^2 - b^2$	Length of side a
$b^2 = c^2 - a^2$	Length of side b

Michelle walks 40 yards, turns right, and walks another 30 yards. What is the shortest distance she would walk to return to her point of origin? ☐

To answer this question, you first need to realize that the two legs of Michelle's short walk form the two short sides of a right triangle and that drawing a line from her destination to her point of origin forms the hypotenuse. Then, all you have to do is plug the numbers into the Pythagorean formula and do the math:

$$c^2 = 30^2 + 40^2 = 900 + 1600 = 2,500$$

If $c^2 = 2,500$, then $c = \sqrt{2500} = \sqrt{5 \times 5 \times 10 \times 10} = 5 \times 10 = 50$.

You may be able to save yourself precious minutes on the test by memorizing a few Pythagorean triples, such as (3, 4, 5); (9, 16, 25); (5, 12, 13); and (8, 15, 17). If you plug these numbers into the Pythagorean formula, using the largest number of each as the hypotenuse, and you do the math, you find that these triples are Pythagorean ratios for the sides of right triangles. If you come across a problem that provides a hypotenuse of 25 with one side being 16, you know immediately that the other side must be 9 without having to do the math.

Another unique property of right triangles is that they're essentially half of a rectangle. If you draw a line from one corner of a rectangle to the opposite corner, you form two identical right triangles. Because of this, you can determine the area of a right triangle simply by multiplying the lengths of its two shortest sides and dividing the total by 2. You can represent the equation as $A = \frac{1}{2}ab$, where A is the area of a right triangle and a and b are the lengths of the two shorter sides (*not* the hypotenuse).

Solving Problems with Volume and Surface Area

The GED Math test is likely to ask a few questions that involve volume and surface area. *Volume* is a measure of space inside a three-dimensional object, such as a bathtub or a box of cereal. *Surface area* is a measure of the outside part of a three-dimensional object, such as the front, sides, top, and bottom of that cereal box. In the following sections, we present the formulas for calculating the volume and surface area of three-dimensional objects and provide some sample problems for practice.

You don't need to memorize these formulas. When taking the computer version of the GED test, you can click the "Formula Sheet" button just above the question to display the formulas.

Calculating the volume of 3D objects

The GED Math test doesn't expect you to memorize the formulas for calculating volumes of three-dimensional objects, but you need to be able to look at an object or imagine the object based on the description provided in a word problem and choose the right formula to use. Table 7-1 presents the formulas along with an image of each shape to help you match the formulas to their three-dimensional objects.

Table 7-1	Formulas for Calculating Volume	
Shape	**Image**	**Volume Formula**
Rectangular prism		$V = lwh$, where l is one side of the base, w is the adjacent side, and h is the height

Shape	Image	Volume Formula
Right prism		$V = Bh$, where B is the area of the base and h is the height of the prism
Cylinder		$V = \pi r^2 h$, where r is the radius of the circular base and h is the height
Pyramid		$V = \frac{1}{3} Bh$, where B is the area of the base and h is the height, measured from the tip of the pyramid straight down to the base
Cone		$V = \frac{1}{3} \pi r^2 h$, where r is the radius of the circular base and h is the height, measured from the tip of the cone straight down to the base
Sphere		$V = \frac{4}{3} \pi r^3$, where r is the radius measured from the center of the sphere to its outside edge

When calculating the volume of a prism or cylinder, you calculate the area of the base and multiply it by the height. If the prism has a rectangular bottom, use the formula for calculating the area of a rectangle to find the area of the base: $A = lw$. Then, multiply the result by the height. If the base is a triangle, use the formula for the area of a triangle instead: $A = \frac{1}{2}bh$.

To calculate the area of the base for a cylinder, use the formula for calculating the area of a circle: $A = \pi r^2$. Then multiply the area of the base by the height of the prism or cylinder to find its volume.

Practice with the following problems.

A rectangular car-top carrier holds 18 cubic feet. Which of the following can be its dimensions?

(A) 3 feet by 3 feet by 3 feet

(B) 3 feet by 2 feet by 2 feet

(C) 3 feet by 3 feet by 2 feet

(D) 6 feet by 3 feet

A rectangular car-top carrier is the shape of a rectangular prism, so use the formula $18 = lwh$. From the answer choices, you simply need to find the values that fit in the equation and equal 18. Choice (A) is wrong because $3 \times 3 \times 3 = 27$. Choice (B) is wrong because $3 \times 2 \times 2 = 12$. Choice (D) is clearly wrong because multiplying two values results in area, not volume. Choice (C) is correct because $3 \times 3 \times 2 = 18$.

An ice cream cone is 4 inches deep and 3 inches across at the top. How many cubic inches of ice cream can it hold? Round your answer to the nearest tenth: ⬚ cubic inches of ice cream.

For this problem you use the formula for the volume of a cone: $V = \frac{1}{3}\pi r^2 h$. Keep in mind that radius is half the diameter, so the radius of the base is 1.5 inches. Plug the numbers into the equation and do the math:

$$V = \frac{1}{3} \times 3.14 \times 1.5^2 \times 4 = \frac{28.26}{3} = 9.42$$

Round your answer to the nearest tenth, and you have 9 cubic inches.

Computing the surface area of 3D objects

The GED test also expects you to be able to calculate the surface area of three-dimensional objects. Fortunately, it supplies you with the formulas for calculating surface areas. The tricky part is figuring out which formula to use. Table 7-2 presents the formulas along with an image of each shape to help you match the formulas to their three-dimensional objects.

Table 7-2	Formulas for Calculating Surface Area (SA)	
Shape	**Image**	**Surface Area Formula**
Rectangular prism		$SA = 2lw + 2lh + 2wh$, where SA stands for surface area, l is one side of the base, w is the adjacent side, and h is the height
Right prism		$SA = ph + 2B$, where SA stands for surface area, p is the perimeter of the base, h is the height of the pyramid, and B is the area of the base
Cylinder		$SA = 2\pi rh + 2\pi r^2$, where SA stands for surface area, r is the radius of the circular base, and h is the height
Pyramid		$SA = \frac{1}{2} ps + B$, where SA stands for surface area, p is the perimeter of the base, s is the *slant length* (distance from the tip of the pyramid to the base along one of its sides), and B is the area of the base

continued

Table 7-2 *(continued)*

Shape	Image	Surface Area Formula
Cone		$SA = \pi rs + \pi r^2$, where SA stands for surface area, r is the radius of the circular base, and s is the distance from the tip of the cone down to the base along its slope
Sphere		$SA = 4\pi r^2$, where SA stands for surface area and r is the radius measured from the center of the sphere to its outside edge

Finding height, radius, or diameter using volume or surface area

The GED Math test literally expects you to be able to calculate volume and surface area forward and backward. Not only do you have to be able to calculate volume and surface area when given an object's dimensions, but you also must be able to calculate a missing dimension when given an object's volume or surface area. To solve problems such as these, plug in the values you have and then solve the equation for the unknown. Here's an example:

A rain barrel holds 7 cubic feet of water. If its diameter is 24 inches, what is its height? Round your answer to the nearest one hundredth: ☐ feet.

Because you're asked to enter the answer in feet, convert the diameter to feet by dividing 24 inches by 12 inches per foot to find that the diameter is 2 feet. Divide the diameter in half to find the radius: $2 \times \frac{1}{2} = 1$. The barrel holds 7 cubic feet of water. Plug the numbers you have into the volume formula for a cylinder and you have

$$7 = \pi r^2 h = 3.14(1^2)(h)$$
$$\frac{7}{3.14} = h = 2.229$$

Round up to the nearest hundredth and you get 2.23 feet.

Here's another example using surface area:

A pyramid has a square base with one of its sides being 3 feet long and a total surface area of 39 square feet. What is the slant length of one of its sides? ☐ feet.

To answer this question, use the surface area formula for a pyramid, $SA = \frac{1}{2}ps + B$, and plug in the values you have: The area of the base is $3 \times 3 = 9$, the perimeter is $3 \times 4 = 12$, and the surface area is 39 square feet, so you have $39 = \frac{1}{2}12 \times s + 9$. Do the math:

$$39 - 9 = \frac{12}{2}s + 9 - 9$$
$$30 = 6s$$
$$\frac{30}{6} = s = 5$$

Calculating the volume and surface area of composite figures

To calculate the volume or surface area of composite figures or objects, break the composite image or object into its component parts, figure the volume or surface area of each component part, and then do the math to add or subtract volumes or surface areas as necessary.

Volume is always in cubic measurements, dimensions are linear, and the units used must all be the same.

Challenge yourself with the following practice problems:

Ken places a 6-inch-diameter solid glass ball into a cylinder with a radius of 1 foot and a height of 2 feet. How many cubic inches of water can the cylinder hold? Round your answer to the nearest cubic inch: ☐ cubic inches.

To answer this question, you need to determine the volume of the cylinder and the volume of the glass ball and subtract the volume of the glass ball from the volume of the cylinder, and you have to do it all in inches. Because 12 inches = 1 foot, the radius is 12 and the height is 24. The volume of the cylinder in inches is $V = \pi \times 12^2 \times 24 = 3.14 \times 144 \times 24 = 10,851.84$. To determine the volume of the glass ball, you first need to divide the diameter in half to find the radius: $6 \div 2 = 3$. The volume of the glass ball is $V = \frac{4}{3}\pi 3^3 = \frac{4}{\not{3}} \times 3.14 \times \not{9}^3 = 12 \times 3.14 = 37.68$.

Subtract the volume of the glass ball from the volume of the cylinder: $10,851.84 - 37.68 = 10,814.16$. That rounds down to 10,814 cubic inches.

Interpreting and Presenting Data Graphically

Part of the GED Math test focuses on your ability to understand data presented graphically in the form of graphs, plots, histograms, and tables, and to plot data points on a coordinate plane. In the following sections, we explain how to read and interpret visual representations of data and how to plot data points on graphs in response to questions on the Math test.

Reading graphs

Graphs (also referred to as *charts*) communicate data through pictures. The most common graphs you'll see on the test are bar or column graphs, line graphs, and pie graphs (also known as *circle graphs* or *pie charts*). You may also bump into the occasional histogram or scatter plot. Regardless of the type of graph presented in a question, take the following steps to read it (see Figure 7-5):

1. **Read the title carefully because it describes what the data presented in the graph represents.**

2. **Look carefully at all labels, especially along the axes — the lines at the left and bottom of most graphs that indicate the variables being plotted, such as days or dollars.**

   Axis labels indicate the type of data displayed in the graph. (In a pie graph, the labels are inside or near each "slice" of the pie.)

3. **Read the legend, if provided.**

   The legend describes what each grouping of data represents.

4. **Read the question and answer choices to find out which data or aspect of that data you need to focus on.**

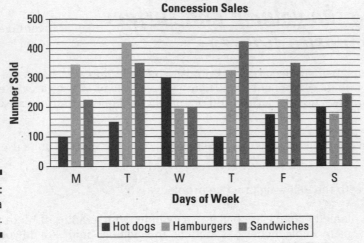

Figure 7-5:
Reading a
graph.

John Wiley & Sons, Inc.

 Graphs are used more for revealing the significance of data and spotting trends and less for presenting precise values. During the actual test, you may be instructed to click an area of the graph to plot a point; you just need to get pretty close to the precise spot.

In the following sections, we present common graph types along with guidance on how to read and interpret the data displayed in each type.

Bar or column graph

Bar graphs and *column graphs* typically show relationships among items. Figure 7-5 shows a column chart, which displays data in vertical columns. A bar chart is very similar but represents data using horizontal bars instead. To figure out what the bars or columns represent, read the axis labels or legend, if provided.

Histogram

Histograms look like column graphs, but on the histogram, the numbers representing the data are grouped into ranges, and the columns stand shoulder-to-shoulder. The histogram in Figure 7-6, for example, shows number of cars that get gas mileage in various ranges: 10–15 mpg, 15–20 mpg, 20–25 mpg, 25–30 mpg, and over 30 mpg.

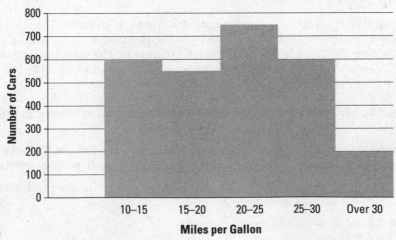

Figure 7-6:
A histogram.

John Wiley & Sons, Inc.

Line graph

Line graphs (see Figure 7-7) are used primarily to track data that changes over time. They're made up of a series of plotted points joined by a "best fit" line. The information is most accurate at the points. You can gain information from the points and observe trends from the lines. Read the axis labels carefully to ensure that the information you think you're reading is what's being presented.

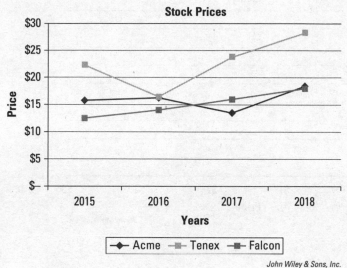

Figure 7-7:
A line graph.

John Wiley & Sons, Inc.

Pie graph

Pie graphs (see Figure 7-8) are useful for showing parts or percentages of a whole. To read a pie graph, look at the "slices" of the pie and look for labels that indicate what each slice of pie represents.

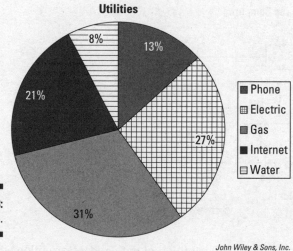

Figure 7-8:
A pie graph.

John Wiley & Sons, Inc.

Scatter plot

A *scatter plot* is a graph in which data points are plotted based on the values of two variables to determine whether the two variables are related. If a relationship exists, you should see an upward or downward trend in the data points, as shown in Figure 7-9, through which you can draw an imaginary line.

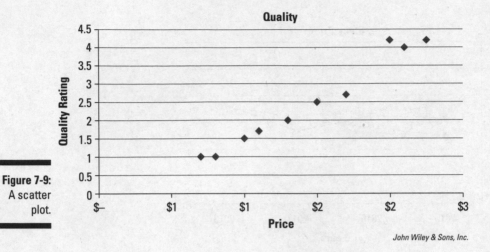

Figure 7-9:
A scatter plot.

John Wiley & Sons, Inc.

Box plot

Box plots (see Figure 7-10) divide data into four *quartiles*. The box represents the distribution of data over the two middle quartiles (second and third) divided by a vertical line inside the box that represents the median (see the later section "Calculating Mean, Median, Mode, Range, and Weighted Average"). Lines (called *whiskers*) extend to the left and right of the box to represent data over the first and fourth quartiles. Extreme data points that fall outside the typical range are called *outliers* (represented as asterisks in the figure).

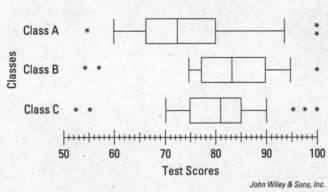

Figure 7-10:
A box plot.

John Wiley & Sons, Inc.

Box plots are excellent tools for examining distribution of data and determining whether results are skewed one way or another. When you encounter a box plot, questions typically ask for the following:

✔ **Range:** To determine the range, subtract the highest value from the lowest value plotted on the graph. The outliers count, so if you have an upper and lower outlier, subtract the lower from the upper outlier.

✔ **Interquartile range:** The box represents the interquartile range. To determine the range, subtract the lower from the upper value represented by the box.

✔ **Skewedness:** The box location relative to the upper and lower limits of the whiskers may indicate whether the data distribution is skewed positively (high box) or negatively (low box). If the plot is horizontal, a far left box means the data is skewed right because more data is to the right of the box. If the box is far right, the data is skewed left.

The location of the median line may also indicate whether data is skewed.

✔ **Spread:** A relatively big box (tall or wide depending on the orientation) and short whiskers indicate a wide spread of data. A small box (short or narrow depending on the orientation) indicates a narrow spread.

Extracting data from tables

Tables (see Table 7-3) present data in columns and rows to make the data more easily accessible. You've probably used tables without even knowing it, such as when you look in the TV listings to find programs to watch or look at a scoreboard. On the GED Math test, however, tables do more than merely help you find pieces of data; they often contain details for analyzing that data.

Table 7-3	Distribution of Digital Video Downloads in 2015 and 2016 (in Millions)	
Category	*2015*	*2016*
Rock	50	45
Blues	35	30
Country	30	32
Folk	15	13
Jazz	12	11
Hip-hop	45	60
R&B	38	50
Alternative	40	75

Sample questions

Try your hand at the following questions.

A rocket launches and accelerates as shown in the following graph. At what altitude does the rocket's speed begin to level off?

(A) 100 meters

(B) 300 meters

(C) 500 meters

(D) 700 meters

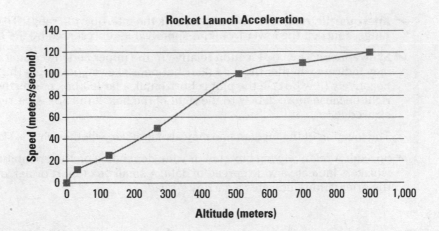

Rocket Launch Acceleration

Speed is measured along the *y* (vertical) axis, while acceleration is measured along the *x* (horizontal) axis. Follow the line from left to right, and you see that the rocket's speed steadily increases until the rocket reaches 500 meters, at which point the increase in speed slows. The correct answer is Choice (C).

City planners have been tracking population growth in their town. They have collected the data shown in the following table and have started to plot it on a chart. They start by plotting the points for years 2 and 6. Plot those data points on the following chart.

Year	Population (in Thousands)
1	15
2	15.3
3	16
4	17
5	18.3
6	19.4
7	21
8	23.2

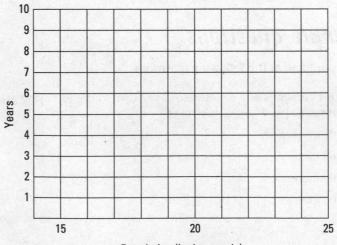

Population (in thousands)

Find the year 2 on the *y*-axis and follow the line across to where it crosses 15. Place your first dot on the year 2 line just a little to the right of where it crosses the population 15 line. Find the year 6 line and follow it to the right to where it crosses the population 19 line, and place your point just to the left of the middle point between 19 and 20. Your points should appear on the coordinate plane as shown in the following figure.

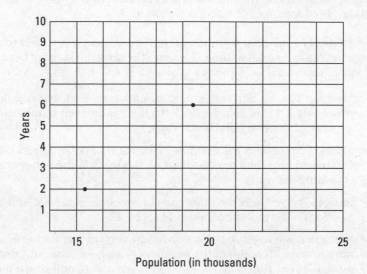

Based on the following chart, approximately what percentage of sales is comprised of T-shirts and socks?

(A) 50%

(B) 15%

(C) 75%

(D) 35%

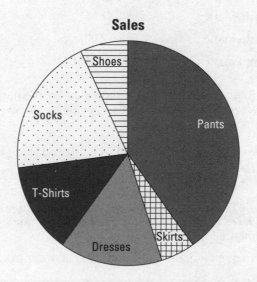

Based on the size of the slices, sales of T-shirts and socks comprise about one-third of the pie, which is close to 35%, Choice (D).

Calculating Mean, Median, Mode, Range, and Weighted Average

Certain questions on the Math test may require you to find the mean, median, mode, range, and weighted average for a series of values:

- **Mean:** The *mean* of a group of numbers is usually referred to as the *average* and is calculated by adding the values and dividing the sum by the number of values. For example, the mean of 12, 23, and 44 is $\frac{12+23+44}{3} = \frac{79}{3} = 26.33$.

- **Median:** The *median* is the middle number of a list that has been placed in order. In the preceding list, the median is 23. If a list has an even number of values, the mean is the average of the two middle numbers.

- **Mode:** The *mode* is the number in the list that occurs most often. A series of numbers can have more than one mode or no mode, as in the sequence 12, 23, 44, which has no repeating values.

- **Range:** The *range* is the difference between the smallest and largest number. In the previous example, the range is 44 – 12 = 32.

- **Weighted average:** A *weighted average* is an average where, instead of treating each number equally, each of the numbers is assigned a weight depending on a predetermined set of criteria. If, for example, Pierre were entering a mathematics contest and had to submit his average grades over his four years of high school, his math marks may be given a higher weighting than marks from other subjects, as shown here.

Subject	Mark (Weighting)
Grade 10 English	83% (1.00)
Grade 10 History	76% (1.00)
Grade 10 Physics	91% (1.25)
Grade 9 Mathematics	96% (1.50)
Grade 10 Mathematics	98% (1.75)
Grade 11 Mathematics	97% (2.00)
Grade 12 Mathematics	100% (2.50)

Instead of adding Pierre's grades and dividing by the number of grades (a normal average), a weighted average first multiplies each grade by the weight it's given. Pierre's weighted average is:

$$\text{Weighted Average} = \left[83(1.00)+76(1.00)+91(1.25)+96(1.50)+98(1.75)+97(2.00)+100(2.50)\right] \div 7$$
$$= \left[83+76+113.75+144+171.5+194+250\right] \div 7 = 147.46$$

A junior league basketball team scored the following for its first 8 games: 45, 67, 55, 44, 32, 44, 58, and 49. Determine the mean, median, and mode for that series of numbers. Mean: ☐. Median: ☐. Mode: ☐.

To answer the question, first put the values in order from least to greatest:

32, 44, 44, 45, 49, 55, 58, 67

You can instantly tell that the mode is 44 because it's the only number that appears more than once in the series. You have an even number of values, so to determine the median, you must add the two middle values and divide by two: $(45+49) \div 2 = 94 \div 2 = 47$. And the mean is the average of all the values, so total the values and divide by 8: $(32+44+44+45+49+55+58+67) \div 8 = 394 \div 8 = 49.25$.

Using Counting Techniques to Solve Problems

If you encounter a problem on the test asking you to determine the number of ways two or more items can be arranged or combined, you're looking at a *combinations* or *permutations* problem. With combinations, order doesn't matter; for example, you can combine oranges, apples, and lemons in any order. With permutations, order does matter; for example, if five people run a race and the top three finish first, second, and third, order does matter. In either case, if the numbers are small, you can figure the answer simply by writing down all the possible combinations or permutations.

Note: When you look at the formula sheet, you won't find anything about permutations and combinations, and that is because you only need to demonstrate mastery of this topic to pass with honors. If passing with honors is your goal or if you just want to do as well as you possibly can, study the following sections and memorize any formulas you think you may need. If might be worthwhile entering "permutations and combinations" into your favorite search engine to get more information and practice.

For more complicated problems with bigger numbers, you can use various formulas, as explained in the following sections.

Calculating combinations

If you have 2 pairs of pants and 3 shirts, you can create 6 different outfits. Combining 1 pair of pants with each of the 3 shirts gives you 3 outfits, and combining the other pair of pants with each of the 3 shirts gives you 3 more outfits. Fortunately, there's an easier way to calculate combinations that comes in handy when you're dealing with larger numbers. According to the *counting principle*, if one event has *m* possible outcomes and another event has *n* possible outcomes, then together the two events have $m \times n$ outcomes. So, if you have a walk-in closet with 40 shirts, 15 pairs of pants, and 10 pairs of shoes, your total number of different outfits is $40 \times 15 \times 10 = 6,000$. The same is true of any number of items in combination. Suppose you have 4 dice, and each die has 6 numbers on it; the total possible number of combinations is $6 \times 6 \times 6 \times 6 = 1,296$.

At a local ice cream store, you can choose from 35 flavors of ice cream, 12 different toppings, and 2 containers — dish or cone. How many different combinations do you have to choose from? ☐

To answer this question, simply multiply all the numbers: $35 \times 12 \times 2 = 840$

Using factorials

A *factorial* is a convenient way to represent the product of integers up to and including a specific integer, so 5!, which stands for "5 factorial," is $5 \times 4 \times 3 \times 2 \times 1 = 120$. Factorials play a key role in calculating possible permutations and combinations, as explained in the following sections.

0! breaks the rule. 0! = 1.

When order matters: Permutations

If the order in which items are arranged or events occur matters, you're looking at a *permutations* problem. For example, if 5 people run a race, how many different ways can they finish first, second, and third? To reason this problem out, follow the logic:

1. Five people have a chance to win first.

2. After 1 person wins, only 4 people have a chance to win second place.

3. After someone wins second, only 3 are left to win third place.

4. You have 5 different people who can win first, 4 who can win second, and 3 who can win third, so you have $5 \times 4 \times 3 = 60$ different ways the contestants can finish first, second, and third.

The formula to solve permutations problems such as this is $_nP_r = \dfrac{n!}{(n-r)!}$, where P stands for permutations, n is the total number of things to choose from, and r is the number chosen.

Try it:

How many different 4-letter combinations can be formed from the word STUMPED? ☐

To answer this question, count the number of letters in STUMPED, and you get 7. That's n. You're choosing only 4 letters, so r is 4. Plug the numbers into the permutations equation, and you get your answer:

$$_7P_4 = \frac{7!}{(7-4)!} = \frac{7!}{3!} = \frac{7 \times 6 \times 5 \times 4 \times \cancel{3!}}{\cancel{3!}} = 840$$

To find out the number of ways all items can be arranged, you have no r value to subtract. For example, if 9 horses are running a race and you're asked how many different ways they can finish the race, the answer is $9! = 362,880$.

When order doesn't matter: Combinations

If the order in which items are arranged or events occur does not matter, you're looking at a *combinations* problem. These problems usually involve choosing items from a group; for example, choosing 4 pieces of fruit from a selection of 20 different types. To solve a combinations problem, use the following formula:

$$C_r^n = \frac{n!}{r!(n-r)!}$$

where C is the number of combinations you're trying to determine, n is the total number of objects or events, and r is the number of objects or events you're choosing.

From a group of 15 colleagues, Sally must choose 5 to serve on a committee. How many possible combinations does she have to choose from?

Because the order doesn't matter, this is a combination problem, so proceed as follows:

$$C_{15}^5 = \frac{15!}{5!(15-5)!} = \frac{15!}{5!(10!)} = \frac{\overset{3}{\cancel{15}} \times \overset{7}{\cancel{14}} \times 13 \times \overset{1}{\cancel{12}} \times 11 \times \cancel{10!}}{\cancel{5} \times \overset{1}{\cancel{4}} \times 3 \times \overset{1}{\cancel{2}} \times 1(\cancel{10!})} = 3,003$$

Computing Probability

Probability is the likelihood of one or more events occurring. The probability of the sun rising tomorrow morning is almost a certainty. The probability of your winning the lottery tomorrow is much less likely (and is zero if you didn't buy a ticket). In the following sections, we explain how to calculate probability for *simple* (one-time) events and *compound* (two or more) events.

Simple events

Simple events are independent. No matter how many coins you toss or how many times you flip a coin, with each toss of the coin, you have a 1 in 2 chance of it landing on heads.

To calculate probability, divide the number of ways the desired outcome can happen by the total number of outcomes possible. For example, a die has 6 sides marked with dots representing the numbers 1 through 6, so the total number of outcomes possible is 6. The chances of rolling a 5 (desired outcome) are 1 in 6, or $\frac{1}{6}$, because it can happen only one way — if the die shows a 5. A 52-card deck of playing cards has 4 aces, so there are 4 ways to draw an ace (desired outcome) and 52 possible outcomes when you draw a card from the deck, so the possibility of drawing an ace is $\frac{4}{52} = \frac{1}{13}$.

To calculate the probability of either of two or more events occurring, add the probabilities of the two events. For example, what are the chances of rolling a die and having it come up a 2 or a 5? Each event has a one in six chance, so add the probabilities:

$$\frac{1}{6} + \frac{1}{6} = \frac{2}{6} = \frac{1}{3}$$

Compound events

Compound events are two or more events occurring at the same time or sequentially. For example, what are the odds of a coin landing on tails 6 times in a row? To calculate probability for compound events, multiply the probabilities of each event occurring. For example, each time you toss a coin, you have a $\frac{1}{2}$ chance it'll land on tails, so the chance of tossing 6 tails in a row is:

$$\frac{1}{2} \times \frac{1}{2} \times \frac{1}{2} \times \frac{1}{2} \times \frac{1}{2} \times \frac{1}{2} = \frac{1}{64}$$

Calculating probability of compound events becomes more complicated when an event changes the odds for the next event. For example, to determine the probability of drawing 4 hearts from a standard 52-card deck of playing cards, you need to subtract the number of cards drawn from the total. The odds of drawing a heart on the first draw is 13 in 52. Assuming you drew a heart with your first draw, there are now 12 hearts and a total of only 51 cards in the deck, so the chance of drawing a heart on the second draw is 12 in 51. On the third draw, you have an 11 in 50 chance.

Practice Session

Time for additional practice. Try your hand at the following sample questions.

1. Shirley wants to build steps down from the 6-foot-high porch behind her house. The bottom step should be 7 feet away from the house to allow for a gentle slope. How long, in feet, will the steps be?

   (A) 13.00

   (B) 2.92

   (C) 13.22

   (D) 9.22

2. Jack and Petra compare their report cards.

Subject	Jack's Grades	Petra's Grades
Mathematics	76%	82%
Social Studies	66%	71%
Science	58%	73%
Language Arts	84%	75%
Physical Education	87%	78%

   The teacher tells them that the ratio of their total marks is very close. What is the ratio of Petra's marks to Jack's marks on these report cards, recorded to one decimal point?

   (A) 9:10

   (B) 18:19

   (C) 10:9

   (D) 1:1

3. Jeremy wants to paint his room, which is 9 feet 5 inches long, 8 feet 3 inches wide, and 8 feet 2 inches high. The label on the paint can cautions that air must be exchanged in the room every 12 minutes. When Jeremy looks for exhaust fans to keep the air moving, he finds one that is capable of moving 5 cubic feet of air per minute. Would this fan serve Jeremy's needs? Yes or No: _____.

4. Miriam and Jonathan just bought a small circular swimming pool for their children to play in. The diameter of the pool is 16 feet, and the pool can be filled safely to a depth of 9 inches. If a cubic foot of water weighs 62.42 pounds, how many pounds does the water in their pool weigh?

   (A) 4,907.94

   (B) 7,904.94

   (C) 9,704.94

   (D) 9,407.94

5. An international survey found the following information about participation in adult education:

Denmark	62.3
Hungary	17.9

Norway   43.1

Portugal   15.5

United States   66.4

Approximately how many times more is the participation rate in the country with the highest participation rate than in the country with the lowest participation rate?

(A) 4

(B) 6

(C) 8

(D) not enough information given

6. Catherine follows the stock market very carefully. She has been following Isadora's Information Technology Corporation the last few months, keeping track of her research in the following table.

Date	Closing Price
August 7	$15.03
August 17	$16.12
September 1	$14.83
September 9	$15.01
September 16	$14.94
September 20	$15.06
September 23	$15.17
September 24	$15.19

She bought shares of the stock on September 24 and wants to make money before selling it. She paid 3% commission to her broker for buying on August 7 and will pay the same again when she sells. The lowest price for which Catherine can sell each of her shares in order to break even is $☐ .

Check your work:

1. (D) Use the Pythagorean theorem and imagine the staircase, house, and ground as forming a right triangle. A line from the ground running along the house and straight up to the porch forms one side of the triangle and is 6 feet. A line running along the ground between the house and the end of the staircase forms another side of the triangle and is 7 feet. The staircase forms the hypotenuse.

   If the length of the staircase is represented by L, then $L^2 = 6^2 + 7^2 = 85$, and the square root of 85 is 9.22 feet.

   This is a good question on which to use the calculator because it involves squaring, adding, and calculating the square root.

2. (D) Because Petra and Jack have the same number of grades, you can compare their totals or their averages. (If they had a different number of grades, you'd need to calculate their averages.)

   Petra's grades: $82 + 71 + 73 + 75 + 78 = 379$

   Jack's grades: $76 + 66 + 58 + 84 + 87 = 370$

   The ratio is 379:370, which is very close to 1:1 (actually 1.02:1).

3. Yes. First, calculate the volume of the room in cubic inches:

$$9\frac{5}{12} \times 8\frac{3}{12} \times 8\frac{2}{12} = \frac{113}{12} \times \frac{99}{12} \times \frac{98}{12} = \frac{1,096,326}{12} = 91,360.5$$

Now, convert cubic inches into cubic feet. Each cubic foot contains $12 \times 12 \times 12 = 1,728$ cubic inches. Divide the volume of the room in cubic inches by the number of cubic inches in a cubic foot: $91,360.5 \div 1,728 = 52.87$ cubic feet.

The label on the paint can cautions that air must be exchanged in the room every 12 minutes, so divide the total cubic feet of air in the room by 12 minutes to determine the number of cubic feet of air a fan would need to move per minute: $52.87 \div 12 = 4.41$ cubic feet per minute. A fan that moves 5 cubic feet of air per minute would be sufficient.

4. (D) First, calculate the total gallons of water in the pool by using the volume of a cylinder equation. The pool's diameter is 16 feet, its radius is 8 feet, and the pool is filled to a depth of 9 inches, which is $\frac{9}{12} = \frac{3}{4}$ feet deep:

$$V = \pi r^2 h = 3.14 \times 8^2 \times \frac{3}{4} = 3.14 \times \overset{16}{\cancel{64}} \times \frac{3}{\cancel{4}_1} = 3.14 \times 48 \doteq 150.72$$

Because 1 cubic foot of water weighs 62.42 pounds, the weight of 150.72 cubic feet of water is $150.72 \times 64.42 = 9,407.94$ pounds when rounded to two decimal places.

5. (A) The country with the highest participation rate, 66.4%, is the United States. The country with the lowest participation rate, 15.5 %, is Portugal. Because you're asked for an approximation, you can say that the participation rate in the United States is 60 and in Portugal is 15, so the rate in the United States is 4 times higher than the rate in Portugal.

6. 16.13. Most of the information given is irrelevant, except to decide that Catherine may have bought at a high point. The important price to consider is $15.19. In addition to this price per share, she has to pay her broker a 3% commission.

Her final price per share on September 24 is $15.19 + \$.03(15.19) = \$15.6457$. Her final price per share including commission is $15.65 rounded to the nearest penny.

To break even, Catherine must receive at least $15.65 per share after the commission is paid, so the share price minus the commission must be equal to $15.65. Write your equation, using s to represent share price, and do the math:

$$1s - 0.03s = \$15.65$$
$$0.97s = \$15.65$$
$$s = \frac{\$15.65}{0.97} = \$16.13$$

Chapter 8

Solving Algebraic Problems with Expressions and Equations

In This Chapter

▶ Working with linear expressions and equations

▶ Performing operations on polynomials

▶ Using various methods to solve quadratic equations

▶ Manipulating rational expressions

▶ Answering inequality questions and graphing their solutions

Algebraic equations and expressions are similar to the numeric equations and expressions covered in Chapter 8, but in addition to containing numbers, algebraic equations and expressions contain variables, such as a, b, x, y, and so on, which represent unknown values. An *equation* in math is like a complete sentence in English. It even has a verb in the form of $=$, which means "is equal to." An algebraic equation enables you to solve for the variable. For example, suppose you have twice as many *Star Trek* models as your best friend. If the number of *Star Trek* models owned by your friend is represented by x, then the number of models you have can be represented by $2x$. If the total number of models you have all together is 42, then the algebraic equation can be written as $x + 2x = 42$. You can solve the equation for x and find out how many models you have and your friend has.

An *expression* is like a sentence fragment; it has no verb, no $=$. For example, $x + 2x$ is an algebraic expression. To solve for x, you need more information, and an expression doesn't provide the information you need.

The main difference between an expression and an equation is the solution. An equation can be solved, whereas an expression can only be simplified.

In this chapter, you find out how to answer questions and solve problems that involve various types of algebraic equations and expressions, including linear and quadratic equations, polynomials, rational expressions (algebraic fractions), and inequalities. We explain the various types of equations and expressions, show you how to write them in proper form and simplify them so they're easier to manage, and solve them to answer test questions. You even discover how to plot inequalities on number lines and graphs.

Tackling Linear Expressions and Equations

A *linear equation* is a mathematical statement that can be graphed as a line on the coordinate plane. For example, the equation $y = 2x$ describes a line that rises twice as fast as it runs, as shown in Figure 8-1. It's linear because it defines a line. It's an equation because it can be solved. For example, if x is 0, y is 0. If x is 1, y is 2. Simple linear equations have only one variable; for example, $3x + 15 = 45$ is also a linear equation. (See Chapter 9 for more about how linear equations can be plotted as lines on the coordinate plane.)

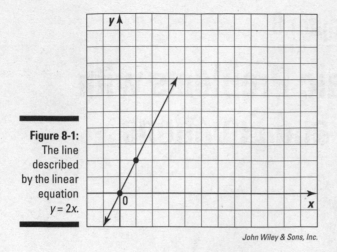

Figure 8-1:
The line
described
by the linear
equation
$y = 2x.$

In this section, you find out everything you need to know about linear expressions and equations to tackle related questions on the GED Mathematical Reasoning test, including how to solve linear equations and simplify linear expressions, write and evaluate linear equations and expressions, solve real-world (word) problems using linear equations, and solve problems that involve the intersection of two lines defined by two linear equations.

Computing linear expressions and equations

The key to solving linear equations and simplifying linear expressions is to isolate the variable — the x, y, or z that represents the unknown value. You want the variable on one side of the equal sign and a numeric value on the other. If you can accomplish that feat, you've "solved for the value of the unknown," which most of the questions on the GED test that involve linear equations direct you to do. To isolate and solve for the variable, take the following steps:

1. **Move all constants to one side of the equal sign.**

   For example, if the equation is $4p - 24 = 88 + 2p$, you can add 24 to both sides of the equation to eliminate −24 on the left, leaving you with $4p = 112 + 2p$.

2. **Move all variables to the other side of the equal sign by performing the same operation on both sides of the equation.**

   In this example, you'd subtract $2p$ from both sides of the equation to get $4p - 2p = 112$.

3. **Combine terms.**

   For example, $4p - 2p = 2p = 112$.

4. **Strip the term of the numerical value that accompanies it.**

   In this example, you divide both sides by 2 to get rid of the 2 next to p, leaving you with $p = 56$.

5. **(Optional) To check your work, plug your answer into the original equation to see whether it works:**

$$4(56) - 24 = 88 + 2(56)$$
$$224 - 24 = 88 + 112$$
$$200 = 200$$

Here's another one: $4x + 23 = 35$. To solve this equation, first subtract 23 from both sides to get $4x + 23 - 23 = 35 - 23 = 12$. Then, divide both sides by 4: $4x \div 4 = 12 \div 4$, so $x = 3$.

Treat a linear *expression* the same way, but keep in mind that an expression doesn't contain enough information for you to solve it. For example, you can simplify the expression $7b + 3b$ by adding them to get $10b$. Likewise, you can simplify $\frac{ab}{b^2}$ by dividing the numerator and denominator by b, leaving you with $\frac{a}{b}$.

Practice solving the following linear equations and simplifying the linear expressions to find the value or possible values of the unknown variable:

1. $25x - 15 = 65$, $x =$ ☐
2. $7k - 23 = 37$, $k =$ ☐
3. $3w(5 + 7) = 108$, $w =$ ☐
4. $7x = (43 + 4) + 2$, $x =$ ☐

Check your work:

1. $x = 2$
2. $k = 2$
3. $w = 3$
4. $x = 7$

Writing linear expressions and equations

Writing a linear equation or expression is like writing a simple sentence or phrase in English. Each tells a story about numbers. Equations are more like mystery stories in which you need to find the unknown. Expressions are like fantasy stories in that they have no single solution but a number of possibilities.

To translate a word problem into a linear expression or equation, assign a variable to the unknown and write the equation or expression that reflects the relationship between the variable (unknown) and the known values. Suppose Frank received a 10-percent discount on 5 books he bought for $3.00 each at a garage sale, and you're asked to write an equation to calculate the discount Frank received in dollars. The first step is to assign a variable to the unknown. You can use any letter, but d is a logical choice, because it stands for "discount." Now you can write your equation starting with $d =$. You know he bought 5 books at $3.00 each, so he paid a total of $5 \times \$3.00 = \$15.00$, and the 10 percent discount was applied to that total, so the equation for determining the discount in dollars is

$$d = 0.10 \times (5 \times \$3.00)$$

You weren't asked to solve the equation — just to write the equation for doing so. (Most questions like this one are multiple choice; you must select the correct equation or expression from a list of choices.)

Try your hand at converting the following word problems into expressions/equations.

1. Jenny has $40 to spend on her cats. She needs a bag of cat food that sells for $20 and wants to buy as many cans of cat food as she can afford. Each can is priced at $0.50. Write an expression or equation to represent the number of cans of cat food she can afford to buy.

_____

2. David is hiking the Appalachian Trail and has agreed to meet his father in 4 days at a checkpoint 150 miles from his current location. Write an expression or equation to determine the number of miles that David must hike each day to meet his father at the agreed-upon place and time.

_____

3. Georgia plans to drive to her parents' home 240 miles away. She knows she can average 60 miles per hour on this highway at this time of day. If she were invited for 4 p.m. and wants to arrive 15 minutes early, write an equation or expression that determines when she should leave.

_____

Check your work:

1. The unknown is the number of cans of cat food, and Jenny has only $40, so her entire purchase must be equal to $40. Assign the unknown the variable c for number of cans of cat food and write your expression:

$$\$20 + (\$0.50c) = \$40$$

2. The unknown is the number of miles that David must hike per day, so assign the unknown the variable m for miles. The number of miles he must walk in 4 days is $4m$, and the total miles he must walk is 150, so your equation looks like this:

$$4m = 150$$

3. The unknown is when Georgia should depart, so let the unknown be d for "depart." She needs to arrive 15 minutes before 4 p.m., so you can start your equation with = 3:45. Her total travel time is 240 miles divided by 60 miles per hour, and her time of departure plus her total travel time must be equal to 3:45, so your equation looks like this:

$$d + (240 \div 60) = 3\!:\!45$$

You can plug in numbers to determine whether your equation is accurate. If Georgia were to leave at noon, she would arrive at 12:00 + 4:00 = 4:00, which is 15 minutes late. She would need to leave at 11:45 to arrive at 3:45 pm.

Evaluating linear expressions and equations

Certain questions on the GED Mathematical Reasoning test provide you with a linear equation along with the value of one or more variables and ask you to solve for the unknown variable, as in the following example:

If $x = 5$ and $y = -2$, evaluate the following expression: $x(y + 5) = \boxed{}$.

To solve equations such as these, plug in the values for the variables and do the math:

$$x(y+5) = 5(-2+5) = 5(3) = 15$$

On the golf course, you'd refer to such questions as gimmes because they're so easy. They're actually pretty easy on the test, as well.

Now, evaluate the following expressions and check your answers using the answer key immediately after:

1. $x = 5$, $y = 23$, evaluate $6x - 5y + 21 = \boxed{}$

2. $a = 4$, $b = 3$, $c = 7$, evaluate $a(c - b) + 12 = \boxed{}$

3. $p = 15$, $r = -4$, $s = 25$, evaluate $2s - 4r + p = \boxed{}$

4. $m = 17$, $n = 12$, $o = 3$, evaluate $\dfrac{o}{n}m = \boxed{}$

5. $f = 3$, $g = 6$, $h = 18$, evaluate $h + \dfrac{f}{g}h = \boxed{}$

Check your work:

1. $6(5) - 5(23) + 21 = 30 - 115 + 21 = -64$

2. $4(7 - 3) + 12 = 4(4) + 12 = 16 + 12 = 28$

3. $2(25) - 4(-4) + 15 = 50 + 16 + 15 = 81$

4. $\dfrac{3}{12} \cdot 17 = \dfrac{1}{4} \cdot 17 = 4\dfrac{1}{4}$

5. $18 + \dfrac{3}{6}18 = 18 + \dfrac{1}{2}18 = 18 + 9 = 27$

Don't overthink these easy problems. Just plug in the numbers and do the math. As long as you insert the correct value for each variable and avoid mistakes in calculations, these are easy questions to boost your score.

Solving real-world problems involving linear equations

When you know how to write linear equations and evaluate them, as explained in the previous two sections, you've mastered the approach to solving a wide range of algebra word problems on the GRE Mathematical Reasoning test. Many of the questions on the test challenge your ability to find the value of an unknown variable using known values presented in the question.

Practice writing and evaluating linear equations as you go about your daily business. For example, if you have $10 in your pocket and you're craving a candy bar priced at $0.88 with 7 percent sales tax, how many candy bars can you afford to purchase?

The unknown is the number of candy bars, c, and the maximum amount you can spend is $10, so place c on one side and $10 on the other. The total price you'll pay for the candy bars before tax is $0.88 per candy bar times the number of candy bars, or $0.88c$. You also need to add in the 7 percent sales tax on those candy bars, so your expression ends up looking like this:

$$\$0.88c + (\$0.88c \times 0.07) = \$10.00$$

To isolate the variable, first multiply $0.88c$ by 0.07, and you get $0.0616c$, which is the amount of sales tax you'll pay. Then add $0.0616c$ to to $0.88c$ and you get $0.9416c$. Divide both sides by 0.9416 and you get $c = 10.62$. Of course, you can't buy 0.62 candy bars, so the most candy bars you could buy is 10.

Try these problems, which are closer to what you may expect on the GED exam. Answers and explanations are provided after the problems. Check your answers and read the explanations, especially if you made an error or don't fully understand how to solve the problem.

1. Gilbert and Sullivan paint houses. Gilbert is faster, so he earns $15.00 an hour, while Sullivan earns only $10.00 an hour. They work the same number of hours painting a house and are paid $1,500. How many hours did they work? ☐

2. The prom committee sold 4 times as many advanced tickets as it sold on the day of the prom. If it sold 200 tickets, how many tickets did it sell on the day of the prom? ☐

3. Kimmie drove from Chicago, Illinois, to Columbus, Ohio, and back on a tank of gas. If she drove a total of 750 miles and her car gets 37 miles per gallon on the highway, what is the least amount of fuel her gas tank can possibly hold? ☐

4. Dan has $15.75 in change consisting solely of dimes and nickels. He knows he has 3 times as many dimes as nickels. How many total coins does he have?

5. Cara pays $15.75 for a book at a 25% discount. What was the price of the book before the discount?

Check your work:

1. Let h be the number of hours Gilbert and Sullivan worked. Gilbert earned $15.00h$, and Sullivan earned $10.00h$, for a total of $1,500. Create your equation and solve for h:

$$\$15h + \$10h = \$1,500$$
$$\$25h = \$1,500$$
$$h = \frac{\$1,500}{\$25} = 60$$

2. Let t be the number of tickets sold on the day of the prom, so $4t$ is the number of advanced tickets. Two hundred total tickets were sold, so your equation looks like this:

$$t + 4t = 200$$
$$5t = 200$$
$$t = 40$$

Note that if the question had asked for the number of advanced tickets, you'd need to multiply 40 by 4 to get 160.

3. Let g be the number of gallons Kimmie's tank holds. She traveled a total of 750 miles using 1 gallon every 37 miles, so your equation looks like this:

$$g = 750 \text{ miles} \times \frac{1 \text{ gallon}}{37 \text{ miles}} = \frac{750}{37} = 20.27 \text{ gallons}$$

4. Use n to represent the number of nickels, so $3n$ is the number of dimes. Each nickel is worth $0.05, and each dime is worth $0.10, and together they total $15.75, so your equation looks like this:

$$\$0.05n + \$0.10 \times 3n = \$15.75$$
$$\$0.05n + \$0.30n = \$15.75$$
$$\$0.35n = \$15.75$$
$$n = 45$$

That's the number of nickels. The number of dimes is 3 times that many, or $45 \times 3 = 135$. To determine the total number of nickels and dimes, add them: $135 + 45 = 180$.

5. The unknown is the original price of the book, which you can set as b. The discounted price is $b - 0.25b$, which equals the price Cara paid, $15.75:

$$b - 0.25b = \$15.75$$
$$0.75b = \$15.75$$
$$b = \frac{\$15.75}{0.75} = \$21.00$$

Solving problems using a system of two linear equations

A *system of two linear equations* is a set of equations, each with two variables that you solve together. Because each equation defines a line on the coordinate plane, the fact that the lines are likely to intersect enables you to use the equations in tandem to solve for both variables in each equation. This concept may be difficult to wrap your brain around without an example, so here's one:

$$y = 3x + 2$$
$$y = -x + 6$$

If you were to plot these two equations on the coordinate plane, you'd see that they intersect at the point $x = 1$, $y = 5$, as shown in Figure 8-2. If you were to plug those two numbers into either equation, you'd see that they work:

$$5 = 3(1) + 2$$
$$5 = -1 + 6$$

To solve problems that consist of systems of linear equations, you have three options:

- ✔ **Plot the two lines and try to figure out where they intersect,** as shown in Figure 8-2. This option may not give you the most precise answer, but if you're given multiple choices, it'll probably get you close enough to choose the correct answer.

- ✔ **Use the substitution method.** Solve one of the equations for one of the variables and then plug your solution into the other equation. Continuing with the previous example, you don't need to solve one of the equations for one of the variables, because the second equation already does that for you: $y = -x + 6$. You can plug $-x + 6$ in for y in the second equation and solve for x:

$$-x + 6 = 3x + 2$$
$$-4x = -4$$
$$x = 1$$

Now, plug 1 in for x in either equation to find the value of y: $y = -1 + 6 = 5$.

- ✔ **Use the elimination method.** The elimination method consists of combining the equations and then canceling out like items. Continuing the example, this one's easy, because y is isolated on the left in both equations. Because $y = 3x + 2$ and $y = -x + 6$, $3x + 2 = -x + 6$, so $4x = 4$, and x is 1. You can then plug 1 in for x in either equation and solve for y.

You may come across a more complex system of linear equations, such as this:

$$4x + 5y = 12$$
$$7x - 5y = 27$$

Whenever you encounter such a system of linear equations, in which the *coefficient* (the number next to) of the *x* or *y* variable in both equations is equal but opposite, as in the case of +5*y* and −5*y* here, you can add the two equations to cancel out one of the variables; for example, $7x + 4x = 11x$, $+5y + (−5y) = 0$, and $12 + 27 = 39$. The reason you can do this is that you're essentially adding the same thing to both sides of the equation. Because $7x − 5y = 27$, you can add $7x − 5y$ to the left side of the first equation and add 27 to the right side without throwing off the balance. You end up with $11x = 39$. Divide both sides by 11 and you find that *x* is approximately 3.54. You can then plug in 3.54 for *x* in either equation and solve for *y*.

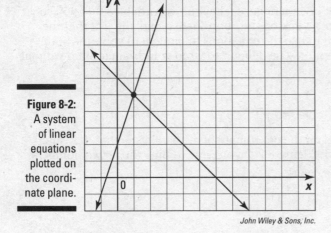

Figure 8-2:
A system of linear equations plotted on the coordinate plane.

John Wiley & Sons, Inc.

Systems of linear equations also come into play with real-world word problems you may encounter on the GED Math test. When you encounter such a problem, translate the words into math and formulate your equations as you normally do. You'll end up with two equations, which is a great clue that you're dealing with a system of linear equations problem. You can then employ one of the methods we just described to solve the problem. Here's an example:

You and your friends have formed a rock band that is becoming increasingly popular. Your group headlined a recent concert and was promised 80% of the gross from the sale of adult tickets priced at $4.00 per person. Your group agreed not to receive any proceeds from the sales of student tickets priced at $1.50. The concert attendance was 220 people of all ages, and gross sales from tickets was $505.00. How much money was your band paid?

To solve this problem, set up two equations, with *S* representing the number of students and *A* representing the number of adults. Gross sales from tickets was $505.00, which is the total received from adult tickets priced at $4.00 and student tickets priced at $1.50, so your first equation is this:

$$\$4.00A + \$1.50S = \$505.00$$

You also know that the total number of tickets sold is the number of adult tickets plus the number of student tickets, so your second equation is this:

$$A + S = 220$$

You can then use the substitution method. Solve for A in the second equation and you have $A = 220 - S$. Plug that in for A in the first equation and you have

$$\$4.00(220 - S) + \$1.50S = \$505.00$$
$$\$880.00 - \$4.00S + \$1.50S = \$505.00$$
$$\$880.00 - \$2.50S = \$505.00$$
$$\$2.50S = \$375$$
$$S = 150$$

If 150 student tickets were sold, then $220 - 150 = 70$ adult tickets were sold at \$4.00 each, bringing in \$280. Your band received only 80 percent of that amount, or $\$280 \times 0.80 = \$224$.

Here's another system of linear equations problem:

Bonny has invented a new game. It involves throwing two dice one after the other. If the difference between the numbers thrown is zero, the player wins. What are the chances of winning at Bonny's new game? 1 in ☐.

The chances of throwing any number with a die is 1 in 6 (a die has 6 faces). Having done so, the chances of throwing the same number with the same die is 1 in 6. In throwing the second die, the chances of any one number coming up is 1 in 6, but to win the player must get the same number as they got on the first throw. The chances of this are 1 in 36 (6×6).

To express this as an equation, let C = the chance of a player winning in each turn be C, the chance of a player throwing a particular number be F and the chance of the player throwing the same number on the second turn be S, then $C = F \times S$, then C = 1 in 36.

Computing with Polynomials

A *polynomial* is a mathematical expression containing one or more terms, two or more of which must be *algebraic* (containing a variable). A term can be a variable, a combination of a variable and a numeric value called a *coefficient,* or a numeric value alone (a *constant*). In the example $6x + y - 8$, x and y are variables, 6 is a coefficient of x, and -8 is a constant.

On the test, you may not be required to solve polynomial expressions unless the question provides you with a value to plug in for the variable. Instead, you're expected to know how to work with and simplify polynomial expressions. In the following sections, we explain how to add, subtract, multiply, and divide polynomial expressions and, in the process, simplify them.

Writing polynomial expressions

When writing polynomials, you're expected to follow standard form by placing the terms in descending order of magnitude from left to right:

1. **Terms with exponents come first and are arranged in descending order of magnitude.**

   For example, $2x^5$ comes before $9x^3$ because its exponent is larger. Keep in mind that a variable without an exponent really has an exponent of 1.

2. **Constants come last in descending order of magnitude.**

If a question prompts you to solve a problem with a polynomial, make sure the terms are in the right order before trying to tackle the problem. For example, if you're given a polynomial such as this:

$$8x^2 + 30 + 5x^5 + 3x$$

rearrange the term so it looks like this:

$$5x^5 + 8x^2 + 3x + 30$$

Doing so will make your life a whole lot easier.

Adding polynomials

Adding polynomials is just combining *like terms* — terms that are constants or that have the same variables raised to the same power. For example, you can combine $4x^3$ and $2x^3$ to get $6x^3$ because they contain the same variable raised to the same power. However, you can't combine $4x^2$ and $2x^3$ or $2y^2$. You can add polynomials horizontally or vertically.

To add polynomials horizontally, work from left to right. For example, to add $3x + 2y$ to $5x - 4y$, first you add $3x$ and $5x$ to get $8x$, and then you add $2y$ and $-4y$ to get $-2y$. The resulting expression is $8x - 2y$.

You can also add the two polynomials vertically by writing like terms under like terms:

$$\begin{array}{r} 3x + 2y \\ \underline{5x - 4y} \\ 8x - 2y \end{array}$$

Solve $(3r + 8p) + (9r - 6p) = $.

To solve this equation, add $3r$ and $9r$ to get $12r$, and then add $8p$ and $-6p$ to get $2p$:

$$3r + 9r + 8p - 6p = 12r + 2p$$

Subtracting polynomials

Just as you can add polynomials either horizontally or vertically, you can subtract polynomials horizontally or vertically. The only difference is that when you subtract, you need to account for the fact that the minus sign applies to anything inside the parenthesis enclosing the polynomial you're subtracting. For example, if given $(9m - 4n) - (6m + 9n)$, the minus sign before the second polynomial applies both to $6m$ and $9n$. To perform the subtraction, you have $9m - 6m = 3m$ and $-4n - 9n = -13n$, so the result is $3m - 13n$.

To subtract vertically, stack the two equations and remember to apply the minus sign to the entire second polynomial:

$$\begin{array}{r} 9m - 4n \\ \underline{-6m - 9n} \\ 3m - 13n \end{array}$$

Solve $(12k - 11m) - (9k - 3m) = \boxed{}$.

To solve this equation, $12k - 9k = 3k$ and $-11m - 3m = -11m + 3m = -8m$, so the result is $3k - 8m$.

Multiplying polynomials

To multiply polynomials, multiply each term in the first polynomial by each term in the second polynomial, as shown in Figure 8-3. When multiplying terms, multiply the coefficients (the numbers) and add the exponents. Here's an example of adding the exponents:

$$4x \times 5x = 4x^1 \times 5x^1 = 20x^{1+1} = 20x^2$$

When you're done multiplying, try to combine terms to simplify the result. In the second equation shown in Figure 8-3, for example, you can simplify by adding $9mn$ and $-56mn$ to get $-47mn$.

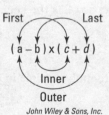

Figure 8-3:
Multiplying
polynomials.

$$5x(2x + 7y) = 10x^2 + 35xy$$

$$(3m - 8n) \times (7m + 3n) = 21m^2 + 9mn - 56mn - 24n^2$$

John Wiley & Sons, Inc.

Some teachers recommend the FOIL method, as shown in Figure 8-4. FOIL stands for First, Outer, Inner, Last. What's important is that you have a system to follow that ensures you don't overlook anything when you're multiplying terms.

Figure 8-4:
Multiplying
polynomi-
als using
the FOIL
method.

First · · · Last

$$(a - b) \times (c + d)$$

Inner

Outer

John Wiley & Sons, Inc.

You can multiply polynomials using various systems that are either horizontal or vertical, but the two systems in this section are sufficient for answering questions on the GED test. Just be sure that each term in one factor is multiplied by each term in the other factor.

Solve $4y(7x + 6y) = \boxed{}$.

To solve this equation, multiply $4y$ by both terms inside the parentheses: $4y \times 7x = 28xy$ and $4y \times 6y = 24y^2$, so your equation is $28xy + 24y^2$.

Solve $(14x - 17y) \times (8x + 3y) = \boxed{}$.

To solve this equation, start by multiplying the first term in the first polynomial by the two terms in the second polynomial: $14x(8x+3y) = 112x^2 + 42xy$. Multiply the second term in the first polynomial by the two terms in the second polynomial: $112x^2 + 42xy + 136xy + 51y^2 = 112x^2 - 51y^2 + 136xy$. Now, put it all together and simplify:

$$112x^2 - 94xy - 51y^2$$

Dividing polynomials

Dividing polynomials ranges from easy to very difficult. If you're dividing a polynomial by a *monomial* (a single term), you simply divide the monomial into each of the terms that comprise the binomial. The easiest approach for such problems is to convert the expression into a fraction and then do the math.

Solve $(21x^3 - 35x^2) \div 7x$

To solve this problem, rewrite it as a fraction:

$$\frac{21x^3 - 35x^2}{7x}$$

Then solve it in steps: $21x^3 \div 7x = 3x^2$ and $-35x^2 \div 7x = -5x$, so your answer is $3x^2 - 5x$.

To divide a polynomial by another polynomial, you may need to use long division (see Chapter 5), which can get very messy, as in the following example.

Solve $(x^2 + 3x - 10) \div (x + 5)$

You can reason your way to the answer of this problem. Instead of looking at it as a division problem, ask yourself, "What do I need to multiply $(x+5)$ by to get $(x^2 + 3x - 10)$?" You know you're going to have to multiply $(x+5)$ by another polynomial that contains x to get the x^2 in $(x^2 + 3x - 10)$, so start with that: $(x+5)(x \pm ?)$.

You also know that you need to multiply $(x+5)$ by -2 to get -10, so -2 is the second term, giving you $(x+5)(x-2)$. Now test to see whether it works:

$$(x+5) \times (x-2) = x^2 - 2x + 5x - 10 = x^2 + 3x - 10$$

You'll get better at using this method after you practice factoring polynomials in the next section.

The other approach is to use long division (ugh!):

$$x+5\overline{)\begin{array}{l} x \\ x^2 + 3x - 10 \\ x^2 + 5x \end{array}}$$

But you need to subtract the $x^2 + 5$ from what's above it, so change the signs to negatives:

$$x+5\overline{)\begin{array}{l} x \\ x^2 + 3x - 10 \\ \underline{-x^2 - 5x} \\ 0 - 2x \end{array}}$$

Drop down the −10 to get:

$$\begin{array}{r} x \phantom{{}+3x-10} \\ x+5{\overline{\smash{\big)}\,x^2+3x-10}} \\ \underline{-x^2-5x} \\ 0\;-2x-10 \end{array}$$

Now you need to subtract −2*x* from −2*x* to cancel it out, so you have:

$$\begin{array}{r} x-2 \\ x+5{\overline{\smash{\big)}\,x^2+3x-10}} \\ \underline{-x^2-5x} \\ 0\;-2x-10 \\ -2x-10 \end{array}$$

But you must *subtract* −2*x* −10, so change the signs to get:

$$\begin{array}{r} x-2 \\ x+5{\overline{\smash{\big)}\,x^2+3x-10}} \\ \underline{-x^2-5x} \\ 0\;-2x-10 \\ \underline{+2x+10} \\ 0 \end{array}$$

Here's a polynomial division problem to try on your own.

Solve $(ab-2a+5b-10) \div (b-2) = \boxed{}$.

To solve this problem, use long division:

$$\begin{array}{r} a \\ b-2{\overline{\smash{\big)}\,ab-2a+5b-10}} \\ \underline{ab-2a} \end{array}$$

Change the signs to subtract:

$$\begin{array}{r} a \\ b-2{\overline{\smash{\big)}\,ab-2a+5b-10}} \\ \underline{-ab+2a} \\ 0 \end{array}$$

Carry down 5*b* −10 to get:

$$\begin{array}{r} a \\ b-2{\overline{\smash{\big)}\,ab-2a+5b-10}} \\ \underline{-ab+2a} \\ 0+5b-10 \end{array}$$

You can see that the next term will be +5:

$$\begin{array}{r} a+5 \\ b-2{\overline{\smash{\big)}\,ab-2a+5b-10}} \\ \underline{-ab+2a} \\ 0+5b-10 \\ 5b-10 \end{array}$$

You have your answer. Change the signs to subtract and make sure you have no remainder:

$$b-2 \overline{)\begin{array}{l} a+5 \\ ab-2a+5b-10 \end{array}}$$
$$\underline{-ab+2a}$$
$$0+5b-10$$
$$\underline{-5b+10}$$
$$0$$

Factoring polynomials

Factoring is a way to simplify a polynomial by breaking it down into its smallest parts. As explained in Chapter 5, you must factor whole numbers to find a least common denominator (LCM) of two fractions before adding them. You also factor whole numbers to simplify radical expressions. The same is true of polynomials; sometimes you need to factor polynomials to simplify an expression or make it more manageable in an equation.

You can use various methods to factor polynomials. One of the most common methods is the guess-and-test method, which is more like reason-it-out-and-test. You guess what the factors are and then multiply them to test your guess. Guess-and-test works well on simple expressions, such as $x^2+3x-10$. For example, just by looking at x^2 you can tell that the first term in each factor will be x, so jot those down:

$$(x\pm?)(x\pm?)$$

You can also tell from the -10 that the last two terms in the two factors when multiplied together must return a result of -10, so they can be -2 and 5, 2 and -5, -1 and 10, or 1 and -10. And you know that added together, the correct number pair must equal the coefficient in the middle term, which is 3. The only number pair that works is 5 and -2 because $5-2=3$. Now for the test:

$$(x+5)(x-2)=x^2+5x-2x-10=x^2+3x-10$$

More complex polynomials, such as $12y^4+46y^3+40y^2$, require a more systematic approach to factoring, such as this:

1. **Identify the greatest common factor (GCF) of all terms in the polynomial, keeping in mind that they may not have a GCF.**

   Although you can factor each term in the expression, that can become very messy, so try reasoning it out. In this example, you can tell that 2 is a common factor of all three coefficients (12, 46, and 40) and that 2 goes into 46 23 times, which is a prime number, so the greatest common factor of all those coefficients is 2. You also can tell that y^2 is a factor of each term. So the GCF is $2y^2$.

2. **Divide each term by the GCF:**

   $12y^4 \div 2y^2 = 6y^2$, $46y^3 \div 2y^2 = 23y$, $40y^2 \div 2y^2 = 20$

3. **Use the distributive property to write the polynomial as a product of factors:**

   $2y^2(6y^2+23y+20)$

4. **Start factoring inside the parentheses by creating two factors.**

   You know that the first term in each factor must begin with y to produce y^2, so start with that: $(y\pm?)(y\pm?)$.

5. **Factor the coefficient of the first term in parentheses, the 6 in $6y^2$, to find out which two numbers when multiplied together equal 6.**

   The values can be 2 and 3 (or –2 and –3). Plug in the positive values first because all operations inside the parentheses are positive: $(2y \pm ?)(3y \pm ?)$.

6. **Factor the constant, 20, and you get 2 and 10, 1 and 20, and 4 and 5.**

   Each pair could also work if both numbers are negatives, but again, because all operations in parentheses are positive, that's highly unlikely.

7. **Figure out which factor pair from Step 6 when multiplied by a factor pair from Step 5 and then added together results in the coefficient of the middle term, 23.**

   The only factor pair from Step 5 is 3 and 2. Using the factor pairs from Step 7, you can instantly rule out 1 and 20 because $20 \times 2 = 40$ and $20 \times 3 = 60$, both of which are larger than 23. Likewise, you can rule out 10 and 2 because $10 \times 3 = 30$ (too big) and $(10 \times 2) + (2 \times 3) = 26$ (also too big). That leaves you with 4 and 5. Take those for a spin: $(4 \times 3) + (5 \times 2) = 12 + 10 = 22$ (too small), but $(5 \times 3) + (4 \times 2) = 15 + 8 = 23$ works!

8. **Use the number pair identified in Step 7 to complete the factors you started in Step 4:**

   $(2y + 5)(3y + 4)$

9. **Put it all together and you have you have the factors for your polynomial:**

   $2y^2(2y + 5)(3y + 4)$

   Technically speaking, you could break this down even further by factoring $2y^2 = (2 \times y \times y)$, but that wouldn't exactly simplify the expression.

   Try your hand at factoring the following expressions.

1. $49b^3a^2 + 35b^2a - 63$

   _____

2. $10a^2 + a - 21$

   _____

3. $15m^5 + 18m^4 - 45m^3 - 27m^2$

   _____

   Check your work:

   1. $7\left(7b^3a^2 + 5b^2a - 9\right)$
   2. $(2a + 3)(5a - 7)$
   3. $3m^2(5m^3 + 6m^2 - 15m - 9)$

Writing and Solving Quadratic Equations

A *quadratic equation* is a mathematical statement in the following standard form:

$$ax^2 + bx + c = 0$$

where a, b, and c are constants, x is a variable, and a can't be zero.

It's referred to as a *quadratic* equation because "quad" means square, and one of the variables is squared. Like a linear equation, a quadratic equation can be plotted on the coordinate plane, but instead of forming a line, it forms a parabolic curve, as shown in Figure 8-5.

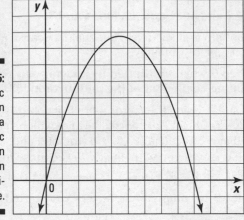

Figure 8-5:
A quadratic equation forms a parabolic curve when plotted on the coordinate plane.

John Wiley & Sons, Inc.

Writing quadratic equations

You may encounter quadratic equations on the GED Math test that don't appear to be quadratic equations at first glance. When you do, you usually need to convert the equation into its quadratic form before you can answer the question. Table 8-1 provides some examples of quadratic equations that don't appear to be quadratic, along with guidance for converting them into standard form.

Table 8-1	Converting Quadratic Equations into Standard Form	
Nonstandard	**Solution**	**Standard Form**
$7x + 3x^2 + 3 = 0$	Rearrange terms	$3x^2 + 7x + 3 = 0$
$7y(y-3) = 9$	Expand and move 9 to the left	$7y^2 - 21y - 9 = 0$
$5m = 13 - m^2$	Move everything to the left with the squared variable first	$m^2 + 5m - 13 = 0$
$8 + \frac{3}{x} - \frac{5}{x^2} = 0$	Multiply both sides by x^2	$8x^2 + 3x - 5 = 0$
$z^2 = 3z$	Move everything to the left and add a zero	$z^2 - 3z + 0 = 0$

Time for some practice. Write the following quadratic equations in their proper form.

1. $(4x + 2)(3x - 1) = 0$

2. $9t^2 = 13t - 5$

3. $9m(m + 2) = 27$

4. $y^2 - 5y = 0$

Check your work:

1. $12x^2 + 2x - 2 = 0$
2. $9t^2 - 13t + 5 = 0$
3. $9m^2 + 18m = 27$
4. $y^2 - 5y + 0 = 0$

Solving quadratic equations in one variable

If you're asked to solve a quadratic equation on the test, the equation contains only one variable, which simplifies the task quite a bit. To solve quadratic equations in one variable, you have three options, as explained in the next three sections:

- Factor the quadratic.
- Complete the square.
- Use the quadratic formula.

Regardless of which option you choose, the ultimate goal is to isolate the variable x (or whatever it happens to be) and solve for it.

The solution for almost all quadratic equations consists of two numbers called *roots* or *zeros,* which helps to explain the parabolic nature of the curve formed when a quadratic equation is plotted on the coordinate plane. As you can see in Figure 8-5, the curve intersects the x-axis at two points, which represent the two answers to the equation — points where $y = 0$.

Factoring the quadratic

The easiest and fastest way to solve a simple quadratic equation in one variable in standard form is to factor the equation, as explained earlier in the "Factoring polynomials" section, and then solve for the variable.

For example, suppose you're asked to solve for x in the equation $x^2 - 5x + 6$. You know that the two factors each must start with x to produce x^2, so start with that:

$$(x \pm ?)(x \pm ?) = 0$$

Now you want to find the two factors of 6 that added together equal –5, and those would be –2 and –3. Complete your factors:

$$(x - 3)(x - 2) = 0$$

Here's where that 0 on the other side of the equation comes into play. Knowing that $(x - 3)(x - 2) = 0$, you can insert a number for x into either factor to make the equation equal to 0. If $x = 3$, then $(x - 3) = (3 - 3) = 0$, and if you multiply $(x - 2)$ times 0, the equation equals 0. Likewise, if you substitute 2 for x in $(x - 2)$, you also get 0, and $(x - 3) \times 0 = 0$.

The solution to the problem is the two values of x that make the left side of the equation equal to 0, and those two numbers are 3 and 2, commonly presented as (3, 2).

Completing the square

The completing the square approach adds to the left side of the equation to create a factor such as $(x+5)^2$ on the left side of the equation and a constant on the right side, so you can find the value of variable by calculating the square root of both sides.

For example, if you're asked to solve for y in the equation $y^2 + 8y - 20 = 0$, you can take the following steps to complete the square:

1. **Move the constant to the right side of the equation to get $y^2 + 8y = 20$.**

2. **Take half of the y coefficient and square it.**

    Half of 8 is 4, and 4 squared is 16.

3. **Add the result from Step 2 to both sides of the equation to get**

    $y^2 + 8y + 16 = 16 + 20 = 36.$

4. **Factor the left side of the equation to create two identical factors (a square):**

    $(y+4)(y+4) = (y+4)^2 = 36.$

5. **Take the square root of both sides and you find that $(y+4) = \pm\sqrt{36} = \pm 6$.**

    The $\pm$ before the radical sign indicates that 6^2 and -6^2 both work because they produce the same value, 36.

6. **For $y + 4 = 6$, y must be 2, and for $y + 4 = -6$, y must be -10, so the solution is (2, -10).**

Using the quadratic formula

The quadratic formula is the quadratic equation rewritten to isolate the variable on the left side of the equation and the constants on the right:

$$x = \frac{-b \pm \sqrt{b^2 - 4ac}}{2a}$$

With the quadratic formula, you can solve the equation for x simply by plugging in values for a, b, and c.

Use the quadratic formula to solve the following equation: $x^2 + 4x = 5$.

To solve this problem, take the following steps:

1. **Put the equation in standard form: $x^2 + 4x - 5 = 0$.**

2. **Insert the values $a = 1$, $b = 4$, and $c = -5$ into the quadratic formula:**

    $x = \dfrac{-4 \pm \sqrt{4^2 - 4(1)(-5)}}{2(1)}$

3. **Simplify the equation:**

    $x = \dfrac{-4 \pm \sqrt{16 + 20}}{2} = \dfrac{-4 \pm \sqrt{36}}{2} = \dfrac{-4 \pm 6}{2}$

4. **Calculate the two values of x:**

    $\dfrac{-4 + 6}{2} = \dfrac{2}{2} = 1$ and $\dfrac{-4 - 6}{2} = \dfrac{-10}{2} = -5$

When you're taking the test, you can click "Formula Sheet" in the upper left of the screen to access a pop-up window that contains the quadratic formula.

Simplifying and Computing with Rational Expressions

Rational expressions are fractions that contain variables. They're called "rational" because they represent a *ratio* of two polynomials. Here's an example of a rational expression at work:

$$\frac{5x}{3x-2} + \frac{2x+1}{2x+3}$$

You manipulate rational expressions in exactly the same manner as you do numeric fractions (see Chapter 5), but if you're unaccustomed to working with variables, rational expressions can be confusing, and if there's anything you don't need during the test, it's more confusion.

In this section, we explain how to simplify rational expressions to make them more manageable and how to perform basic mathematical operations with rational expressions: addition, subtraction, multiplication, and division.

Many of the skills required to work with rational expressions are covered earlier in this chapter and in Chapter 5. If you're skipping around the book and landed here before mastering addition, subtraction, multiplication, division, and factoring of algebraic expressions, work through those sections of the book first. Otherwise, you'll be totally lost here.

Simplifying rational expressions

Before you set out to perform mathematical operations in rational expressions, you should know a little about simplifying rational expressions to make them easier to manage. To simplify a rational expression, here's what you do:

1. **Factor the numerator and denominator.**

2. **Cancel common factors.**

3. **Multiply any remaining factors in the numerator and those in the denominator.**

For example, to simplify $\frac{3y^2}{y^3}$, you factor the numerator and the denominator and cancel common factors:

$$\frac{3y^2}{y^3} = \frac{3 \times y \times y}{y \times y \times y} = \frac{3}{y}$$

The expression has no remaining factors, so you're done.

Cancel factors, but *never* cancel terms being added or subtracted. For example, in the expression $\frac{3 \times 13}{13 \times 5}$, you can cancel the 13 in the numerator and denominator without affecting the value of the fraction. However, if you have $\frac{3+13}{13-5}$, canceling the 13s would change the value of the expression; $\frac{3+13}{13-5} = \frac{16}{8}$, which is nowhere close to the $\frac{3}{5}$ you'd get if you canceled the 13s.

Try your hand at a more difficult expression:

$$\frac{2x^2 - 7x - 15}{6x^2 + 13x + 6}$$

In this example, you must factor the numerator and the denominator first, as explained in the earlier "Factoring polynomials" section. When you factor the numerator and denominator, you get:

$$\frac{\cancel{(2x+3)}(x-5)}{\cancel{(2x+3)}(3x+2)}$$

The factor $(2x+3)$ appears in both the numerator and denominator, so you can cancel it out. You can't simplify any further because the remaining terms in the numerator and denominator are added or subtracted, not multiplied.

Simplify the following rational expressions:

1. $\dfrac{7x^7}{3x^3+5x^4}$

2. $\dfrac{m^3+2m^5+1}{3m^3+4m}$

3. $\dfrac{7b^4-21b}{14b^5+7b^3+28b^2}$

4. $\dfrac{15x^2+4x-4}{6x^2+19x+10}$

Check your work:

1. $\dfrac{7x^7}{3x^3+5x^4}=\dfrac{\cancel{x^3}7x^4}{\cancel{x^3}(3+5x)}=\dfrac{7x^4}{3+5x}$

2. $\dfrac{m^3+2m^5+1}{3m^3+4m}=\dfrac{\cancel{m^3}(1+2m^2)+1}{\cancel{m^3}(3+4)}=\dfrac{1+2m^2+1}{3+4m}=\dfrac{2m^2+2}{4m+3}$

   $\dfrac{m^3+2m^5+1}{3m^3+4m}=\dfrac{\cancel{m^3}(1+2m^2)+1}{\cancel{m^3}(3+4m)}=\dfrac{1+2m^2+1}{3+4m}=\dfrac{2m^2+2}{4m+3}$

3. $\dfrac{7b^4-21b}{14b^5+7b^3+28b^2}=\dfrac{\cancel{7b}(b^3-3)}{\cancel{7b}(2b^4+b^2+4b)}=\dfrac{b^3-3}{2b^4+b^2+4b}$

4. $\dfrac{15x^2+4x-4}{6x^2+19x+10}=\dfrac{\cancel{(3x+2)}(5x-2)}{\cancel{(3x+2)}(2x+5)}=\dfrac{(5x-2)}{(2x+5)}$

Computing with rational expressions

You can perform addition, subtraction, multiplication, and division with rational expressions, as you can with numeric fractions. This section explains how and provides plenty of practice to hone your skills.

When working with rational expressions, maintain balance in the expression. Whatever you do to the numerator, you must do to the denominator.

Addition

You can add fractions as long as the fractions you're adding have the same denominator (see Chapter 5). If they have different denominators, you must adjust one or both fractions, so they have the same denominator before proceeding with the addition. In the following example, the two denominators are the same, so you can simply add the numerators:

$$\frac{2x}{3x^3}+\frac{3}{3x^3}=\frac{2x+3}{3x^3}$$

On the other hand, if the rational expressions have different denominators, you must find the least common denominator (LCD) first. As explained in Chapter 5, the LCD is the least common multiple (LCM) of the two denominators. To find the LCM, factor the two denominators and then multiply each factor the greatest number of times it occurs in either number. Here's an example:

$$\frac{7x}{6x^2 - 2x} + \frac{3}{12x - 4}$$

Factor the denominators and you get:

$$\frac{7\cancel{x}}{2 \times \cancel{x} \times (3x - 1)} + \frac{3}{2 \times 2 \times (3x - 1)}$$

You can cancel x in the numerator and denominator of the first rational expression. Now, 2 appears twice in the second denominator, and $(3x - 1)$ appears once in both, so the common denominator is $2 \times 2 \times (3x - 1) = 4(3x - 1)$ or $12x - 4$. To get that LCD in the first fraction, you must multiply both the numerator and denominator by 2:

$$\frac{2 \times 7}{4(3x - 1)} + \frac{3}{4(3x - 1)} = \frac{14}{12x - 4} + \frac{3}{12x - 4} = \frac{17}{12x - 4}$$

Subtraction

As with addition, to subtract rational expressions, the expressions must have the same denominator. After you find the LCD of the two fractions, as explained in the preceding section, and multiply the numerator and denominator by the factor required to make their denominators identical, all you do is subtract the values in the two numerators.

For example, to calculate $\dfrac{12 + y}{2x^2} - \dfrac{3 + y}{4x^3}$, you first need to find their LCD, which in this case is pretty easy. Multiply $2x^2 \times 2x = 4x^3$, so all you need to do is multiply the first fraction by $\dfrac{2x}{2x}$:

$$\left(\frac{2x}{2x} \times \frac{12 + y}{2x^2} \right) - \frac{3 + y}{4x^3} = \frac{24x + 2xy}{4x^3} - \frac{3 + y}{4x^3} = \frac{24x + 2xy + y + 3}{4x^3}$$

Practice time. Solve the following rational expression addition and subtraction problems.

1. $\dfrac{5}{x} + \dfrac{2}{3x} + \dfrac{3}{x^2}$

2. $\dfrac{3b^2}{4a + 8} - \dfrac{b^2}{3a + 6}$

Check your work:

1. The LCD is $3x^2$, so multiply the first fraction by $\dfrac{3x}{3x}$, the second fraction by $\dfrac{x}{x}$, and the third fraction by $\dfrac{3}{3}$ to get

$$\frac{15x}{3x^2} + \frac{2x}{3x^2} + \frac{9}{3x^2} = \frac{17x + 9}{3x^2}$$

2. Factor the denominator in both rational expressions and you have:

$$\frac{3b^2}{4(a + 2)} - \frac{b^2}{3(a + 2)}$$

Multiply the first expression by $\dfrac{3}{3}$ and the second fraction by $\dfrac{4}{4}$ and you have:

$$\frac{9b^2}{12(a + 2)} - \frac{4b^2}{12(a + 2)} = \frac{5b^2}{12(a + 2)}$$

Multiplication

In many ways, multiplying rational expressions is easier than adding or subtracting. All you do is multiply the numerators and the denominators and simplify the result. The denominators don't need to be identical.

Before multiplying two rational expressions, simplify them as much as possible to reduce the clutter. You can cancel any identical terms that appear in the numerator of one rational expression and the denominator of the other, as in the following example:

$$\frac{5x^3}{\cancel{7}^1} \times \frac{\cancel{14}^2}{3x^2} = \frac{10x}{3} = 3\frac{1}{3}x$$

When the rational expressions are more complex, try factoring the numerators and denominators to find factors that cancel out, as in the following example:

$$\frac{14b^2 + 29b - 15}{4x + 6} \times \frac{6x + 9}{2b^2 + 7b + 5}$$

You can factor the numerator and denominator in both expressions and then cancel out common factors to get:

$$\frac{(7b - 3)\cancel{(2b + 5)}}{2\cancel{(x + 3)}} \times \frac{3\cancel{(x + 3)}}{(b + 1)\cancel{(2b + 5)}} = \frac{21b - 9}{2b + 2}$$

Division

To divide rational expressions, invert the second expression and multiply, as in the following example:

$$\frac{a}{b} \div \frac{c}{d} = \frac{a}{b} \times \frac{d}{c} = \frac{ad}{bc}$$

Reduce the clutter by simplifying the two expressions as much as possible before multiplying. You can cancel any identical factors that appear in the numerator of one expression and the denominator of the other. Invert before simplifying.

Try your hand at the following rational expression multiplication and division problems:

1. $\dfrac{3x^2}{2x + 6} \times \dfrac{x + 3}{2x^2} =$

2. $\dfrac{3m^2 + 3m}{2m^3} \div \dfrac{5m + 5}{5m^2} =$

3. $\dfrac{3x + 1}{6x^2 - 11x - 10} \times \dfrac{2x - 5}{6x^2 + 2x}$

4. $\dfrac{7a}{12a^2 - 18a} \div \dfrac{21a^3 + 35a}{6a^2 - 5a - 6}$

Check your work:

1. $\dfrac{3x^2}{2x + 6} \times \dfrac{x + 3}{2x^2} = \dfrac{3\cancel{x^2}}{2\cancel{(x + 3)}} \times \dfrac{\cancel{x + 3}}{2\cancel{x^2}} = \dfrac{3}{4}$

2. $\dfrac{3m^2 + 3m}{2m^3} \div \dfrac{5m + 5}{5m^2} = \dfrac{3m^2 + 3m}{2m^3} \times \dfrac{5m^2}{5m + 5} = \dfrac{3m\cancel{(m + 1)}}{2\cancel{m^3}} \times \dfrac{5\cancel{m^2}}{5\cancel{(m + 1)}} = \dfrac{15}{10} = 1\dfrac{1}{2}$

3. $\dfrac{3x + 1}{6x^2 - 11x - 10} \times \dfrac{2x - 5}{6x^2 + 2x} = \dfrac{\cancel{3x + 1}^1}{\cancel{(2x - 5)}(3x + 2)} \times \dfrac{\cancel{2x - 5}^1}{2x\cancel{(3x + 1)}} = \dfrac{1}{6x^2 + 4x}$

4. $\dfrac{7a}{12a^2-18a} \div \dfrac{21a^3+35a}{6a^2-5a-6} = \dfrac{7a}{12a^2-18a} \times \dfrac{6a^2-5a-6}{21a^3+35a} =$

$\dfrac{^1\cancel{7a}}{6a\cancel{(2a-3)}} \times \dfrac{\cancel{(2a-3)}(3a+2)}{\cancel{7a}(3a^2+5)} = \dfrac{3a+2}{18a^3+30a}$

Solving Real-World Problems Involving Inequalities

In mathematics, an *inequality* is a relationship between two values that aren't necessarily equal. These relationships are shown using the inequality symbols, as shown here:

Symbol	Example	Meaning
>	$a > b$	a is greater than b
<	$a < b$	a is less than b
≥	$a \ge b$	a is greater than or equal to b
≤	$a \le b$	a is less than or equal to b

The GED Math test may include one or more questions that involve inequalities. You may be asked to read a word problem and choose the expression that best describes the inequality in mathematical terms. One or more questions may ask you to solve or graph an inequality or present an inequality that contains a variable and instruct you to identify which inequality best represents the value of that variable. In the following sections, we provide guidance on how to answer inequality questions.

Writing inequalities

On the test, you need to be able to spot inequalities in word problems. You may be asked to read a word problem and identify the inequality that most accurately expresses the situation in mathematical terms, as in the following example:

Cindy has $20 in her pocket and is heading to the fair. Admission is $3.50, and tickets for food and games are $1.00 each. Which of the following inequalities represents the number of tickets that Cindy can afford to buy if t represents the number of tickets?

(A) $\$20.00 \le \$3.50 + \$1.00t$

(B) $\$3.50 - \$1.00t \le \$20.00$

(C) $\$1.00t \le \$20.00 - \$3.50$

(D) $\$20 - \$3.50 - \$1.00t = 0$

To answer questions such as this one, reason it out. Cindy starts with $20.00 and spends $3.50 getting in, so she now has $20.00 − $3.50. She wants to buy t number of tickets at $1.00 each, making the total she ultimately spends on tickets 1.00t$. The total she spends on tickets plus the admission price must be less than or equal to $20.00, which can be expressed as: $\$3.50 + \$1.00t \le \$20.00$. Unfortunately, that's not one of the choices, but Choice (C) looks promising. The amount she can spend on tickets, 1.00t$, must be less than or equal to the $20.00 she started with minus the $3.50 admission. Choice (C) is correct! By the way, Choice (D) is obviously incorrect because it's not an inequality.

Here's a more complex inequality problem:

David is a prolific stamp collector. When asked how large his collection is he replies that he has nearly 2,000 stamps. He has 780 Canadian stamps and 910 U.S. stamps with an average value of $5.00 each, and 310 stamps from other countries around the world with an average value of less than $3.00 each. Which of the following inequalities most accurately expresses the total monetary value of David's stamp collection if S represents the total value of his collection?

(A) $\$9,380 > S > \$8,450$

(B) $\$8,450 > S > \$9,380$

(C) $\$10,000 > S > \$9,380$

(D) $\$10,000 > S > \$8,450$

David has $780 + 910 = 1,690$ total Canadian and U.S. stamps that average $5.00 each for a total of $8,450. Additionally, he has 310 stamps with an average value of less than $3.00, so the total value of those must be less than $930. $\$8,450 + \$930 = \$9,380$, so the total value of his collection must be more than $8,450 and less than $9,380. Choice (A) is correct. Choice (B) has the possibility of the value being less than $8,450 and possibly exceeding $9,380. Choice (C) also has the possibility of the collection's value exceeding $9,380. And Choice (D) has a range of values that's too broad; although it's correct, it's not as accurate as Choice (A).

Solving inequalities

Solving inequalities typically involves finding the range of values that works for the variable in the inequality. The process for solving an inequality is very similar to the process you follow to solve any equation; you try to isolate the variable on one side of the inequality symbol and solve for the variable. You can simplify the inequality by performing the same operations on both sides of the inequality symbol.

However, the one huge difference between solving equations and inequalities is that if you multiply or divide both sides of the inequality by a negative value, you must flip the inequality sign so it points in the opposite direction, because multiplying by a negative changes a positive value to a negative value and a negative value to a positive value.

Here's an example of an inequality similar to one you may need to solve on the test:

$3x + 7 < 4x - 8$

(A) $x < 1$

(B) $x > -1$

(C) $x > 15$

(D) $x < 15$

To answer this question, treat the inequality as you would an equation. Get the variables on one side of the symbol and the constants on the other and then simplify:

$$3x + 7 < 4x - 8 \leq\leq$$
$$3x - 4x < -8 - 7$$
$$-x < -15$$
$$x > 15$$

Practice solving the following inequalities:

1. $5x - b < 7x - b$
2. $5x - 5 < 3x + 20$
3. $3n^2 - 4 \le 2n^2 + 5$
4. $-5 < \dfrac{3 - 2x}{7} < 15$

Check your work:

1. $5x - b < 7x - b$

   $5x - 7x < -b + b$

   $-2x < 0$

   $x > 0$

   This one is tricky because at the end you must divide both sides by –2, meaning that you must flip the inequality sign.

2. $5x - 5 < 3x + 20$

   $5x - 3x < 20 + 5$

   $2x < 25$

   $x < 12.5$

3. $3n^2 - 4 \le 2n^2 + 5$

   $3n^2 - 2n^2 \le 5 + 4$

   $n^2 \le 9$

   $n \le 3$

4. $-5 < \dfrac{3 - 2x}{7} < 15$

   $-35 < 3 - 2x < 105$

   $-38 < -2x < 102$

   $19 > x > -51$

Graphing inequalities

Graphing inequalities involves plotting a point on a number line or plotting a line on the coordinate plane and then shading the area on one side of the point or line to show that the possible answers are greater than or less than, or include values that are greater than or less than, what the point or line represents.

To plot an inequality on the number line, first mark the point on the number line where the variable is equal to the value on the other side of the inequality. For greater-than and less-than inequalities, circle the point to indicate that it's not included. For greater-than-or-equal-to or less-than-or-equal-to values, fill in the circle. Then, draw an arrow pointing to the left to indicate values that are less than that point or to the right to indicate values that are greater than that point. For example, if the inequality is $x > 2$, you'd plot the point and draw the arrow shown in Figure 8-6. You circle the 2 to exclude it because x must be greater than 2 and can't be equal to 2.

To plot a linear inequality, first plot the line to represent the linear equation (see Chapter 9). For greater-than and less-than inequalities, use a dashed line to indicate that values on the line are not included. For greater-than-or-equal-to or less-than-or-equal-to values, use a solid line to indicate that values on the line are included. Then, shade above or below the line to indicate values that are greater than or less than the values represented by the line.

Figure 8-6:
x > 2 plotted on the number line.

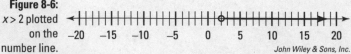

John Wiley & Sons, Inc.

When plotting a linear equation, rewrite the equation, if necessary, to isolate *y* to the left of the equal sign. Doing so makes it easier to plug in a value for *x* and see what the corresponding *y* value is.

For example, if the inequality is $y > 2x + 1$, you'd plot the dashed line and shade above it, as shown in Figure 8-7.

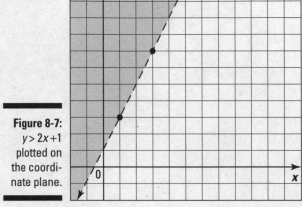

Figure 8-7:
$y > 2x + 1$ plotted on the coordinate plane.

John Wiley & Sons, Inc.

Chapter 9

Solving Algebraic Problems Involving Lines and Functions

- -

In This Chapter
▶ Plotting points, lines, and slopes on a coordinate plane
▶ Charting linear and nonlinear relationships on graphs
▶ Answering math questions that involve functions

- -

*Y*ou're likely to encounter several questions on the GED Mathematical Reasoning test that present mathematical relationships graphically. These questions may ask you to calculate the slope of a line, write the linear equation for a line plotted on the coordinate plane, or plot linear or nonlinear equations on the coordinate plane based on their equations. In addition, questions may challenge your understanding of and ability to work with mathematical functions. A *function* is a mathematical device that performs one or more operations on an input to produce an output. (Fuzzy, we know. You find out more about functions later.)

In this chapter, we introduce the coordinate plane and explain everything you need to know to tackle any linear equation question you're likely to encounter on the test, even questions that don't look like linear equation questions. We also introduce you to the wonderful world of functions, so you can answer function questions with confidence.

Connecting the Dots: Points, Lines, and Slopes

Certain mathematical relationships, particularly those that show a change in rate, are easier to grasp when they're plotted on a coordinate plane. For example, if you're using straight-line depreciation to track the depreciation of a business asset over the course of ten years, you could look at a bunch of numbers like these:

Year	*Asset Value*
0	$25,000
1	$22,500
2	$20,000
3	$17,500
4	$15,000
5	$12,500
6	$10,000
7	$7,500
8	$5,000
9	$2,500
10	$0

Or you could plot a line that illustrates depreciation over time, as shown in Figure 9-1. Note that the dollar figures are more precise, but the line graph provides a snapshot of the asset's declining value over time.

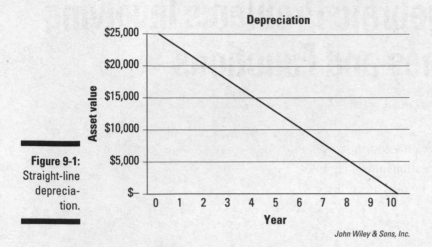

Figure 9-1:
Straight-line
deprecia-
tion.

John Wiley & Sons, Inc.

In this section, you find out all you need to know to successfully answer questions on the GED Math test that involve points, lines, and slopes and how they relate to linear equations. (See Chapter 8 for additional details about linear equations.)

Locating points on a coordinate plane

A *coordinate plane* is like two number lines at right angles that intersect at point 0 on both lines. Each number line is referred to as an *axis,* and the coordinate plane has two axes. The horizontal (across) line is the *x*-axis, and the vertical (up-and-down) line is the *y*-axis. Lines extend from the hash marks on the number lines and intersect to form a grid, as shown in Figure 9-2.

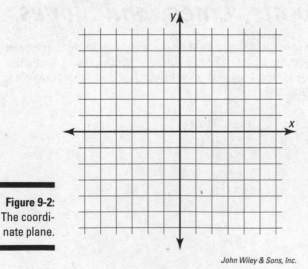

Figure 9-2:
The coordi-
nate plane.

John Wiley & Sons, Inc.

If you've ever played the game Battleship, you appreciate the usefulness of the coordinate plane in locating specific positions on the grid. In the game, letters appear along the left side of the grid, and numbers appear across the top. You position your ships on the grid, and your opponent calls out letter-and-number combinations, such as B5 or E7, in an attempt to hit and eventually sink your battleships. Of course, you return the favor, taking turns to fire your next volley.

As in Battleship, you can locate points on the coordinate plane by specifying x and y values *(coordinates)* for the point. The proper format for these "addresses" is (x, y), where x is the value along the x-axis and y is the value along the y-axis. If the y value is positive, the point appears above the x-axis. If y is negative, the point is below the x-axis. Likewise, if x is positive, the point is to the right of the y-axis, and if x is negative, the point is to the left of the y-axis.

To locate a point when given the point's x and y coordinates, follow these steps:

1. **Find the point where the *x*- and *y*-axes intersect, which is point (0, 0).**

2. **Go left or right to the *x* value. (Left is negative; right is positive.)**

3. **Go straight up or down to the *y* value. (Up is positive; down is negative.)**

For example, if a question instructs you to plot the point $(5, -3)$, find where the x and y axes intersect, which is point $(0, 0)$, go right 5 ticks and down 3 ticks, and plot your point, as shown in Figure 9-3.

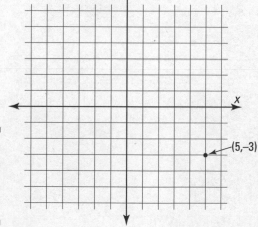

Figure 9-3:
Point (5, –3) plotted on the coordinate plane.

John Wiley & Sons, Inc.

To present the location of a point on the coordinate plane in the proper format, enclose the x and y coordinates in parentheses. Write the x coordinate first, followed by a comma and space, followed by the y coordinate.

Plot the following points on the coordinate plane, and label each point using the letter provided.

Letter	A	B	C	D	E	F	G	H	I
Coordinates	(5, –4)	(–6, 4)	(6, 5)	(0, 0)	(3, 0)	(–3, –5)	(–3, 3)	(2, 4)	(–5, –2)

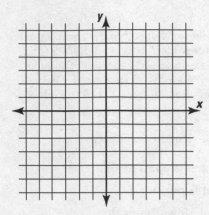

Use the following coordinate plane to check your answers.

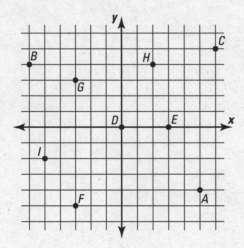

Plotting a linear equation

A *linear equation* is an algebraic statement that describes the relationship between the *x* and *y* coordinates that form a line and is commonly presented in the following standard form known as the *slope-intercept form:*

$$y = mx + b$$

where *x* and *y* are the coordinates of any point on the line, *m* is the slope, and *b* is the *y* intercept (the point where the line crosses the *y*-axis). See the next section for more about slope.

If you're given the slope-intercept form of a line, you have all the information you need to plot the line on the coordinate plane. You just plot a couple points and connect the dots:

1. **Plot the point (0, *y*) where *y* is *b* in the slope-intercept form.**

   For example, if the equation is $y = 5x + 6$, the *y* intercept is 6, and the coordinate for the point is (0, 6).

2. Substitute 0 for y and solve the equation for x.

This gives you the point $(x, 0)$ where x is the value you just calculated.

3. Plot the point whose coordinates you determined in Step 2.

4. Draw a line connecting the two dots.

Plot the following linear equations on the coordinate plane provided.

1. $y = 2x + 2$
2. $y = -1.5x - 3$

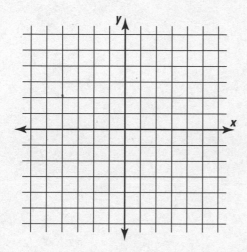

1. The y intercept is 2, so the coordinates of the first point are $(0, 2)$. Substitute 0 for y, in which case $0 = 2x + 2$, $-2 = 2x$, $x = -1$, which gives you the coordinates of the second point $(-1, 0)$, and your line should look like line A in the following figure.

2. The y intercept is -3, so the coordinates of the first point are $(0, -3)$. Substitute 0 for y, in which case $0 = -1.5x - 3$, $3 = -1.5x$, $x = -2$, giving you the coordinates of the second point, $(-2, 0)$, and your line should look like line B in the following figure.

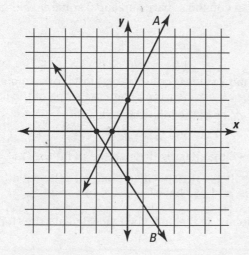

Finding the slope of a line

Slope is defined as "rise over run"; that is, the distance the line travels up compared to the distance it travels across, as shown in Figure 9-4. The slope of the line in Figure 9-4 is $\frac{5}{3}$. The slope may be written as a whole number, a fraction, or a decimal. Sometimes the slope is easiest to work with as a fraction, sometimes as a decimal. You have to decide based on the question.

If the slope is positive, the line goes up from left to right, as in Figure 9-4. If the slope is negative, it goes down from left to right.

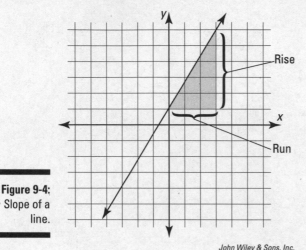

Figure 9-4:
Slope of a
line.

John Wiley & Sons, Inc.

You can find the slope of a line using various methods, as described next.

Using a graph

If you have the line plotted on graph paper or a question on the test displays the line plotted on a coordinate plane, you can determine the line's approximate slope by counting squares. In Figure 9-4, for example, you can count 5 squares up and 3 squares over and see that rise over run (slope) is $\frac{5}{3} = 1\frac{2}{3}$.

Using a formula

If you have a line's *x* intercept and the *x* and *y* values (coordinates) for another point on the line, you can use the slope-intercept form, $y = mx + b$, to calculate the slope of the line. Just plug in the values you have and solve for *m*, as in the following example.

Find the slope of a line defined as $y = mx - 2$ that passes through the point (3, 7): ⬚.

To answer this question, plug the coordinates of the specified point into the equation provided: $7 = m(3) - 2$. Add 2 to both sides, and you have $9 = m(3)$, so $m = 3$.

If you know the coordinates of any two points on the line, you can calculate the slope of the line by using the *slope formula:*

$$m = \frac{y_2 - y_1}{x_2 - x_1}$$

where m is the slope, x_1 is the x coordinate of the first point, x_2 is the x coordinate of the second point, y_1 is the y coordinate of the first point, and y_2 is the y coordinate of the second point.

Find the slope of a line that passes through the points (15, –12) and (–12, 15): ☐.

To answer this question, you simply plug the x and y coordinates into the slope formula and solve it:

$$m = \frac{15-(-12)}{-12-15} = \frac{27}{-27} = -1$$

Using a table

A slope question may provide you with a table of x and y values and ask you to determine the slope of the line, as in the following example.

Find the slope of a line with the following (x, y) coordinates: ☐.

x	–7	–4	–1	2	5	8
y	13	11	9	7	5	3

Of course, you could plug any two of the (x, y) coordinates into the slope formula and solve for m, but the table makes it easier than that. Think of the slope formula like this:

$$m = \frac{\text{change in } y}{\text{change in } x}$$

Any two consecutive y values in the table indicate the change in y. For example, 13 and 11 show that the change in y is 2; 9 and 7 show that the change in y is 2; and 5 and 3 show that the change in y is 2. Likewise, any two consecutive x values indicate the change in x: –7 and –4 show a change in x of 3; –4 and –1 show a change in x of 3; and –1 and 2 show a change in x of 3. Just plug in the change in y over the change in x and you have your answer:

$$m = \frac{\text{change in } y}{\text{change in } x} = \frac{2}{3}$$

Grasping the relationship between unit rate and slope

You may encounter questions on the test that challenge your ability to transfer your knowledge and skills from working with slopes to unit rate problems, so you need to grasp how the two are related. Just as a line's slope can be expressed as

$$m = \frac{\text{change in } y}{\text{change in } x}$$

unit rates can be expressed as a change in one quantity over a change in another. For example, if you drive 500 miles in 10 hours, your unit rate can be expressed as a slope:

$$m = \frac{\text{change in miles}}{\text{change in hours}} = \frac{500 \text{ miles}}{10 \text{ hours}} = \frac{50 \text{ miles}}{1 \text{ hour}}$$

You could graph the change in miles against the change in hours, as shown in Figure 9-5, to see that, indeed, the line has a slope of $\frac{50}{1}$.

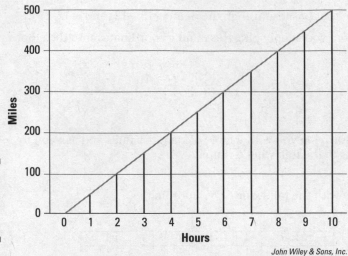

Figure 9-5:
A unit rate expressed as a slope.

Certain questions on the test may not even mention the word "slope," but don't be fooled. If you see a question with a graph that looks like the following one, you're looking at a slope question.

George used the following graph to plan his speed and distance for an upcoming bicycle race.

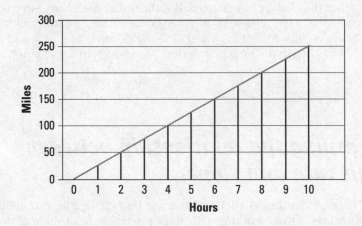

How fast is George planning to ride?

(A) 10 miles per hour

(B) 15 miles per hour

(C) 20 miles per hour

(D) 25 miles per hour

If the race covers 200 miles, how long will it take George to complete it?

(A) 6 hours

(B) 7 hours

(C) 8 hours

(D) 9 hours

To answer the first question, you can tell from the graph that George rides 250 miles in 10 hours, so he rides $\frac{25\not0}{1\not0} = 25$ miles per hour. Choice (D) is correct. To answer the second question, simply follow the 200-mile line across, and you see that it intersects the 8-hour line. Choice (C) is correct.

Other questions on the test may present you with a rate problem that challenges your ability to convert rate into a linear equation.

Carey started a trip with 20 gallons of fuel in the tank of his car. After driving 300 miles, he had half a tank of fuel. He charts his fuel consumption against the miles he traveled to project how far he can drive on a tank of fuel.

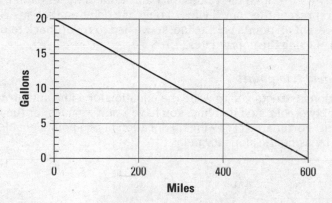

Find the slope of the line: ☐.

To find the slope of the line, place change in y over change in x. Gallons are plotted along the y-axis, and miles along the x-axis. Use the slope formula:

$$m = \frac{y_2 - y_1}{x_2 - x_1} = \frac{10 - 20}{300 - 0} = \frac{-1\not0}{30\not0} = -\frac{1}{30}$$

Note that the line goes down from left to right, so the slope is negative.

Writing the equation for a line

You may encounter a question on the test that requires you to write the equation of a line that has a certain slope and passes through a certain point, or the equation of a line that passes through two specific points. The equation such questions ask for is the slope-intercept form:

$$y = mx + b$$

However, solving these problems isn't a simple matter of plugging in given values. They typically involve a two-step process that requires finding the slope or y intercept first to complete the equation. In this section, we explain how to solve the two most common versions of these question types: when you're given the slope and the coordinates of one point, and when you're given the coordinates of two points.

When you know the slope and a given point

When a question instructs you to write the equation for a line and provides you with the slope and the coordinates of one point, you have y, x, and m and need to find b to complete the equation, as in the following example.

Find the equation of the line with slope -3 that passes through the point $(-5, 8)$.

To answer this question, use the slope-intercept form to find the value of b:

$$y = mx + b$$
$$8 = -3(-5) + b = 15 + b$$
$$b = 8 - 15 = -7$$

Insert the y intercept you just found into the equation, and you have $y = -3x - 7$. If you're wondering why we dropped the values for y and x out of the equation, the reason is that those values represent the coordinates of only one point on that line. The equation for the line must represent all points on the line, so we had to revert back to using the variables x and y instead of using the coordinates $(-5, 8)$.

When you know two points

When a question instructs you to write the equation for a line and provides you with the coordinates of two points on that line, you have x and y values for the linear equation but no m or b value. Fortunately, knowing the location of two points enables you to calculate the slope, m, by using the slope formula:

$$m = \frac{y_2 - y_1}{x_2 - x_1}$$

Knowing the slope, you can then use that value along with the coordinates of one of the points you used to calculate the slope to calculate the value for b (the y intercept, as explained in the previous section). Here's an example.

Find the equation of a line that passes through points $(-4, -7)$ and $(7, 3)$.

To solve this problem, use what you know to find out what you don't know. Using the coordinates of the two points, use the slope formula to determine the slope:

$$m = \frac{3 - (-7)}{7 - (-4)} = \frac{10}{11}$$

Next, plug the coordinates of one point and the slope into the slope-intercept form and solve for b:

$$3 = \frac{10}{11}(7) + b = \frac{70}{11} + b$$
$$b = 3 - \frac{70}{11} = \frac{33}{11} - \frac{70}{11} = -\frac{37}{11} = -3\frac{4}{11}$$

Knowing the line's slope and y intercept, you can now write the equation for the line:

$$y = \frac{10}{11}x - 3\frac{4}{11}$$

Again, you don't plug in any values for x and y from the question, because the equation must describe all points on the line, not just one point.

Practice session

Now for some practice. (You'll probably need some scratch paper.)

1. Write the equation of a line with slope 0.5 that passes through point (3, 5).

   _____

2. Write the equation of a line that passes through points (4, 7) and (2, 5).

   _____

3. Write the equation of a line with slope 2 that passes through point (4, 7).

   _____

4. Write the equation of a line that passes through points (−5, −2) and (4, 4).

   _____

1. $y = 0.5x + 2.5$. Use the slope-intercept form to find the value of b and then insert the value of b, along with the slope provided in the question, into the slope-intercept form.

   $b = 3.5$

2. $y = x + 3$. Solving this problem is easier if you put the second set of coordinates first and use the equation for change in y over change in x to find the slope. Change in y is $7 - 5 = 2$, and change in x is $4 - 2 = 2$, so the slope is $\frac{2}{2} = 1$. Plug the slope and the coordinates (2, 5) into the equation, and you find that $b = 5 - 2 = 3$.

3. $y = 2x - 1$. Use the slope-intercept form to find the value of b and then insert the value of b, along with the slope provided in the question, into the slope-intercept form.

4. $y = \frac{2}{3}x + 1\frac{1}{3}$. Use change in y over change in x to find the slope, and you get $\frac{6}{9} = \frac{2}{3}$. Use the slope-intercept form. Plug in $\frac{2}{3}$ for m, 4 for x, and 4 for y. Do the math, and you find that $b = 1\frac{1}{3}$. You now have all the information to write the equation.

Solving geometry problems on the coordinate plane

Certain problems on the test may present geometry problems on the coordinate plane. For example, a question may ask whether two lines intersect or whether they're perpendicular to each other. You may be asked to determine the perimeter or area of a shape that's superimposed on the coordinate plane. In this section, we show you what to expect and how to tackle a few of the more common types of such questions.

Using slopes to identify parallel and perpendicular lines

You can determine whether lines are parallel (never cross) or perpendicular (cross at right angles) by comparing their slopes:

✔ Two parallel lines have the same slope. For example, if each line has a slope of 0.5, the two lines are parallel. (If the lines don't have identical slopes, then they cross at some point.)

✓ The slopes of two perpendicular lines are reciprocals with opposite signs; for example, if one line has a slope of 3 and the other has a slope of $-\frac{1}{3}$, then the two lines are perpendicular to each other.

Here are a couple sample questions.

1. What is the slope of a line perpendicular to the line that passes through points (5, −3) and (−5, 10)? ☐

2. One line passes through the points (0, 5) and (−3, 6). Another passes through points (3, −5) and (6, −6). Do these two lines intersect? Yes or No: ☐.

1. $\frac{10}{13}$. The slope of the line described is $\frac{10-(-3)}{-5-5} = -\frac{13}{10}$, so a line perpendicular to it must have a positive reciprocal slope.

2. No. The slope of the first line is $\frac{6-5}{-3-0} = -\frac{1}{3}$. The slope of the second line is $\frac{-6-(-5)}{6-3} = -\frac{1}{3}$. Because the slopes are identical, these lines are parallel and never intersect.

Finding where two lines intersect

If a question asks you to determine where two lines intersect, determine the slope-intercept form for the two lines and then set the equations equal to each other and solve for x. Insert the value you found for x into either equation and solve for y.

A line with slope $-\frac{2}{3}$ passes through point (−4, 3). Another line with a slope of $-\frac{3}{4}$ passes through point (−2, −3). What are the coordinates of the point where the two lines intersect? ☐

First, write the equation for each line as explained in the earlier section "Writing the equation for a line." The equation for the first line is $y = -\frac{2}{3}x + \frac{1}{3}$. The equation for the second line is $y = -\frac{3}{4}x - 4\frac{1}{2}$. Set the equations equal to each other and solve for x:

$$-\frac{2}{3}x + \frac{1}{3} = -\frac{3}{4}x - \frac{9}{2}$$

$$-\frac{2}{3}x + \frac{3}{4}x = -\frac{9}{2} - \frac{1}{3}$$

$$\frac{1}{12}x = -\frac{29}{6}$$

$$x = -\frac{29}{\cancel{6}} \times \cancel{12}^2 = -58$$

Plug −58 into either line's equation and solve for y: $y = -\frac{3}{\cancel{4}_2}\left(\cancel{-58}^{-29}\right) - \frac{9}{2} = \frac{87}{2} - \frac{9}{2} = \frac{78}{2} = 39$,

so the coordinates of the point where the two lines intersect are (−58, 39).

Solving problems involving shapes

Certain questions challenge your ability to apply your knowledge of geometry to the coordinate plane. We can't possibly cover all the various types of such problems you're likely to encounter, but as long as you have a solid grasp of geometry (see Chapter 7) and are familiar with the coordinate plane, you should have no trouble solving such problems.

Calculate the area of the circle shown here. Round your answer to the nearest hundredth. ☐

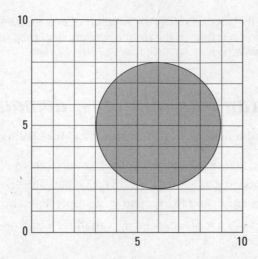

The area of a circle is πr^2, and $\pi = 3.14$. Count the squares, and you know that the radius is 3. It could be 3 inches or 3 miles, but it doesn't matter, because the question doesn't specify. Plug in 3 for the radius and do the math: $\pi r^2 = 3.14 \times 3^2 = 3.14 \times 9 = 28.26$.

Getting Up to Speed with Functions

Think of functions as tiny mathematical manufacturing plants; you feed raw material in one end, and a finished product comes out the other. If the machine squares numbers and you feed x into one end, x^2 comes out the other. If you feed 5 into one end, 25 comes out the other. More formally, a *function* is a mathematical relationship between an input and an output in which each input produces only one output. The function we just described would be written as $f(x) = x^2$:

- ✔ f stands for "function," but other letters, such as $g(x)$ or $m(x)$, work as well.

- ✔ (x) indicates the input. Again, it doesn't have to be x; it could be some other letter. x is also referred to as the *independent variable* because its value doesn't depend on the value of another variable.

- ✔ x^2 is the output, which varies depending on what the function does to the input to create the output. The output is referred to as the *dependent variable* because its value depends on the value of the input.

The easiest function problems on the test provide you with the function and an input and ask you to "evaluate the function," which means you need to plug in the value for the independent variable and do the math.

Diana's take-home pay is described by the function $f(h) = 2,000h - 0.15(2,000h)$. Evaluate $f(\$25)$: ☐ .

To solve this problem, insert $25 for h and do the math:

$$f(\$25) = 2,000(\$25) - 0.15(2,000(\$25)) = \$50,000 - \$7,500 = \$42,500$$

More difficult questions may ask you to identify the function that expresses a certain mathematical relationship.

A car rental company charges $50 per day plus $0.40 per mile traveled. Write the function that represents the daily cost of the car rental: ☐ .

In this problem, the variable is the number of miles traveled, so use *m* for miles. The charge is $50/day, so place that to the right of the equal sign, plus 40 cents for every mile traveled, or $0.40 per mile. You then have $f(m) = \$50 + \$0.40m$.

Understanding relations, domains, and ranges

To understand functions, you must also grasp three other important concepts:

- ✔ A *relation* is a set of ordered pairs. For example, the function $f(x) = x^2$ has the following relation: {(2, 4), (3, 9), (4, 16), (5, 25)}. The first value in each ordered pair represents the input, and the second value represents the output.

- ✔ A *domain* is a set of independent variables. In the preceding example, the domain is the *x* variable {2, 3, 4, 5}.

- ✔ A *range* is a set of dependent variables. In the preceding example, the range is the *y* variable {4, 9, 16, 25}.

Ordered pairs are often displayed in a table to make them easier to evaluate, as shown here:

x	x^2
2	4
9	81
4	16
5	25

On the test, you may be provided with a relation displayed as a series of ordered pairs and asked to identify the function that represents the relationship, as in the following example.

Which of the following functions produces the relation {(0, 0), (1, 1), (−1, 1), (5, 5), (−5, 5)}?

(A) $f(x) = \pm x$

(B) $f(x) = |x|$

(C) $f(x) = xy$

(D) $f(x) = \sqrt[3]{x^3}$

The series of ordered pairs are absolute values: $|0| = 0$, $|1| = 1$, $|-1| = 1$, $|5| = 5$, $|-5| = 5$, so the function is $f(x) = |x|$, Choice (B). By the way, $f(x) = \sqrt{x^2}$ would also produce the ordered pair presented in the question, but $f(x) = \sqrt[3]{x^3}$ does not.

Determining whether a relation is a function

A function is a special type of relation in which each input has only one output. To test whether a relation is a function, check its ordered pairs to make sure every input has only one output. An output may have more than one input, but for a relation to be a function, each input must have only one output. For example, $f(x) = x^2 + 2$ *is* a function and generates the following ordered pairs:

x	x^2+2
1	3
−1	3
2	6
−2	6

Note that each input has only one output. No number in the input column (the domain) repeats. Repetition in the output column (the range) is acceptable.

However, the equation $y = \pm2x$ is not a function, because each value for x can produce two different outputs, as shown here:

x	$\pm2x$
1	$2x$
1	$-2x$
2	$4x$
−2	$-4x$

Note that numbers in the input column repeat, an indication that the relation is not a function.

You can also determine whether a relation is a function by looking at a graph of the relation, as explained next.

Graphing functions

Because functions generate ordered pairs, you can plot the points that represent the ordered pairs on the coordinate plane. On the test, you may encounter a question that includes a graph of a function. The question may ask whether the graph represents a function, or you may be asked to identify the function that produces a certain graph.

To answer such questions, keep the following facts in mind (see Figure 9-6):

✔ To determine whether a graph represents a function, apply the *vertical line test*. If the vertical line intersects the line that defines the relation at more than one point, the relation is *not* a function. Why? Because a given x value would produce two y values, disqualifying the relation as a function.

✔ A linear equation produces a line.

✔ A quadratic equation produces a parabolic curve. (See Chapter 8 for more about quadratic equations.) See the following graph of a parabola.

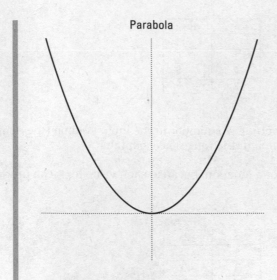

Parabola

✔ An absolute value produces a V shape.

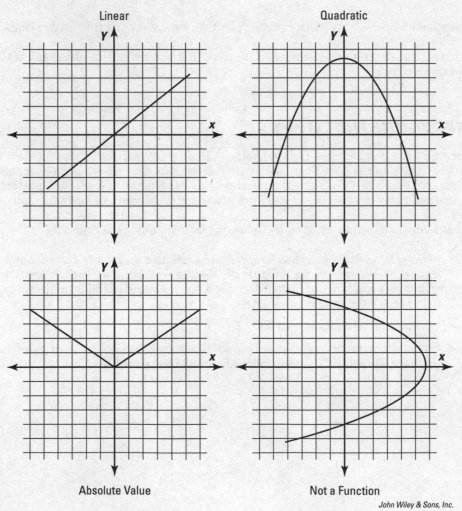

Linear

Quadratic

Figure 9-6:
Determining
whether
a graph
represents
a function.

Absolute Value

Not a Function

John Wiley & Sons, Inc.

Which of these functions produces the graph shown here?

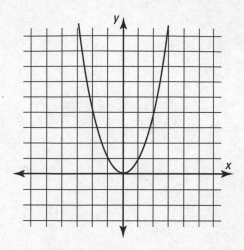

(A) $f(x) = x^2$

(B) $f(x) = 2x$

(C) $f(x) = x + 2$

(D) $f(x) = |2x|$

The only quadratic is Choice (A), which is the correct answer. This is the standard equation of a parabola. Choices (B) and (C) produce straight lines, and Choice (D) produces a V-shaped line.

If you need to graph a function to answer a question on the test, input several positive and negative values for x and use the function to generate corresponding y values. This gives you several ordered pairs that you can plot on the coordinate plane.

Part III

Putting Your Math Knowledge and Skills to the Test

Five Ways to Simulate the GED Math Test Environment

✔ Find a quiet place to work where you won't be distracted or interrupted. Put away cellphones, music players, and all other electronic devices. They aren't permitted on test day.

✔ Don't use a calculator on the first five questions. You may use a calculator to help answer the remaining questions. For the most accurate simulation, use the calculator on a computer screen.

✔ Use a separate pad of paper to draw shapes, coordinates, and other figures or work other math problems that aren't suitable for figuring on a calculator.

✔ Set a timer to count down from the 115 minutes allocated for the math section of the test.

✔ Don't take a break during the test.

Check out the Cheat Sheet for this book at www.dummies.com/cheatsheet/gedmathtest for helpful tips and tidbits to increase your knowledge and confidence for taking the GED Mathematical Reasoning test.

In this part . . .

✔ See how your stamina measures up by taking a full-length practice GED Math test.

✔ Score your test quickly with the answer key.

✔ Discover how to improve your performance by reading through the answer explanations for all practice test questions.

Chapter 10

Practice Test: Mathematical Reasoning

. . . .

On the Mathematical Reasoning test, you have 115 minutes to solve a series of questions involving general mathematical skills and problem solving. These questions may be based on short passages, graphs, charts, or figures. You must do the first five questions without a calculator, but after that, you can use a calculator for the rest of the test. You also have at your fingertips a list of formulas to help you with some of the questions. Remember that the calculator and list of formulas aren't magic solutions. You have to know how to use them.

Memorizing the formulas and knowing how and when to use them will speed things up and can give you valuable time at the end to go over any questions you had trouble with. Answer the easy questions first to give yourself more time at the end for the more difficult ones.

Unless you require accommodations, you'll take the actual GED test on a computer, where you use the mouse and the keyboard to select and enter your answers. We formatted the questions and answer choices in this book to make them appear as similar as possible to what you'll see on the computerized test, but we had to retain some A, B, C, and D choices and provide an answer sheet for you to mark your answers. The skills required to correctly answer the questions are the same, but the format may be different.

Answer Sheet for Practice Test, Mathematical Reasoning

1. ☐
2. Ⓐ Ⓑ Ⓒ Ⓓ
3. Ⓐ Ⓑ Ⓒ Ⓓ
4. Ⓐ Ⓑ Ⓒ Ⓓ
5. Ⓐ Ⓑ Ⓒ Ⓓ
6. Ⓐ Ⓑ Ⓒ Ⓓ
7. ☐
8. ☐
9. Ⓐ Ⓑ Ⓒ Ⓓ
10. Ⓐ Ⓑ Ⓒ Ⓓ
11. ☐
12. Ⓐ Ⓑ Ⓒ Ⓓ
13. Ⓐ Ⓑ Ⓒ Ⓓ
14. Ⓐ Ⓑ Ⓒ Ⓓ
15. Ⓐ Ⓑ Ⓒ Ⓓ
16. ☐
17. Ⓐ Ⓑ Ⓒ Ⓓ
18. Ⓐ Ⓑ Ⓒ Ⓓ
19. Ⓐ Ⓑ Ⓒ Ⓓ
20. Ⓐ Ⓑ Ⓒ Ⓓ
21. Ⓐ Ⓑ Ⓒ Ⓓ
22. ☐
23. ☐ ☐
24. Ⓐ Ⓑ Ⓒ Ⓓ
25. Ⓐ Ⓑ Ⓒ Ⓓ
26. Ⓐ Ⓑ Ⓒ Ⓓ
27. Ⓐ Ⓑ Ⓒ Ⓓ

28. Ⓐ Ⓑ Ⓒ Ⓓ
29.
30. Ⓐ Ⓑ Ⓒ Ⓓ
31. Ⓐ Ⓑ Ⓒ Ⓓ
32. Ⓐ Ⓑ Ⓒ Ⓓ
33. Ⓐ Ⓑ Ⓒ Ⓓ
34. ☐
35. ☐
36. Ⓐ Ⓑ Ⓒ Ⓓ
37. Ⓐ Ⓑ Ⓒ Ⓓ
38. ☐
39. Ⓐ Ⓑ Ⓒ Ⓓ
40. ☐ ☐
41. ☐ ☐
42. Ⓐ Ⓑ Ⓒ Ⓓ
43. Ⓐ Ⓑ Ⓒ Ⓓ
44. ☐
45. Ⓐ Ⓑ Ⓒ Ⓓ
46. Ⓐ Ⓑ Ⓒ Ⓓ
47. Ⓐ Ⓑ Ⓒ Ⓓ
48. ☐
49. ☐
50. ☐

Mathematics Formula Sheet

Area	
Square	$A = s^2$
Rectangle	$A = lw$
Parallelogram	$A = bh$
Triangle	$A = \frac{1}{2}bh$
Trapezoid	$A = \frac{(b_1 + b_2)}{2}h$
Circle	$A = \pi r^2$

Perimeter	
Square	$P = 4s$
Rectangle	$P = 2l + 2w$
Triangle	$P = s_1 + s_2 + s_3$
Circumference	$C = 2\pi r$ or $C = \pi d$, $\pi = 3.14$

Surface area and volume	Surface area	Volume
Rectangular prism	$SA = 2lw + 2lh + 2wh$	$V = lwh$
Right prism	$SA = ph + 2B$	$V = Bh$
Cylinder	$SA = 2\pi rh + 2\pi r^2$	$V = \pi r^2 h$
Pyramid	$SA = \frac{1}{2}ps + B$	$V = \frac{1}{3}Bh$
Cone	$SA = \pi rs + \pi r^2$	$V = \frac{1}{3}\pi r^2 h$
Sphere	$SA = 4\pi r^2$	$V = \frac{4}{3}\pi r^3$
(p = perimeter of base with area B; $\pi = 3.14$)		

Data	
Mean	Mean is the average.
Median	Median is the middle value in an odd number of ordered values of a data set or the average of the two middle values in an even number of ordered values in a data set.

Algebra	
Slope of a line	$m = \frac{y_2 - y_1}{x_2 - x_1}$
Slope-intercept form of the equation of a line	$y = mx + b$
Point-slope form of the equation of a line	$y - y_1 = m(x - x_1)$
Standard form of a quadratic equation	$y = ax^2 + bx + c$
Quadratic formula	$x = \frac{-b \pm \sqrt{b^2 - 4ac}}{2a}$
Pythagorean theorem	$a^2 + b^2 = c^2$
Simple interest	$I = Prt$ (I = interest, P = principal, r = rate, t = time)
Distance	$D = rt$ (D = distance, r = rate, t = time)
Total cost	total cost = (number of units) × (price per unit)

GED Mathematics Practice Test

Time: 115 minutes for 50 questions

Directions: Mark your answers on the answer sheet provided. You must do the first five questions without a calculator but may use one for the rest of the test.

1. Forgetful Frank goes grocery shopping without remembering to go to the bank to get some money first. He puts the following items in his cart:

1 jar salad dressing	$1.97
1 jug laundry detergent	$4.97
3 yogurt cups	$0.79 each

   When he gets to the cashier, he looks in his wallet and discovers he only has a $10 bill. Does Forgetful Frank have enough money to buy the contents of his cart? Yes or No: [   ].

2. Georgio is out on a first date with Helen and wants to impress her by paying for dinner. The bill comes to $27.63, and he wants to leave the server a 15% tip. After dinner, he notices two things. One, he forgot to bring money. Two, there is an ATM machine in the restaurant, but it only dispenses $20 bills. How many bills will he have to withdraw from the ATM machine to pay for his meal and the tip?

   (A) 1

   (B) 2

   (C) 3

   (D) 4

3. Alvin is always lost because he has no sense of direction and pays no attention to where he is going. After class on Tuesday, Alvin's buddy invites him over to prepare for the science test the next morning. He tells Alvin to walk 3 blocks north and 4 blocks west after he leaves the bus and look for 388 on a red brick house. When Alvin leaves the bus, he walks 3 blocks south and 4 blocks west. Realizing he is completely lost, he starts asking passers-by for directions to the bus stop, hoping he can find his friend's house from there. A good-hearted elderly man walks him the 3 blocks north and 4 blocks east to get back to the bus stop. He then walks Alvin to his friend's house and leaves Alvin with a comment that Alvin makes him feel young again. How many extra blocks did Alvin walk?

   (A) 7

   (B) 14

   (C) 3

   (D) 21

4. Sally is an avid player of any game involving dice. To win the game she is presently playing, she needs to roll a 5 with 6 rolls. What are the odds of her rolling a 5 on her fourth roll?

   (A) 1:24

   (B) 1:6

   (C) 4:6

   (D) 4:24

5. What is the equation of a line with slope 0.75 and y-intercept 6 if you express the slope as a rational number?

   (A) $3x - 4y = 24$

   (B) $4x - 3y + 24 = 0$

   (C) $3x + 4y = -24$

   (D) $3x - 4y + 24 = 0$

Go on to next page

> *You may now use the calculator.*
>
> *Questions 6 and 7 refer to Alex working in the clothing store.*

6. Alex is working in a clothing store. While he is busy pricing stock from the wholesalers' invoices, he notices something interesting. Slacks are marked up by 50%, while shirts are marked up by 45%. Being interested in mathematics, he wonders whether he could create equations to calculate the retail price if he knew the wholesale price and the markup. Which of these equations would work to calculate the retail price *(R)* given the wholesale price *(W)* and the markup *(M)* percentage?

   (A) $R = W - (M)(W)$

   (B) $W = R + (M)(W)$

   (C) $R = W + (M)(W)$

   (D) $R = W + M$

7. The store Alex is working at is planning to have a sale with 15% off all merchandise. Alex has a customer who buys 3 shirts at $45.99 each and 2 pairs of slacks at $99.99 each all on sale. Over lunch, Alex wonders how much less his employer made on that sale and does the calculation using his formula and knowing the discount. His employer made _____ less on these items on sale than if the merchandise had been sold at the regular price.

8. Calculate: $3(24 - 35) + 21^2 \times 5 \div 14 = $ _____ .

9. David is very involved with speed walking. To keep from getting too bored, he has started counting how many breaths he takes for each of his steps. He figured that he takes 3 breaths for every 24-inch step. How many breaths does he take in a 1,500-yard walk?

   (A) 6,750

   (B) 2,250

   (C) 1,875

   (D) not enough information given

10. If the slope of a line is 0.67, and $y_2 = 33$, $y_1 = 19$, and $x_1 = 14$, what is the value of x_2?

    (A) 14

    (B) 23.38

    (C) 34.90

    (D) 43.90

11. Harry has a propane-powered car. He was told it was safe to fill his cylindrical propane tank at a rate of $1\frac{3}{4}$ cubic feet per minute. If the propane tank measures 5.2 feet long and 2.4 feet in diameter and is empty, it would require _____ dollars to fill it at $0.79 per cubic foot.

12. Matilda invested the $2,587.00 she got as gifts for graduating from elementary school in a Guaranteed Investment Certificate. If the certificate pays 2.75% compound interest calculated annually for the 7 years until after she graduates from high school, how much money would she have?

    Use the formula for calculating compound interest:

    $$A = P(1 + \frac{r}{n})^{nt}$$

    Where A = future value of the loan, P = the principal (Amount borrowed), r = annual interest rate, n = number of times interest is compounded per year and t = the number of years the money is borrowed for

    (A) $1,806.00

    (B) $3,281.43

    (C) $2,036.67

    (D) $3,128.02

Go on to next page

13. Harry was interested in the lottery draws and compiled the following table of winning numbers.

Summary of Winning Numbers in Seven Consecutive Lottery Draws

Draw Number	Winning Numbers
1	8, 10, 12, 23, 25, 39
2	1, 29, 31, 34, 40, 44
3	1, 14, 26, 38, 40, 45
4	1, 6, 14, 39, 45, 46
5	10, 12, 22, 25, 37, 44
6	13, 16, 20, 35, 39, 45
7	10, 16, 17, 19, 37, 42

Assuming that there are 49 possible numbers in the set to be drawn, what are your chances of drawing a 1 in your first draw?

(A) 1 in 343

(B) 3 in 343

(C) 3 in 7

(D) 1 in 49

14. Jerry has started a business selling tablet computers. He can buy a good used tablet for $279.00 and sell it for $409.00. The only question he has is whether he will make money. If his overhead (rent, light, heating, and cooling) amounts to $48 per unit, and his taxes amount to $3 per unit, how many tablets will he have to sell to make $850.00 profit per week?

(A) 9

(B) 10

(C) 11

(D) 12

15. Mr. Blain's classes were given an assignment regarding Geothermal-Electric Capacity in several countries in the year 2014. In order to begin the assignment, they had to compile this table:

Geothermal-Electric Capacity in Selected Countries in 2014

Country	Installed Capacity (Megawatts)
China	24
Italy	502
New Zealand	248
Russia	47
United States	1,848

What is the approximate ratio of installed capacity of the largest to the smallest?

(A) 77:1

(B) 1,848:47

(C) 248:502

(D) 1:77

16. Eric wanted to write the population of China in scientific notation for an article he was working on for the school website. If the population of China is 1,361,512,576 and he wrote it out as $1.3 \times 10x$, the value of x is _____.

17. Kevin bought an apartment near an industrial plant. The total floor area is 1,150 square feet. If the ceilings are 9 feet high and his air system withdraws and replaces 57 cubic feet of air each minute, how long, in hours, does it take to withdraw and replace all the air in his apartment?

(A) 6

(B) 3.03

(C) 181.58

(D) 18

18. As part of a mathematics test, Ying was given the following equations to solve:

$$4x + 2y = 20$$
$$2x + 6y = 35$$

What is the value of y?

(A) 3

(B) 4

(C) 5

(D) 6

Go on to next page

19. Vivienne is studying a map. She is 53 miles due south of where she wants to go, but the road goes 15 miles due west to an intersection that then goes northeast to her destination. Approximately how much longer, in hours, must she travel if she can average 50 miles per hour following the way the road goes?

    (A) 1.10

    (B) 0.09

    (C) 1.19

    (D) 0.11

20. As an experiment, a class flips three coins 50 times each and charts the results. What are the odds of the second coin landing on its head during the 37th toss?

    (A) 50:1

    (B) 1:3

    (C) 1:2

    (D) 37:1

Questions 21 and 22 refer to the following table.

Room Level Dimensions

Room	Measurement (in Feet)
Dining room	9.71 x 8.01
Living room	19.49 x 10.00
Kitchen	13.78 x 7.09
Solarium	19.00 x 8.01
Master bedroom	13.78 x 12.40
Second bedroom	11.42 x 8.60

21. Matilda has bought a new apartment and wants to carpet the living room, master bedroom, and second bedroom. If she budgets $27.50 per square yard for carpeting and installation, how much should she budget for these rooms?

    (A) $1,340

    (B) $12,870

    (C) $1,430

    (D) $1,287

22. The carpet installer tells Matilda that he will give her a 15% discount on the carpet and installation if she puts down outdoor floor covering in the solarium for only $25.25 per square yard installed. Will she save money accepting the discount and installing the extra carpeting? Yes or No: ☐.

23. The probability of an event taking place, *P*, is equal to the number of ways a particular event can occur, *N*, divided by the total number of ways, *M*, or $P = N/M$. To test this theory, a student removes all the picture cards from a 52-card deck with 4 cards representing each of 1 to 10. What is the probability that a card less than the number 6 will be drawn? (Aces are low in this case.) Probability: ☐ in ☐.

24. Consider the equation $E = mc^2$. If the value of *m* triples and the value of *c* remains constant, the effect on *E* would be how many times larger?

    (A) 2

    (B) 3

    (C) 6

    (D) 9

25. Coal is considered a major air pollutant, and the South Derward Clean Air Society was trying to draw attention to this fact and created the following table to bring along on their talks:

Coal Consumption by Country

Country	Consumption (Tons)
China	1.31 billion
Greece	70.5 million
Australia	144.17 million
Russia	298 million
Canada	67 million

What is the approximate ratio of coal consumption of the largest to the smallest?

    (A) 70.5:67

    (B) 298:70.5

    (C) 1,310:67

    (D) 144.17:67

Go on to next page

26. Jerry wants to buy a new fuel-efficient car. He notices that a new car is advertised as saving a minimum of 35% in city driving and 25% on the highway. After a week of record keeping, he produces the following table for his old car.

Day	City Driving (Miles)	Highway Driving (Miles)
Monday	32	8
Tuesday	34	21
Wednesday	22	12
Friday	18	5
Saturday	7	70
Sunday	5	75

Calculate the average mileage Jerry gets in his old car and compare that with the new fuel-efficient model to see how much Jerry might save in the new car if gas costs $2.70 a gallon. How much would he save in a week by buying this new fuel-efficient car?

(A) $127.00

(B) $93.00

(C) $15.00

(D) not enough information given

27. If you open a can flat along the seam and cut almost all the way around each end, what shape would you end up with?

(A) a circle

(B) a rectangle with a circle on each end

(C) a rectangle

(D) a circle with two rectangles on each end

28. If a can is designed to contain 24 cubic inches of coconut water and has to be 6 inches tall to fit on the shelves in a store, what would be its diameter in inches?

(A) 1.72

(B) 1.27

(C) 1.79

(D) 2.26

29. A circle is drawn with its center at the origin and a radius of 5 units. Where will the circumference intersect the negative y-axis? Circle this point on the graph.

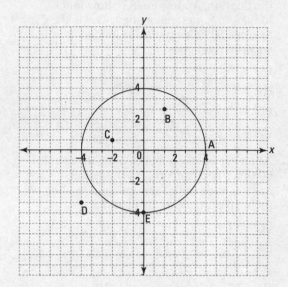

30. Alice's car uses gasoline in direct proportion to her speed. If she increases her average speed by 10 miles per hour to save time, the consequence is:

(A) She would save money.

(B) She would spend more money on fuel.

(C) She would spend the same amount as before.

(D) Not enough information is given.

Questions 31 and 32 refer to the information given in Question 31.

31. In researching fuel consumption for her car, Alice discovers that increasing her speed from 30 to 50 miles per hour would increase her fuel consumption by 18%. If gasoline is selling for $3.50 a gallon, how much could she save by traveling on roads with speed limits of 30 mph instead of 50 mph?

(A) $14.00

(B) $6.78

(C) $8.00

(D) not enough information given

Go on to next page

32. How much time, in minutes, would Alice save by taking a 78-mile-long route with the higher speed limit?

    (A) 62.4

    (B) 1.04

    (C) 60

    (D) 78

Questions 33 and 34 refer to information given in Question 33.

---

33. Sam is making a circular carpet, using small pieces of carpeting glued onto a backing. If he wants a carpet that is 7 feet 8 inches across, including a 2-inch fringe all around the carpet backing, how many square yards of backing does he need to cover the carpet, rounded to the second decimal place?

    (A) 45.9

    (B) 5.10

    (C) 5.15

    (D) 5.14

34. If backing costs $2.75 per square yard but only comes in rectangular sizes, how much would Sam have to pay in dollars for the backing? $ [_____]

35. Gloria and Betty are eating ice-cream cones. Betty wonders what volume of ice cream her cone would hold if filled to the top. Gloria measures the cone and finds it to be $2\frac{1}{4}$ inches across the top and $5\frac{3}{4}$ inches high. The cone would hold [_____] cubic inches of ice cream, rounded to one decimal place, if it were filled to the top.

36. Betty is looking up some information on the Internet and finds out that her ice-cream cone holds 4 ounces of ice cream and that the manufacturer states that every 2.54 ounces of its ice cream contains 145 calories. She also knows that consuming 3,500 calories can cause a weight gain of 1 pound. If Betty treats herself to ice-cream cones 5 days a week in addition to her regular diet, which stabilized her weight, how many pounds might she gain in a week?

    (A) 0.33

    (B) 0.31

    (C) 0.35

    (D) 1.0

37. Carol wants to buy a used car. She has been told that a car loses 4.3 cents from its book value for every mile over 100,000 that it has traveled. She sees just the car she wants, but it has 143,185 miles on the odometer. The book value of the car is $14,750. Estimate the realistic value of the car to the nearest $10.

    (A) $12,890

    (B) $8,593.04

    (C) $5,890.00

    (D) $8,590.00

38. Tom and Gary are having a height contest. Tom is 6 feet 1 inch tall, and Gary is 5 feet 9 ½ inches tall. What is the ratio of Gary's height to Tom's? [_____]

39. Elena wants to draw a mural on the wall of her house. The wall is 3 yards high and 21 feet 8 inches long. To plan the mural, she draws a scale drawing of the area for the mural on a piece of paper 11 inches long, leaving a half-inch margin at each end. How high, in inches, should the drawing be to maintain scale?

    (A) 0.14

    (B) 4.2

    (C) 3.0

    (D) 2.8

40. Solve for $3x^2 + 3x - 36 = 0$. $x =$ [_____] or [_____].

41. Solve for x and y:

    $$7x + 13y = 21$$
    $$21x - 4y = 12$$

    $x =$ [_____] and $y =$ [_____].

42. An accident investigator calculates a car's speed during a skid by multiplying the following: the square root of the radius of the curve that the center of mass, r, follows times a constant, k, times the drag factor of the road, m. If the speed is 47 miles per hour and the drag factor is 0.65, what is the radius of the curve?

    (A) 0.27

    (B) 0.33

    (C) 17

    (D) not enough information given

Go on to next page →

43. To be recommended for a scholarship at College of the Americas, a student must score above the median of all the students in his or her final year and have a mean mark of at least 90 percent. Delores is hoping for a scholarship recommendation with these marks:

Mathematics	90
Applied Science	93
English	89
Spanish	96
Physics	90

The median mark for the graduating students is 86.5. How many percentage points above the required minimum mean score did Delores score?

(A) 1.6

(B) 2.6

(C) 3.0

(D) 0.5

44. $24x^3 - 24x^2 - 30x + 18 \div (6x - 9) = \boxed{}$.

45. Clara is shopping for a new car, but different dealerships offer different rates of interest to finance the car. In order to make a rational decision, she summarized the interest rates in the following table:

Interest Rates Offered by Different Car Dealerships

Dealer	Interest Rate Offered
A	Prime + 2%
B	7.5%
C	½ of prime + 5%
D	Prime + 20% of prime for administrative costs

Clara is confused. She is looking for a new car, but each dealership offers her a different interest rate. If the prime lending rate is 7 percent and she is willing to give the dealer a 10% down payment, which dealer is offering her the best terms to finance her car?

(A) dealer D

(B) dealer C

(C) dealer B

(D) dealer A

46. Morrie and Samantha are planning a 900-mile trip. Morrie says that he can drive the distance at an average speed of 45 miles per hour with only 4 half-hour rest breaks. Samantha says that she will fly, but it takes her 45 minutes to get to the airport and 1 hour and 15 minutes to get from the airport to her destination after she lands. If she has to be at the airport 4 hours before takeoff and the airplane travels an average of 506 miles per hour, how many hours will Samantha have to wait for Morrie?

(A) 12.248

(B) 7.78

(C) 14.22

(D) 22

47. The Haute Couture Hat Company of Lansing, Michigan, produces designer hats for women who feel that they require a hat to complete an outfit. The company's sales vary from quarter to quarter and factory to factory. The following chart reflects its sales for one year:

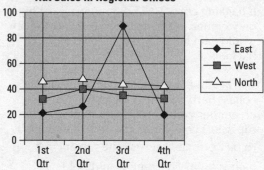

Hat Sales in Regional Offices

John Wiley & Sons, Inc.

In which of the three factories and in which quarters are sales figures approximately in the ratio of 2:1?

(A) east and west in second quarter

(B) west and north in third quarter

(C) east and north in third quarter

(D) west and east in first quarter

Go on to next page

48. To complete a school project on longevity and gender, Miss Kelin's class assembled the following table:

Life Expectancy for Urban Dwellers

Age (in Years)	Males	Females
10	61.4	67.3
20	50.3	55.1
30	40.4	45.1
40	32.8	36.5
50	22.1	26.4
60	15.2	17.8
70	9.9	10.7

What is the ratio of the average life expectancy between men and women in the age range 30 to 60? [　　　]

49. Paul is emptying his swimming pool. He can pump 11 cubic feet of water per minute. If his pool measures 16 yards by 5 yards with an average depth of 4 feet, when will his pool be empty if he starts pumping at noon on Tuesday? [　　　] p.m.

50. Pedro works in sales. He compares his commissions for the four-week period when bonuses were being given and finds that he has earned an average of $424.50 per week for the four weeks. He earned $485.00 the first week, $257.00 the second week, $410.00 the third week, and $546.00 the final week. Pedro's company offered sales staff an incentive bonus of 15% for each week their commissions exceeded $475.00. How much did he earn in dollars that four-week period, including commissions and bonuses? $[　　　]

STOP DO NOT TURN THE PAGE UNTIL TOLD TO DO SO. DO NOT RETURN TO A PREVIOUS TEST.

Chapter 11

Checking the Answers and Explanations

• •

This chapter gives you the answers and explanations for the Mathematical Reasoning practice test in Chapter 10. The first question you may ask yourself is why you should bother with the explanations if you got the answers right. The simple answer is: The explanation walks you through the problem, from the question to the correct answer. The solutions are like a roadmap leading from the question to the answer. They won't show you every twist and turn, but they will give you general directions on how to get to the answer. If you made an error in the question and got it wrong, the explanation can save you from a lot of frustration. By following the steps, you can discover why and where you went wrong and figure out a way not to repeat the error on similar questions on the real test.

Answers and Explanations

1. **Yes.** The easiest way to do this problem is with mental math. Round all the prices: salad dressing $2, detergent $5, yogurt $3 \times \$0.80 = \$2.40$. Total is $9.40, which is less than the money Frank has in his wallet.

2. **(B) 2.** The bill came to $27.63 and the tip would be $4.14 for a total of $31.77. Because Georgio can only withdraw $20 bills, he would need two of them, or $40, to pay the bill and the tip.

3. **(B) 14.** This is a good place for a quick sketch:

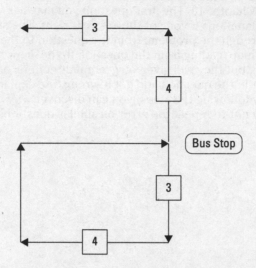

Assuming the streets run parallel, Alvin would have traveled 3 + 4 +3 +4 +4 +3 = 21 blocks instead of the 7 blocks he would have had to travel. He traveled 14 extra blocks.

4. **(B) 1:6.** As long as Sally is rolling just one die, and most games stipulate that, she has a one in six chance of rolling any number.

5. **(D)** $3x - 4y + 24 = 0$. Using the general equation of a line $y = mx + b$ and substituting the
$$y = \frac{3}{4}x + 6$$
given values, you would arrive at $4y = 3x + 24$
$$3x - 4y + 24 = 0$$

6. **(B)** $W = R + (M)(W)$. The reality is that the retail price is made up of the wholesale price plus the markup, both in dollars. You calculate the markup in dollars by multiplying the markup in percent (as a decimal) by the wholesale price. Choice (B) is that as an equation. The others if you read them as English sentences or Mathematical equations would produce incorrect results in the calculations.

7. **$432.05.** This question requires you to use information in Questions 6 and 7. Always be careful of questions in groups because you may need to use information from other passages or, even worse, use a correct answer from one of the questions. If you put the information in a table, you would get:

Item	Number	Sale Price	Regular Price	Unit Loss	Total Loss
Shirt	3	$45.99	$100.00	$54.01	$162.03
Slacks	2	$99.99	$235.00	$135.01	$270.02
TOTAL					$432.05

The store would have made $432.05 less by selling at the sale price than by selling at the regular price. (For the realists in the group, this would not have taken into account the wholesale price he paid for them originally. Most stores, when they have a sale, would make sure that they had made a profit on the total number of items before selling them at substantial markdowns.) The 15% discount is extraneous information; the sale price would already include the discount.

8. **124.5.** Do the math, remembering PEMDAS:

$$3(24-35)+21^2\times5\div14$$
$$(3)(-11)+441\times\frac{5}{14}$$
$$-33+\frac{2,205}{14}$$
$$-33+157.5=124.5$$

9. **(A) 6,750.** 1,500 yard walk = 54,000 inches = 2,250 steps = 6,750 breaths.

10. **(C) 34.90.** $\dfrac{33-19}{x_2-14}=0.67$

$$x_2=34.90$$

11. **$18.57.** Volume of tank $=V=\pi r^2h=(3.14)(1.2\times1.2)(5.2)=23.51$ cubic feet.

    Propane is $0.79 per cubic foot.

    Cost of filling tank $=23.51\times\$0.79=\$18.57$

12. **(D) $3,128.02.** $A=P(1+r)^t$ is the formula for compound interest compounded annually.

$$A=(\$2,587)(1+0.0275)^7=\$3,128.02$$

13. **(D) 1 in 49.** If there are 49 possible numbers that can be drawn and 1 is one of the possibilities, your chances are 1 in 49 to draw 1 in your first draw. The table is extra information, and if you read the question carefully, you would see that the answer is in the question and not in the table.

14. **(C) 11.** Jerry's base cost per tablet is $279.00, his overhead per unit is $48, and the taxes per unit are $3, which means his gross cost per unit is $279 + $48 + $3 = $330.00.

    His selling price is $409.00, which means his profit is $409.00 − $330.00 = $79.

    To make $850.00 profit per week, he would have to sell $850.00 ÷ $79 = 10.76 tablets, or, rounded up, 11 tablets.

15. **(A) 77:1.** The largest installed capacity is the United States at 1,848.

    The smallest installed capacity is China at 24.

    The ratio of the largest to the smallest is 1,848 to 24.

    Because the ratio can be simplified by dividing both by 24, the ratio is 77:1.

    Choice (D) is the correct numbers for the ratio, but the question asks for largest to smallest, not the other way around.

16. **9.** The value for x is 9 because you would have to move the decimal point 9 places to the right to get the equivalent number in Scientific Notation.

17. **(B) 3.03.** The volume of air in the apartment is $1,150\times9=10,350$ cubic feet.

    The air system withdraws and replaces 57 cubic feet per minute, and it would take $10,350\div57=181.58$ minutes, or $181.58\div60=3.03$ hours, to withdraw and replace all the air in the apartment.

18. **(C) 5.** Multiply the second equation by 2: $4x + 12y = 70$. Subtract the new second equation from the first (remember your signs):

$$\begin{aligned} 4x + 2y &= 20 \\ -(4x + 12y &= 70) \\ \hline 0x - 10y &= -50 \\ y &= 5 \end{aligned}$$

19. **(A) 1.10.** Draw a sketch map. Due south and west are at right angles, and the course of the road is the hypotenuse of a right-angled triangle. Here you can use the Pythagorean theorem. Let the length of the road be x:

$$x = \sqrt{53^2 + 15^2} = \sqrt{3034} = 55.08$$

If Vivienne can travel an average of 50 miles an hour, she can travel 55.08 miles in 1.10 hours.

20. **(C) 1:2.** Each toss is an independent event and has no relationship with the others. Therefore, the odds are the same as tossing a single coin once — in other words, 1:2 of it landing heads.

21. **(C) $1,430.**

Area of living room $= 19.49 \times 10.00 = 194.49$ square feet $= 21.66$ square yards.

Area of master bedroom $= 13.78 \times 12.40 = 170.87$ square feet $= 18.99$ square yards.

Area of second bedroom $= 11.42 \times 8.60 = 98.21$ square feet $= 10.91$ square yards.

She would need a total of $21.66 + 18.99 + 10.91 = 51.56$ square yards of carpeting.

Because carpeting is sold in even square yards, rounded up, Matilda would have to budget 52 square yards of carpeting at $27.50 per square yard = $1,430.

22. **Yes.** A 15% discount on the carpeting Matilda wanted would be $1,430 \times 0.15 = 214.50$, which is more than the cost of 1 square yard of outdoor floor covering. Yes, she would save money on this deal.

23. **1 in 40.** With the picture cards removed, 40 cards remain. Twenty of those cards are less than 6. The odds of drawing a card with a value less than 6 is 1 in 40.

24. **(B) 3.** This is basically a linear equation if c remains constant; therefore, E would be three times larger.

25. **(C) 1,310:67.** The largest consumer is China at 1.31 billion tons, and the smallest consumer is Canada at 67 million tons. Therefore, the ratio is 1,310 to 67. Because these two numbers have no common factors, you can't simplify the ratio.

26. **(D) not enough information given.** To answer this question, you would need to know the gas mileage of the old car for both city and highway driving. Neither is given, so this question can't be answered.

27. **(B) a rectangle with a circle on each end.** The easiest way to answer this is to draw a sketch of what the opened can would look like.

28. **(D) 2.26.** Substituting in the formula for the volume of a right cylinder $24 = (\pi r^2)6$ divide both sides by 6 to simplify

$$4 = (\pi r^2)1 \text{ or}$$

$$r^2 = \frac{4}{\pi} \text{ and}$$

$r = 1.13$ and the diameter would be 2.26 inches

29. **(0, –5).** The circumference would intersect the negative y-axis at a point 5 units below the origin, or at (0, –5) since the y-axis goes from top to bottom.

30. **(B) She would spend more money on fuel.** According to the problem, this is a linear relationship. The faster Alice goes, the more fuel she uses per mile, and the more money she would spend on fuel.

31. **(C) not enough information given.** Without an indication of how far Alice was traveling, there's no way to calculate cost savings or extra expenditures.

32. **(A) 62.4.** A 78-mile-long route would take 1.56 hours at 50 mph and 2.6 hours at 30 mph. Alice would save 1.04 hours at the higher speed, but the question asks for the answer in minutes: 1.04 hours = 62.4 minutes.

33. **(B) 5.10.** The diameter of the backing is 7 feet 8 inches, or 7.67 feet. Therefore, the radius is 3.84 feet, or 1.28 yards.

    Substituting in the formula for the area of a circle: $A = \pi(1.28^2) = 3.14(1.64) = 5.14$ square yards, or 5.10 square yards rounded to one decimal point.

34. **$4.51.** Sam would need a square of backing of 1.28 yards on each side. Assuming that the backing can be purchased in that size (the problem doesn't indicate otherwise), the required area would be $A = 1.28^2 = 1.64$ square yards, which would cost $1.64 \times 2.75 = \$4.51$.

35. **7.62 cubic inches.** Use the formula for the volume of a cone and substitute for π, r, and h, remembering that r is half the distance across the cone:

$$\text{Volume} = \frac{1}{3}(3.14)(1.125^2)5.75 = 7.62$$

or 7.62 cubic inches of ice cream rounded to one decimal place.

36. **(A) 0.33 lbs.** If 2.54 ounces of that ice cream contains 145 calories, then 4 ounces of the ice cream would contain $\frac{145}{2.54} \times 4 = 228.35$ calories.

    If Betty ate 5 ice cream cones a week, she would consume an additional $228.35 \times 5 = 1,141.75$ calories per week.

    If consuming an additional 3,500 calories would cause her to gain 1 pound each week, the additional 1,141.75 calories would cause her to gain $\frac{1,141.75}{3,500} = 0.33$ pounds per week.

37. **(A) $12,890.00.** The car Carol is considering has $143,185 - 100,000 = 43,185$ excess miles on it.

    If a car depreciates $0.043 for each excess mile, this car would depreciate $43,185 \times \$0.043 = \$1,856.96$ from its book value of $14,750, which equals a final price of $12,893.04, or $12,890.00 rounded to the nearest $10.

38. **69:73.** If Tom is 6 feet 1 inch = 73 inches and Gary is 5 feet 9 inches = 69 inches, the ratio of Gary's height to Tom's is 69:73, and because there are no common factors, the ratio can't be simplified.

39. **(B) 4.2.** If the wall is 21 feet 8 inches = 260 inches long, and the paper is only 10 inches long (accounting for the half-inch margin at either end), the scale would be 260 to 10, or 26 to 1.

    If the wall is 3 yards high, it is 108 inches high, and the scale drawing of the wall would be approximately 4.2 inches high after rounding 4.15 up to the nearest inch.

40. $x = 3$ **or** -4. Factor:

$$3x^2 + 3x - 36 = 0$$
$$(3x - 9)(x + 4) = 0$$

If x is 3, then $3x - 9 = 0$, and if x is -4, then $-4 + 4 = 0$.

41. $x = \dfrac{240}{301}$ **and** $y = \dfrac{51}{43}$. Multiply $7x + 13y = 21$ by 3 to get $21x + 39y = 63$.
    Then add the second equation:

$$
\begin{array}{r}
21x + 39y = 63 \\
-21x + 4y = -12 \\
\hline
0x + 43y = 51 \\
\end{array}
$$

$$y = \frac{51}{43}$$

This can't be simplified, because 51 and 43 have no common factors. Substitute for y in the first equation to find x:

$$7x + \frac{663}{43} = 21$$
$$7x = 21 - \frac{663}{43} = \frac{903}{43} - \frac{663}{43} = \frac{240}{43}$$
$$x = \frac{240}{43} \times \frac{1}{7} = \frac{240}{301}$$

42. **(D) not enough information given.** Without a value for the constant or the equation for calculating the unknown, this is an impossible question, and the only answer is "not enough information given."

43. **(A) 1.6.** Delores has a mean mark of 91.6, which is 1.6% above the minimum mean score.

44. $4x^2 + 2x - 2$. Factor the first expression using the second expression as one of the factors:

$$\left(24x^3 - 24x^2 - 30x + 18\right) = (6x - 9)(4x^2 + 2x - 2)$$
$$\cancel{(6x - 9)}(4x^2 + 2x + 2) \div \cancel{(6x - 9)} = (4x^2 + 2x - 2)$$

The quotient would be $4x^2 + 2x - 2$.

45. **(C) dealer B.** The down payment is extra information because the interest rate would be based on the same principal, no matter what the uniform down payment was.

46. **(C) 14.2.** Morrie would take $900 \div 45 = 20$ hours to drive the distance, plus 4 half-hour rest breaks for a total of 22 hours.

    Samantha would take 45 minutes = 0.75 hours to get to the airport, 1 hour and 15 minutes = 1.25 hours to get to her destination, 4 hours waiting time at the airport, and 1.8 hours flying time for a total of 7.8 hours for her trip.

    She would have to wait for 14.2 hours for Morrie.

47. **(C) east and north in the third quarter.** Looking at the graph, in the third quarter, the east plant seems to have produced twice (ratio of 2:1) as many hats as the north plant.

   This answer is considered an approximation because the graphs aren't perfectly accurate.

48. **27.63:31.45.** The average life expectancy for men 30 to 60 is 27.63, and for women in the same age range, it's 31.45.

   The ratio is 27.63 to 31.45.

49. **4:22.** The volume of Paul's pool is 16 yards = 48 feet by 5 yards = 15 feet by 4 feet = 2,880 cubic feet.

   His pump can handle 11 cubic feet per minute, and it would take $2,880 \div 11 = 261.82$ minutes, or 4.36 hours, or 4 hours and 22 minutes, to empty the pool. If he started pumping at noon on Tuesday, he would finish at 4:22 p.m.

50. **$1,852.65.** Pedro earned $485 the first week, $257.00 the second week, $410 the third week, and $546 the fourth week. If the bonus is paid for weeks when his commissions exceeded $475.00, he would have earned bonuses for the first and fourth week. His bonus the first week is $(\$485)(0.15) = \$72.75$ and the fourth week is $(\$546)(0.15) = \$81.90$.

   His earnings for the four-week period = $485 + $257 + $410 + $546 + $72.75 + $81.90 = $1,852.65.

Answer Key

1. **Yes**

2. **B**

3. **B**

4. **B**

5. **D**

6. **B**

7. **$432.05**

8. **124.5**

9. **A**

10. **C**

11. **$18.57**

12. **D**

13. **D**

14. **C**

15. **A**

16. **9**

17. **B**

18. **C**

19. **A**

20. **C**

21. **C**

22. **Yes**

23. **1 in 40**

24. **B**

25. **C**

26. **D**

27. **B**

28. **D**

29. **(0, −5)**

30. **B**

31. **C**

32. **A**

33. **B**

34. **$4.51**

35. **7.62**

36. **B**

37. **A**

38. **69:73**

39. **B**

40. $x = 3 \; or \; -4$

41. $x = \dfrac{240}{301}$ **and** $y = \dfrac{51}{43}$

42. **D**

43. **A**

44. $4x^2 + 2x - 2$

45. **C**

46. **C**

47. **C**

48. **27.63:31.45**

49. **4:22**

50. **$1,852.65**

Part IV
The Part of Tens

In this part . . .

✔ Discover ten shortcuts for solving math problems, so you'll have more time to reason through problems, perform calculations, and check your answers.

✔ Take a dry run through ten tricky math problems, so you're not blindsided by them on test day.

Chapter 12

Ten Shortcuts for Solving Math Problems

. . . .

In This Chapter

▶ Saving time with rounding and estimating

▶ Using a calculator or doing the math in your head

▶ Knowing formulas and memorizing common fractions/decimals

▶ Paying attention to units and factoring to solve problems

. . . .

*T*he biggest challenge of the GED Mathematical Reasoning test often has more to do with the limited time you have to solve problems than with actually solving the problems themselves. Given enough time, you could probably figure out a way to solve most problems on the test, but when the clock is ticking and you're under extreme pressure to choose an answer, the anxiety can cloud your thinking.

One way to reduce anxiety is to have some tricks up your sleeve for solving problems more quickly. In this chapter, we provide ten time-saving tips for answering Mathematical Reasoning questions.

Knowing How and When to Round Answers

If you arrive at a numerical answer with a recurring decimal, such as 210.8740921857362, you're not expected to enter all those decimal places. Look at the question to see whether it instructs you to round the answer to a specific decimal place, such as "round to the nearest hundredth" or "round to the second decimal place." Round up if the number in the next decimal place is 5 or more and round down if it's less than 5. For example, 6.235 rounded to the nearest hundredth is 6.24, but rounded to the nearest tenth, it's 6.2.

If no such guidance is provided, then use your common sense. If you're dealing with money, round up or down to the nearest hundredth (second decimal place) because the smallest coin is a penny — one hundredth of a dollar. If the problem deals with buying carpet by the square yard, round up to the next nearest whole yard because you're not going to round down and end up with less carpet than you need; otherwise, the carpet won't cover the entire portion of the floor you need to cover. For example, if you find out you need 6.2 square yards of carpet, round up to 7, not down to 6.

Ballparking Answers through Estimation

When performing calculations, you normally want to arrive at a precise answer, but if you're given four answers to choose from that are very far apart, calculating a ballpark figure will get you close enough to choose the correct answer. In such cases, you can save time by estimating. For example, if carpeting sells for $2.68 a square yard and you need 20 square yards, you can round $2.68 up to $3.00 and then multiply $3.00 by 20 to get $60. Round down to $2.00 and then multiply by 20 to get $40. You now know that you're going to spend a little over $50 for that 20 square yards of carpeting. If the cashier charges you $70, you know right away a mistake has been made.

Using estimating, you can quickly rule out unreasonable answer choices and focus in on the most reasonable of the choices.

Knowing When to Use the Calculator . . . and When Not to

Calculators are wonderful inventions, but the calculator can slow you down on questions that don't require a calculator to answer. Before clicking the calculator, extract details from the question and jot them down on the erasable notepad that's provided. Draw a picture or write an equation if you think it may help. You may be able to figure the answer in your head without using the calculator. On the other hand, if you jot down an equation that contains a series of complex calculations, don't hesitate to reach for the calculator.

The Mathematical Reasoning test is more about figuring out how to solve math problems than about proving that you know how to perform calculations or use a calculator.

Getting to Know the Formulas and How to Use Them

The GED Mathematical Reasoning test provides you with the formulas you need to solve common math problems, such as calculating the area of a triangle or the volume of a cylinder. These formulas make for interesting reading, but not while you're taking the test. Chapter 7 contains the formulas you'll have access to on test day. Prior to test day, make sure you know what the formulas are used for and how to use them. More important, as you use this book and find that you need a formula that's not on the list, write it down and make sure that you understand it and can use it. When you're taking the test, you want to know which formula will solve the problem and how to use it.

Becoming Accustomed to the Computer Version of the Test

If you're proficient in math, you're able to answer questions regardless of whether they're displayed on a computer screen, a piece of paper, or a chalkboard. However, the GED tests are timed, and if you have to spend several minutes getting oriented to the screen layout and figuring out how to use the keyboard and mouse to answer questions, you're wasting precious moments that you could spend more wisely reading and understanding questions, performing calculations, and checking your answers.

As part of your test prep, take at least one free GED-designed practice test online. Go to www.gedtestingservice.com/freepractice/download/GED_Math/ GEDMathPracticeTest.html, click the Start button, read and accept the license agreement (assuming you agree), and follow the on-screen instructions to take the test.

Go to www.gedtestingservice.com/educators/freepracticetest for a link to an additional free practice test that you can download and run on your computer. At the GED Marketplace (www.gedmarketplace.com), you can purchase additional practice tests.

Crunching Numbers in Your Head with Mental Math

Your brain is an infinitely more complex and powerful calculator than any hand-held model on the market. Yet, when it comes to solving equations such as $\dfrac{\sqrt{139} \times 37}{7^3 \div (12-9)} =$, you probably need to use a calculator to figure out the answer.

However, you can do a lot of math in your head and practice. Here are some suggestions on how to improve your brain's ability to do math:

- Memorize multiplication tables from 1 to 12.

- Memorize squares of numbers from 1 to 12 and the square roots of those numbers. You should know immediately that $12^2 = 144$ and that $\sqrt{64} = 8$ without having to do the math.

- Memorize the cubes of numbers up to 5 and their cube roots. For example, you should know that $5^3 = 125$ and that $\sqrt[3]{64} = 4$ without having to use a calculator.

- When you go shopping, as you add items to your grocery cart, try to keep a running tally of your growing grocery bill. If an item is advertised as 10% off, try figuring what you'll actually pay for it.

- When you eat out, figure out the tip amount in your head. Calculate it for a 10%, 15%, and 20% tip. You can use a calculator to check your math.

- When you pay for anything, use cash and try to figure out how much change you're supposed to get back.

Practice using your brain for mental math and you'll get better at it. Pretty soon, you'll be able to figure out a 15% tip at the coffee shop or whether shirts on sale at 3 for $99 is a better deal than $37.99 each. You'll just have to work it out.

Using Units to Solve Problems

When a question asks for an answer in a particular unit (for example, miles, yards, gallons, or pounds), you can often use what you know from the units presented in the problem to develop an equation to solve it. This shortcut is based on the fact that when you multiply fractions, anything that's the same in the numerator and the denominator cancels out. Here's an example:

A machine produces 35 gadgets every 15 minutes. How many gadgets does it produce per hour?

Based on the question, you know that the answer must be in gadgets per hour or $\frac{\text{gadgets}}{\text{hour}}$, you know that the machine produces gadgets per minute, and you know that there are 60 minutes per hour. So your equation without any values plugged in will look like this:

$$\frac{\text{gadgets}}{\text{minutes}} \times \frac{\text{minutes}}{\text{hour}} = \frac{\text{gadgets}}{\text{hour}}$$

Now, you just plug in the values and crunch the numbers:

$$\frac{35 \text{ gadgets}}{^1\cancel{15} \text{ minutes}} \times \frac{^4\cancel{60} \text{ minutes}}{1 \text{ hour}} = \frac{140 \text{ gadgets}}{\text{hour}}$$

Mastering the Fine Art of Factoring

Factoring consists of breaking down a number into the smallest possible values that can be multiplied together to get the number. For example, factor 200 and you get:

$$200 = 2 \times 2 \times 2 \times 5 \times 5$$

Factoring is useful for determining the least common denominator of two fractions when you need to add and subtract fractions. For example, you can't add $\frac{1}{2} + \frac{2}{5}$, but you can add $\frac{5}{10} + \frac{4}{10} = \frac{9}{10}$.

Factoring is also useful for simplifying square and cube roots, which questions on the GED Mathematical Reasoning test may require you to do. Suppose you need to simplify $\sqrt{3,150}$:

$$\sqrt{3,150} = \sqrt{3 \times 3 \times 5 \times 5 \times 2 \times 7}$$

Because 3 is multiplied by itself and 5 is multiplied by itself, you can pull those two numbers out from under the radical sign and simplify the radical:

$$\sqrt{3 \times 3 \times 5 \times 5 \times 2 \times 7} = 3 \times 5 \times \sqrt{14} = 15\sqrt{14}$$

You also use factoring to determine the least common multiple of a number. For example, to find the least common multiple of 32 and 56, you factor each number and then multiply each factor by the greatest number of times it occurs in either number:

$$32 = 2 \times 2 \times 2 \times 2 \times 2$$
$$56 = 2 \times 2 \times 2 \times 7$$

The 2s appear 5 times in 32, and the 7 appears once in 56, so the least common multiple is $2 \times 2 \times 2 \times 2 \times 2 \times 7 = 224$.

Memorizing the Decimal Equivalents of Common Fractions

Sometimes, multiplying or dividing by a fraction is easier than multiplying or dividing by its decimal equivalent, and vice versa. For example, you probably have an easier time calculating $8,764 \times 0.5$ by looking at it as half of 8,764. On the other hand, if you need to calculate a discount of $\frac{1}{5}$ on a bill, you're probably better off treating it as a 20% or 0.20 discount. Here are decimal equivalents (or approximations, indicated by the symbol ≈) of common fractions you should know off the top of your head:

$$\frac{1}{4} = 0.25$$

$$\frac{1}{2} = 0.50$$

$$\frac{3}{4} = 0.75$$

$$\frac{1}{5} = 0.20$$

$$\frac{2}{5} = 0.40$$

$$\frac{3}{5} = 0.60$$

$$\frac{4}{5} = 0.80$$

$$\frac{1}{3} \approx 0.33$$

$$\frac{2}{3} \approx 0.67$$

$$\frac{1}{8} = 0.125$$

$$\frac{3}{8} = 0.375$$

$$\frac{5}{8} = 0.625$$

$$\frac{7}{8} = 0.875$$

Reading the Answers Before Working the Problem

To tackle a multiple choice question, read the question *and* the answer choices first before working the problem. The answer choices often provide clues as to the units or format the answer must be in. For example, if the answer choices all contain radicals, you know that your answer must be in radical form and not calculated out to a whole number or decimal. If answers are in miles per hour or gallons per minute, you have an additional clue to help you solve the problem.

TIP

Answer choices are also useful in helping you make an educated guess when you have no idea about how to solve a problem. Instead of trying to calculate the precise answer, you may be able to rule out ridiculous answer choices and then choose from the remaining choices to improve your odds of choosing the correct answer.

Chapter 13

Ten Tricky Math Problems and How to Solve Them

In This Chapter

▶ Tackling problems that involve increasing an average

▶ Handling questions that involve prime numbers, absolute values, radicals, and scale factors

▶ Figuring out probability and method problems

▶ Mastering distance-rate-time problems and inequalities

Although you may think otherwise when you're taking the GED Mathematical Reasoning test, the people who write the questions for the test don't intentionally try to trick you. In fact, these folks go out of their way to present problems in a straightforward way. The trouble is that certain math problems, by their very nature, are trickier than others to solve. In this chapter, we present ten tricky math problems and explain how to make them more manageable.

Solving Increasing the Average Problems

One of the favorite types of questions among math teachers who create questions for the GED Mathematical Reasoning test is the "increasing the average" question. The question provides you with values that represent anything from grades on a test to amounts of time required to complete a race and asks you to determine how much the average needs to be increased to meet a certain goal, such as a certain grade point average or a certain record time to complete a race. Here's an example:

Jen has been a competitive racer for the last ten years and finally decides that she wants to enter the state finals. Her present running times are 57 seconds, 62 seconds, 59 seconds, and 61 seconds. The current champion runner averages 53 seconds per race. How many seconds faster than her average must Jen complete the course to have a chance of beating the current champ? Round your answer to the nearest whole second: [   ].

To solve increasing the average problems, take the following three steps:

1. **Calculate the average.**

2. **Subtract the average from the target value.**

3. **Round up as necessary to meet or exceed the target value as instructed in the question.**

In this example question, Jen's average running time is $(57 + 62 + 59 + 61) \div 4 = 59.75$ seconds. To beat the present champ, her average time would have to be less than 53 seconds. $59.75 - 53 = 6.75$ seconds, which is the number of seconds she would need to shave off her average time to tie the champ. To beat the champ, she would need to improve her time slightly more, so round your answer up to 7 seconds.

Weeding Out Superfluous Detail

A good mathematics problem has just enough information to solve the problem and not much extra. But some math problems stop just short of providing you with the characters' life stories. Before you can answer the question, you need to decide which details help you solve the problem and which ones to ignore.

When a question buries you in details, skim through it and find out what it's asking for at the end. It may be asking you for a total, an average, or something else, but as soon as you know what the question is asking, you can go back through and pick out only those details you need to calculate the answer.

Here's an example:

Ann and John are talking about doing some renovations to their living room. It has been a long time, and they are ready for a major change. They see new carpeting for $7.65 a square yard including tax for the 120 square yards of carpeting they need and a new couch for just $1,135 including sales tax and delivery. A contractor quotes them $650 to patch and prime the walls and supply two coats of paint in their choice of colors. While shopping one afternoon, they notice a painting by a local artist that seems to be perfect for their living room. At $950 including tax, it seems a bit expensive, but John says that with interest rates so low, they can afford the extra payments. Their friendly local bank manager says that a payment of 12% per month for 18 months would cover principal, interest, bank charges, and registration fee. How much do they pay for all charges except principal for one year?

This question contains enough extra information to occupy three to four times the amount of time you should spend on any one question. To save yourself some time, drop down to the end of the question, where you find out that you need to calculate the total of the charges, not including the principal payments on the loan. Knowing that all you need is a total, you can pull the numbers out of the question and formulate the following equation:

$$(\$7.65 \times 120) + \$1,135 + \$650 + \$950 = \$3,653$$

Dealing with Prime Numbers in Fractions

Standard operating procedure for adding or subtracting fractions calls for determining their *least common denominator* (LCD) because the denominators must be the same to complete the operation. For example, to add $\frac{3}{4} + \frac{1}{2}$, you need to change $\frac{1}{2}$ to $\frac{2}{4}$. To find the LCD, you factor both denominators and then multiply each factor by the greatest number of times it occurs in either number. Factor 4 and you get 2×2. Factor 2 and you get 2×1. The greatest number of times 2 appears as a factor in either number is twice, so multiply $2 \times 2 = 4$, which is the LCD.

When you encounter a denominator that's a prime number, you can't factor it, so just multiply the two denominators to determine the LCD. Here's an example:

$$\frac{7}{51} + \frac{2}{12} = \left(\frac{7}{51} \times \frac{12}{12}\right) + \left(\frac{2}{12} \times \frac{51}{51}\right) = \frac{84}{612} + \frac{102}{612} = \frac{186}{612}$$

When you're finished, calculate the mixed number equivalent and simplify the fractional part if possible. In this example, you divide both the numerator and denominator by 2 and then 3: $\frac{186 \div 2}{612 \div 2} = \frac{93 \div 3}{306 \div 3} = \frac{31}{102}$.

Overcoming Confusion over Absolute Values

Absolute value is the magnitude of a value regardless of whether it's positive or negative. To overcome any confusion that absolute values may stir up, just keep in mind that the absolute value of a number is positive, regardless of whether the number is negative or positive, and that absolute value is indicated by two vertical lines: $|-25|$.

Absolute value is often used in answer choices for problems that ask you to determine which equation helps determine a certain tolerance, as in the following problem:

A manufacturing plant packages 100 marbles per bag. Bags containing 3 too many or too few marbles are rejected. Which of the following equations can be used to determine which bags are rejected when *b* represents the number of marbles in a bag?

(A) $|100 - b| \leq 3$

(B) $|100 - b| \geq 3$

(C) $|b - 3| \leq 100$

(D) $|b - 3| \geq 100$

To solve problems such as these, plug in upper and lower numbers that you know will be rejected, such as 95 and 105:

$$|100 - 95| \leq 3 \text{ and } |100 - 105| \leq 3$$
$$|100 - 95| \geq 3 \text{ and } |100 - 105| \geq 3$$
$$|95 - 3| \leq 100 \text{ and } |105 - 3| \leq 100$$
$$|95 - 3| \geq 100 \text{ and } |105 - 3| \geq 100$$

The only equation that correctly identifies both 95 and 105 to be rejected is Choice (B).

Giving Way to Radicals and Irrational Numbers

Radicals are any values inside the radical sign, such as $\sqrt{15}$. *Irrational numbers* are those that can't be represented as a fraction or that have endless decimals that don't repeat, such as $\pi = 3.141597\ldots$ and $\sqrt{2} = 1.414213\ldots$ When you encounter a radical or irrational number, don't panic. Read the question to find out what to do. The question will instruct you whether to keep the answer in a simplified radical form or round to the nearest decimal.

For example, suppose you solve a problem and end up with $\sqrt{27}$ as the answer. If the question instructs you to round to the nearest tenth, you can use the calculator to find the square root of 27, which is 5.196 . . . , which is 5.2 when rounded to the nearest tenth. If the question instructs you to enter the answer as a simplified radical, then factor and simplify like so: $\sqrt{27} = \sqrt{3 \times 3 \times 3} = 3\sqrt{3}$.

Calculating Scale Factors

A *scale factor* is a value that increases or decreases the dimensions of one shape or object to produce a similar shape or object that's larger or smaller. For example, model cars are commonly advertised as $\frac{1}{18}$ or 1:18 scale, meaning every part of the model car is $\frac{1}{18}$ the size of the comparable part on the real-life version of the car.

To calculate the scale factor, simply divide the measurements of the two comparable dimensions given in a problem. You can then use the scale factor to determine the measurements of the other unknown dimensions of the object. Here's an example:

Assuming the following two rectangles are similar, what is the width of rectangle A?

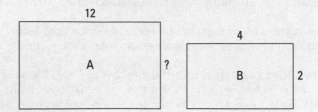

To calculate the scale factor, divide the length of rectangle A by the length of rectangle B, and you get $\frac{12}{4} = 3$. Now, all you need to do is multiply the width of rectangle B by the scale factor to determine the width of rectangle A: $2 \times 3 = 6$.

Scale factors get more complex when the question asks for area or volume because you need to square the scale factor to determine area and cube it to calculate volume. Here's an example:

Assuming the following two boxes are similar, what is the volume of box A?

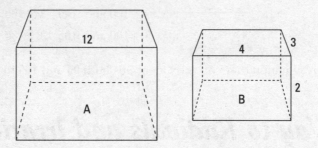

The scale factor is the same as for the preceding question, 3, but you have to cube it: $3 \times 3 \times 3 = 9$. Find the volume of rectangle B, multiply it by the scale factor of 9, and you have your answer:

$$2 \times 3 \times 4 \times 9 = 216$$

Sometimes you want to draw a small diagram of a large object but you want the proportions to be correct. Welcome to the world of scale drawing. If you're given a scale drawing of a living room and the length of the drawing is 6 inches and the width is 4 inches, you would immediately know that this is not an accurate drawing for a room occupied by humans. If you also see a little legend at the bottom that says "Scale: 1 inch = 5 feet," you would know that this drawing represents a living room 30 feet long and 20 feet wide.

Scale drawings are often used in architectural diagrams when the distances are larger than the piece of paper you want to be carrying around. Another use is for a diagram of something very large, such as a ship or an apartment building. The scale drawing allows the architect to communicate with the builder and the developer initially and the real estate agent and the customer after construction. The builder has to know where to put the walls and fixtures, and the potential buyer wants to know if her furniture would fit into the space.

Tackling Playing Card Probability Problems

One of the trickiest problems you're likely to encounter on the GED Mathematical Reasoning test is a question asking the probability of selecting certain cards from a standard 52-card deck of playing cards. When you encounter probability problems with playing cards, you need to remember these three important facts:

✔ The deck has 4 suits: hearts, diamonds, clubs, and spades. If a question asks you to determine the probability of drawing an ace from the deck, you don't have a 1 in 52 chance, you have a 4 in 52 or 1 in 13 chance because the deck has 4 aces.

✔ Each suit contains 13 cards: ace, king, queen, jack, 10, 9, 8, 7, 6, 5, 4, 3, and 2. If a question asks you to determine the probability of drawing a club from the deck, you have a 13 in 52 or 1 in 4 chance.

✔ As you draw cards from the deck, assuming you don't place them back in the deck, the deck has one fewer card for every card you draw. So, if you're asked what your odds are of drawing 3 consecutive aces from the deck, your odds are $\frac{4}{52} = \frac{1}{13}$ for drawing the first ace, and if that card is an ace, your odds that the second card will be an ace fall to $\frac{3}{51} = \frac{1}{17}$, and if that card's an ace, your odds of drawing a third ace drop to $\frac{2}{50} = \frac{1}{25}$. Multiply the probabilities of each of those events occurring and you get the probability of drawing 3 consecutive aces:

$$\frac{1}{13} \times \frac{1}{17} \times \frac{1}{25} = \frac{1}{5,525}$$

Working Out Method Problems

Some GED Math questions ask you to choose the correct method or equation for solving a problem rather than actually calculating the correct answer. When you encounter a problem such as this, instead of reaching for the calculator, reach for the erasable tablet and work on constructing the equation. Here's an example:

On Wednesday, Carol and Tommy picked two dozen tomatoes. On Thursday, they picked half as many as they did on Wednesday. On Friday, they picked 3 times as many as they did on Thursday. How many tomatoes did Carol and Tommy pick? What is the correct solution?

(A) $(2 \times 12) + \left(\frac{1}{2} \times 24\right) + (3 \times 24)$

(B) $24 + \left(\frac{1}{2} \times 12\right) + \left(3 \times \frac{1}{2} \times 24\right)$

(C) $24 + \left(\frac{1}{2} \times 24\right) + \left(\frac{3}{2} \times 24\right)$

(D) $24 + 24\frac{1}{2} + 3 \times 24\frac{1}{2}$

Write the equation step by step:

1. On Wednesday, they picked two dozen tomatoes, which is 24 or 2×12. All the answer choices start correctly.

2. On Thursday, they picked half as many as they did on Wednesday, so that's $\frac{1}{2} \times 24$. That rules out answer Choices (B) and (D).

3. On Friday, they picked 3 times as many as they did on Wednesday, so multiply $\frac{1}{2} \times 24$ by 3 and you get $3 \times \frac{1}{2} \times 24 = \frac{3}{2} \times 24$, which rules out Choice (A) and identifies Choice (C) as the correct answer.

Solving Combined Distance-Rate-Time Problems

Combined distance-rate-time problems present you with two moving people or objects and ask you to determine something related to their distance, rate of speed, or time traveled. To solve these problems, first write down everything you know, including what you know that's not stated in the question. Here's an example:

Two airplanes take off from airports 500 miles away from each other following the same path. One is flying 150 miles an hour, and the other is flying 200 miles an hour. How long will they be in flight before they cross paths?

What this question doesn't tell you but that you can figure out is that they'll travel for the same amount of time when they cross paths. You also know that when the two planes meet, they will have traveled a total of 500 miles, regardless of where they happen to cross paths. For example, if one plane traveled 100 miles, the other would have had to travel 400 miles for them to meet. Now you can develop an equation from what you know:

$$150\text{m/h} \times t + 200\text{m/h} \times t = 500 \text{ miles}$$
$$350\text{m/h} \times t = 500 \text{ miles}$$
$$t = \overset{10}{\cancel{500}} \text{ miles} \times \frac{1 \text{ hour}}{\underset{7}{\cancel{350}} \text{ miles}} = \frac{10}{7} = 1\frac{3}{7} \text{ hours}$$

This equals about 1 hour and 26 minutes.

Grappling with Inequalities

Don't let inequalities put you into a panic. In most cases, you can simply treat the inequality symbol as an equal symbol to find the value of the unknown. For example, treat $5x + 3 \geq 28$ as

$$5x + 3 = 28$$
$$5x = 25$$
$$x = 5$$

Then, replace the equal sign with the inequality sign: $x \geq 5$.

If you multiply or divide both sides of an inequality by a negative value, flip the inequality sign. For example, if you have $-5x \geq -25$ and you must divide both signs by -5 to find x, then flip the sign, so $x \leq 5$.

Index

About the Authors

Murray Shukyn, BA, is a graduate of the University of Toronto with professional qualifications as a teacher at the elementary and secondary levels, including special education. He has taught at the elementary, secondary, and university levels and developed training programs for adult learners in the coffee and food-service industries. During his extensive career, spanning more than 50 years, Murray has taught professional development programs for educators and is acknowledged as a Canadian leader in the field of alternative education. He was instrumental in the creation of such innovative programs for the Toronto Board of Education as SEED, Learnxs, Subway Academy One, SOLE, and ACE. In 1995, Murray became Associate Director of the Training Renewal Foundation, which introduced the GED in the province of Ontario. As a consultant to government, media, and public relations companies, he has coauthored numerous textbooks and magazine and periodical articles with Achim Krull and coauthored several books to prepare adults to take the GED test with both Achim Krull and Dale Shuttleworth.

Achim K. Krull, BA, MAT, is a graduate of the University of Toronto, with specialist qualifications in history and geography. He has taught at both the high school and adult education level. Achim worked for many years in the academic alternative schools of the Toronto District School Board, as administrator/curriculum leader of Subway Academy One and as cofounder of SOLE. He has written textbooks, teachers' guides, and a large variety of other learning materials with Murray Shukyn, including scripts for educational videos, as well as newspaper and magazine articles. Achim designed and currently teaches an academic upgrading program for young adults preparing to enter apprenticeships.

Dedication

From Murray: To Bev, Deb, and Ron, who have always provided ongoing support and encouragement for all the projects I find myself involved in.

Authors' Acknowledgments

We wish to say a special word of thanks to Grace Freedson of Grace Freedson's Publishing Network for all her efforts in negotiating for these books and guiding us through the often murky waters of negotiations.

Thanks to John Wiley & Sons executive editor Lindsay Lefevere for choosing us to write this book and for pulling together a talented team of professionals to help us produce a top-quality product. Thanks to wordsmith Joe Kraynak at joekraynak.com for teaming up with us during the early stages of the project to produce a quality manuscript and deliver it in a timely manner.

We thank Chrissy Guthrie of Guthrie Writing & Editorial, LLC, for shepherding our manuscript through the editorial process and to production and providing the guidance we needed to make a good manuscript great. Thanks also to our copy editor, Todd Lothery, for weeding out any errors in spelling, grammar, and punctuation and, more important, ensuring the clarity of our prose.

Special thanks to our technical editor, Sonia Chaumette, for detecting and eliminating any substantive errors and omissions that would otherwise undermine the accuracy and utility of this book.

Publisher's Acknowledgments

Executive Editor: Lindsay Lefevere

**Editorial Project Manager and
Development Editor:** Christina Guthrie

Copy Editor: Todd Lothery

Technical Editor: Sonia Chaumette

Art Coordinator: Alicia B. South

Project Coordinator: Antony Sami

Cover Image: agsandrew/shutterstock

Anatomy and Physiology For Dummies, 2nd Edition
978-0-470-92326-9

Astronomy For Dummies, 3rd Edition
978-1-118-37697-3

Biology For Dummies, 2nd Edition
978-0-470-59875-7

Chemistry For Dummies, 2nd Edition
978-1-118-00730-3

1001 Algebra II Practice Problems For Dummies
978-1-118-44662-1

Microsoft Office

Excel 2013 For Dummies
978-1-118-51012-4

Office 2013 All-in-One For Dummies
978-1-118-51636-2

PowerPoint 2013 For Dummies
978-1-118-50253-2

Word 2013 For Dummies
978-1-118-49123-2

Music

Blues Harmonica For Dummies
978-1-118-25269-7

Guitar For Dummies, 3rd Edition
978-1-118-11554-1

iPod & iTunes For Dummies, 10th Edition
978-1-118-50864-0

Programming

Beginning Programming with C For Dummies
978-1-118-73763-7

Excel VBA Programming For Dummies, 3rd Edition
978-1-118-49037-2

Java For Dummies, 6th Edition
978-1-118-40780-6

Religion & Inspiration

The Bible For Dummies
978-0-7645-5296-0

Buddhism For Dummies, 2nd Edition
978-1-118-02379-2

Catholicism For Dummies, 2nd Edition
978-1-118-07778-8

Self-Help & Relationships

Beating Sugar Addiction For Dummies
978-1-118-54645-1

Meditation For Dummies, 3rd Edition
978-1-118-29144-3

Seniors

Laptops For Seniors For Dummies, 3rd Edition
978-1-118-71105-7

Computers For Seniors For Dummies, 3rd Edition
978-1-118-11553-4

iPad For Seniors For Dummies, 6th Edition
978-1-118-72826-0

Social Security For Dummies
978-1-118-20573-0

Smartphones & Tablets

Android Phones For Dummies, 2nd Edition
978-1-118-72030-1

Nexus Tablets For Dummies
978-1-118-77243-0

Samsung Galaxy S 4 For Dummies
978-1-118-64222-1

Samsung Galaxy Tabs For Dummies
978-1-118-77294-2

Test Prep

ACT For Dummies, 5th Edition
978-1-118-01259-8

ASVAB For Dummies, 3rd Edition
978-0-470-63760-9

GRE For Dummies, 7th Edition
978-0-470-88921-3

Officer Candidate Tests For Dummies
978-0-470-59876-4

Physician's Assistant Exam For Dummies
978-1-118-11556-5

Series 7 Exam For Dummies
978-0-470-09932-2

Windows 8

Windows 8.1 All-in-One For Dummies
978-1-118-82087-2

Windows 8.1 For Dummies
978-1-118-82121-3

Windows 8.1 For Dummies, Book + DVD Bundle
978-1-118-82107-7

Available in print and e-book formats.

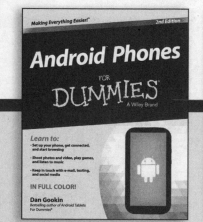

Available wherever books are sold. **For more information or to order direct visit www.dummies.com**

Take Dummies with you everywhere you go!

Whether you are excited about e-books, want more from the web, must have your mobile apps, or are swept up in social media, Dummies makes everything easier.

Leverage the Power

For Dummies is the global leader in the reference category and one of the most trusted and highly regarded brands in the world. No longer just focused on books, customers now have access to the For Dummies content they need in the format they want. Let us help you develop a solution that will fit your brand and help you connect with your customers.

Advertising & Sponsorships

Connect with an engaged audience on a powerful multimedia site, and position your message alongside expert how-to content.

Targeted ads · Video · Email marketing · Microsites · Sweepstakes sponsorship